A Solitary Pillar
Montreal's Anglican Church and the Quiet Revolution

The Anglican Church has played a central role in helping Montreal's anglophone community deal with the social and political upheaval of post–Quiet Revolution Quebec.

In times of uncertainty, threatened populations often turn to key institutions for support. Joan Marshall examines the effect of sociopolitical change on the English-speaking community's use of and relationship to the Anglican Church at both the diocese and parish level. Her argument is based on quantitative measures of attendance, membership, and financial contributions, and qualitative data derived from interviews and participant observation.

Marshall examines such areas as conservatism versus willingness to change, male-female role changes and expectations, the "old order" Book of Common Prayer versus the "new order" Book of Alternate Services, and the role of music to tease out an understanding of the central role of the church vis-à-vis individuals, the parish communities, and the wider Quebec society. Her work makes a significant contribution to an understanding of how our concepts of institutions, community, place, cultural conflict, and cultural survival are interwoven.

JOAN MARSHALL is assistant professor of geography, Carleton University.

McGill-Queen's Studies in the History of Religion
G.A. Rawlyk, Editor

Volumes in this series have been supported by the Jackman
Foundation of Toronto.

A Solitary Pillar

Montreal's Anglican Church and the Quiet Revolution

JOAN MARSHALL

McGill-Queen's University Press
Montreal & Kingston • London • Buffalo

© McGill-Queen's University Press 1995
ISBN 0-7735-1224-1

Legal deposit fourth quarter 1994
Bibliothèque nationale du Québec

∞

Printed in Canada on acid-free paper

This book has been published with the help of a grant from the
Social Science Federation of Canada, using funds provided by the Social
Sciences and Humanities Research Council of Canada.

McGill-Queen's University Press is grateful to the Canada Council
for the support of its publishing program.

Canadian Cataloguing in Publication Data

Marshall, Joan, 1943–
   A solitary pillar: Montreal's Anglican Church and the Quiet Revolution
   Includes bibliographical reference and index.
   ISBN 0-7735-1224-1
   1. Anglican Church of Canada – Quebec (Province) – Montreal
   – History. 2. Quebec (Province) – History – 1960–1976. 3. Anglican
   Church of Canada. Diocese of Montreal – History. I. Title.
   BX5613.M6M67 1994   283'.71428'09046   C94-900581-9

Original line drawings by Nancy Lambert
Maps drawn by Richard Bachand

This book was typeset by Typo Litho Composition Inc.
in 10½/12 Sabon.

Contents

Maps

Tables

Figures

Preface

This book began as an almost intuitive exploration of the meaning of community for anglophones in Quebec. In the spring of 1987 the convergence of a number of personal strands in my life seemed to suggest various meanings for church participation in the context of Quebec society. My involvement in the Anglican Church, my experiences growing up and living in small, semi-rural communities in Quebec, and a long-time commitment to the field of geography all contributed in equal measure to the formulation of this project.

As one who has struggled with the French language while living in predominantly English-speaking communities, I have experienced an ambivalence in my response to the struggles of my francophone neighbours to become "maître chez nous." On the one hand, I sympathize with their goals and support the need for fundamental redress of past injustices. At the same time, lacking confidence in my ability to communicate effectively with them, I have been uncomfortable having to speak French during the course of day-to-day transactions. The concerns of anglophone Quebecers about their "place" in Québécois society are so much part of daily life that they are taken-for granted and usually only consciously perceived when we visit other parts of Canada. For some people these concerns become real fears, touched by resentment. But for most of us who have remained in Quebec through the past twenty-five years, there is a love for the province that transcends definition in terms of landscape, language, or culture. Quebec is home, and within its boundaries – in our communities and churches – we share lives, stories, and histories.

I am indebted to the many people who have given me their trust and who, by sharing their faith with me, have also shared significant parts of their lives. To the members of La Nativité, Church of the Resurrection, St Paul's, Grace Church, and St Matthias, I wish to express my deep appreciation. Their warm welcome included meals, interviews, and even invitations to spend the night when it seemed roads might be closed by snow. I pray that I have not betrayed that trust by even one misplaced word. Not all that I have said will be warmly received, but I have tried to illuminate issues and structures honestly and within as accurate a context as possible. I am grateful too to the rectors of each church, for their cooperation and support, and to the bishop of Montreal Diocese at that time, Bishop Reginald Hollis, to whom I spoke before beginning the original project.

Special thanks must go to Sherry Olson, my thesis adviser, whose ever-cheerful and prompt feedback provided excellent editorial guidance. Her support throughout the project has been greatly appreciated. Appreciation is also extended to Gregory Baum for his thoughtful and articulate comments and suggestions. The financial support for two years provided by the Social Sciences and Humanities Research Council of Canada is deeply appreciated and acknowledged, as is the post-doctoral fellowship awarded by the University of Ottawa (Faculty of Arts) that greatly facilitated the completion of the manuscript.

Most of the data are publicly available through the Anglican Church of Canada. The parish data were collected from individual vestry books, which themselves are the basis of the statistics compiled for the National Synod. The description of the five individual parishes is based upon my experiences over several years as a participant-observer, when I attended meetings, conducted interviews, and generally involved myself in the life of these churches. The documentation (notes) and recorded interviews are all available. Most of this information, while known or intuited by many priests who have wide experience in the diocese, has never before been collected and analysed. To everyone who helped in this project, from the national comptroller who compiled a special listing of mission donations for me, to the parish secretary who helped me locate parishioners on a map, I say thank you.

The personal support and informal suggestions offered by friends can also provide significant guidance. I am especially appreciative of the very early support of professors Jeanne Wolfe and Brian Bird at McGill University, both of whom encouraged me to pursue the idea of church communities in the context of Quebec society. The perceptive comments of the Reverend John Bradley and the Reverend Tony

Grainger and his wife, Dianne, were also helpful in guiding the early formulation of my ideas.

Finally, to my family, thank you, for your patience, your support, and even, on occasion, your culinary masterpieces. We have all learned through this project.

E.J.M.

A Minority Church in Transition

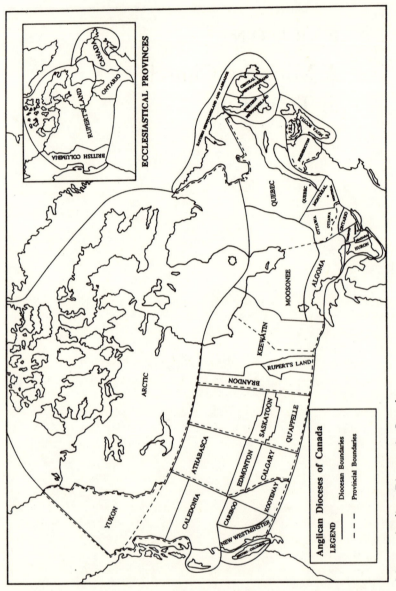

ECCLESIASTICAL PROVINCES

Anglican Dioceses of Canada
LEGEND

Diocesan Boundaries
Provincial Boundaries

Map 1   Anglican Dioceses in Canada

1 Introduction: The Religion-Society Relationship

In every respect except calendar time, centuries – not decades, separate the Quebec of the 1980's from the Quebec of the 1950's.

Hubert Guindon[1]

Beginning with the Quiet Revolution in 1961, fundamental shifts in relationships between English and French Canadians in Quebec have altered forever the majority-minority balance of power and, just as important, the self-defined identities of these two historically dominant cultural groups. Hugh Maclennan's "two solitudes" are no longer characterized by ignorance and isolation, by linguistic hierarchy and English unilingualism. As francophones have reclaimed their status as a majority decision-making group, anglophones have been made increasingly aware of their minority status in the province and have begun to recognize that a defence of anglophone rights "requires patterns of accommodation far different from those that prevailed during the era of the 'two solitudes.'"[2]

It is the "patterns of accommodation" in the particular context of the church that this book will examine. Religion has a socio-political meaning with important implications for personal and collective identities. The following chapters will explore the ways in which the Anglican Church in Montreal has responded to and been affected by the challenges and tensions of social and political change.

I have attempted to clarify some aspects of the religion-society relationship for a specific minority population confronted by an identity crisis. The redefinition of its status within the wider society has raised questions about what it means to be part of Quebec society and what it is that defines the anglophone community. In addition to socio-political change, members of the Anglican Church have also been faced with having to adapt to controversial changes within the church itself. These issues have had an impact upon all aspects of their daily lives, as well as upon their perceptions of control and social power. For anglophones whose very sense of survival seems to be threatened, the need to retain a community of meaning is expressed through a commitment to the church, a commitment that is manifested in very particular ways.

The sources of social power, Michael Mann argues, are the generalized means through which human beings make their own history.[3] These derive from four primary networks: ideological, economic, military, and political. Social power has been an important element in the identities of anglophones, traditionally enabling them to control their major institutions. For most of their history in Quebec, anglophones have dominated and controlled the economic networks and have had significant influence in the ideological and political spheres as well. Since 1961 the balance of power has shifted dramatically.

For English-speaking Quebecers, the structures, rules, and resources that informed their lives have fundamentally changed. Insofar as they have been able to control the transformation, they have been active agents in a restructuring of life-worlds. However, the redefinition of their status and their loss of social power inevitably have severely constrained their ability to exercise control, thereby creating tensions that are manifested in parish churches.

Since 1961 there has been a continuous net out-migration of English-speaking Quebecers. This outflow peaked in the 1976–81 inter-census period, between the election of the separatist Parti Québécois in November 1976 and the rejection of sovereignty-association by a majority of Quebecers in the referendum of May 1980. Membership in the Anglican Church in Montreal Diocese has declined even more precipitously than in Canada as a whole as a result of the combined forces of out-migration of anglophones and, over the longer term, the secularization of society at large. While membership in Canada decreased by 41 per cent between 1961 and 1991, total membership in Montreal Diocese was 24,773 in 1991, down from 94,891 in 1961 and 51,126 in 1976, a decrease of almost 75 per cent in thirty years.

Not only does the Anglican case inform us about the global processes of change in the religion-society relationship, but, as well, the Anglican Church is representative of a Quebec institution that is primarily English speaking and dominantly of British heritage. It

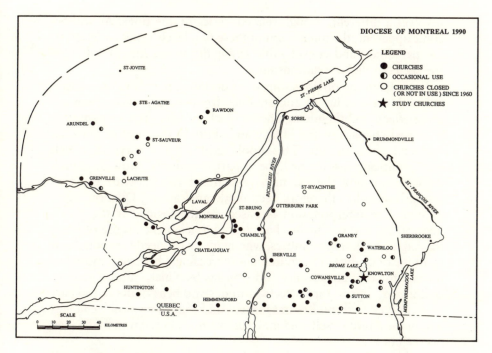

Map 2   Montreal Diocese

includes a significant component of the anglophone minority that has known power and influence.

The Diocese of Montreal, as shown on Map 2, incorporates an area of approximately 120,000 square kilometres, including all of Metropolitan Montreal and extending north of St Jovite in the Laurentians, to Sorel 150 kilometres northeast of Montreal, to Knowlton (Brome) in the Eastern Townships (known also as l'Estrie), and to the Ontario border. It includes 124 congregations within 78 parishes, of which 5 were selected as case studies of distinctive social groups. The time frame presented here is from 1961, when the Quiet Revolution was just beginning, to 1991. Greater emphasis is given to the 1971–91 period, when French Canadian nationalism came to be recognized by anglophones as a significant force redefining traditional relationships.

Two central questions are explored in this book: (1) to what extent has the socio-political milieu had an impact upon the Anglican Church in the province, and (2) do the responses to this milieu vary as a result of the different meaning systems that derive from different life experiences and social groups? The investigation covers two levels of experience, the individual and the collective, each of which involves a different, though related, series of questions. As will become apparent, the interaction of these two levels results in interesting paradoxes and considerable ambiguity in the interpretation of the society-religion relationship.

Apart from the obvious impact of declining membership associated with the exodus of anglophones from the province, there are other effects, subtle but significant, such as distinctive responses to proposed changes in the liturgy and shifts in the level of personal financial commitment. This book explores the ways in which socio-political tensions have been partly mediated through church involvement, and the extent to which the Canada-wide trend to secularization has therefore been moderated among Quebec anglophones. The interpretation is based on the logic that the socio-political context of Quebec has created a heightened sense of place for Anglican Church members, who perceive the need for rootedness in a time of change. The church has increasingly become a more important focus of community and a means by which cultural identity is affirmed. This in turn affects attitudes and behaviours in the parishes, as well as responses of Quebec Anglicans to proposed changes within the church itself, changes, for example, in relation to the new prayer book.

At the level of individuals and their social group, the second part of the book explores patterns of behaviour that reflect the different meaning systems that were incorporated into varying definitions of "community." For individuals, the meaning that their Christian faith, and more particularly their local churches, has for them derives from a complex interaction of community and social values, family experiences, and the broader cultural context. Religion is one important way in which Canadians participate in community life. Personal stories helped to uncover the various meanings people attach to their church and to community.

Religious faith incorporates many dimensions of meaning. While for some people faith affirms identity, rootedness, belonging, and community through the sacralization, myths, and tradition of the collectivity in the institutional church, for others religion is a separate, detached aspect of life, increasingly irrelevant in the secular world of today. Nevertheless, "no matter how spiritual and how private a religious concern may be, it always has a political implication; it is never socially neutral."[4] Late-nineteenth-century thinkers analysed the roles of religious beliefs in different ways: as factors in the development of society (de Toqueville), as expressions of ideological positions (Marx), and as significant conveyors of cultural norms and values (Troeltsch). In this project, the insights of Max Weber and

Emile Durkheim are especially relevant in that they provide frameworks within which we can better understand the complex responses of Quebec Anglicans. Weber, rejecting the alienation paradigm of Marx, argued for the centrality of the individual as creative agent and as a conveyor of values and moral order. He focused on the importance of understanding individuals' subjective meanings and their perceptions of reality, which, he said, would have a profound influence on the constitution of society. Weber showed that religion not only reflects society, but also contains critical and creative elements necessary for change. He also argued that social groups have differing perceptions of reality based on their life experiences and that religious commitment can have different political meanings depending upon the social class of believers. He saw the possibility of change through human agency when people achieve coherence in their lives, combining personal needs with the needs of the community. His discussion of "communal" and "associative" relationships, in which he differentiated between subjective feelings and rationally motivated agreements, recognized distinctive intentions behind ostensibly similar behaviours.

Durkheim, like Marx, began with the broader society, seeing religion as the bond that contributed to the sense of belonging. For him, religion was associated with a community, confirming the members in common values. Whereas Marx argued that religion was a product of alienation, Durkheim saw a functional role for religion, as the symbolic self-manifestation of the community, contributing to the equilibrium of society. The individual is dependent upon the collectivity, he believed, and during times of "creation and renewal" people are led into closer relationships through which the intense exchange of ideas helps in the realization of society's ideals. "Nevertheless these ideals could not survive if they were not periodically revived. This revivification is the function of religious or secular feasts and ceremonies ... whatever draws men together into an intellectual and moral communion."[5]

A frequently acknowledged division in the church is that between those who reach out to the wider society in "mission" and those who focus on the local community. One sociologist and philosopher who has looked at the question of the religion-society interface, with a particular interest in periods of social change, is Karl Mannheim. He saw two significant roles for religion, the ideological and the utopian, the two broadly reflecting the divisions in the church. As did Weber, he recognized the essential ambiguity of religion, arguing that different social groups will have differing life experiences that will affect their mind-sets. He showed that the ideas and ideals of

people evolve as the group to which they belong undergoes significant social changes. In other words, ideas are grounded in social reality, in the life experiences of people and the historical meanings
according to which different groups live. Ideological religion legitimates the existing social order, defends the dominant values,
enhances the authority of the dominant class, and creates the
impression that society is stable and enduring. Utopian religion, on
the other hand, challenges the existing order and offers the possibility of creative change. This fundamental distinction which defines
the ambiguity and paradox of religion, has been the reason for many
of the critiques of religious faith in the modern world.

The nature of the religion-society relationship has changed in the
twentieth century. Nineteenth-century interpretations of the relationship were grounded in the assumption of the undeniable significance of religion. Twentieth-century apologists have had to ask
questions about the relevance of religion, about the meaning of secularization, and about the links between modernity, religion, and
secularization. The assumptions upon which the study of religion
was undertaken were first challenged by Comte when he argued that
the way people perceive the world is the basis on which social organization rests. Therefore, "as man's way of perceiving the world
changed from the theological to the positivistic perspective, so the
social order would also change." [6]

The concept of secularization, like that of community, is difficult
to define because it has been so widely used in different ways. It was
originally used to denote the removal of property from ecclesiastical
control following the Wars of Religion. [7] Today it has evaluative,
ideological connotations, both positive and negative depending
upon the user. In his book *A General Theory of Secularization*,
David Martin begins by describing certain broad tendencies associated with secularization; for example, he points out that "religious
institutions are adversely affected to the extent that the area is dominated by heavy industry" and that "religious practice declines proportionately with the size of the urban concentration." [8] He argues,
however, that while these tendencies tend to be universal processes,
there is no valid reason that they must happen. His thesis is that
these universal processes vary considerably under different cultural
and linguistic situations and that specific "crucial events" shape sets
of tendencies that fructify over time.

Bryan Wilson also challenges the common perception that secularization connotes an evolutionary process inevitably associated with
industrial societies. He emphasizes that secularization is "not only a
change occurring 'in' society, it is also a change 'of' society in its
basic organization." [9] Secularization occurs in diverse ways and con-

texts, and it relates to a diminution in the social significance of religion. It does not mean that everyone acquires a secularized consciousness under modern industrial conditions. "The actual patterns in which [secularization] is manifested are culturally and historically specific to each context and in accordance with the particular character of the conceptions of the supernatural that were previously entertained, and of the institutions in which they were enshrined." [10]

It is this position that is adopted here. There has been an undeniable decline in church membership and attendance, as described in chapter 3. It is demonstrated, however, that despite this trend in Canada, the particular historical and cultural conditions in Quebec have contributed to particular regional responses in the Anglican Church.

One of the key arguments against conventional usage of the term secularization is that it usually refers to the decline of the institutional manifestations of religious practice, rather than to the decline of beliefs and symbols held sacred by individuals. Two important observers of the nature of religion in the twentieth century, Paul Tillich and Mercea Eliade, both argue that religion continues as a significant force in people's lives and that its disappearance is illusory. While accepting the many variations in religious experience "explained by differences in economy, culture and social organization," [11] Eliade posits the existence of "homo religiosus," which is evidenced in characteristic behaviour that reflects the importance of particular sacred places, spaces that are qualitatively different. [12] For those who are members of the church today, their places of worship and the artifacts within them constitute important centres of meaning. Their significance relates to a sacralization of objects that is tied to their belief in God and Christ, but also incorporates historical memories of events, rites, and rituals shared by family and community in the context of a global church. An intimate link between the local and the global provides both rootedness and universality in belonging. The place-centredness of religious faith, which may appear overly concerned with material objects, is a reflection of the significance of symbols of continuity and rootedness, both of which affirm identity. Religion is both spiritual and private, as well as adaptive, radical, and collective. Eliade shows that even people who consider themselves to be non-believers continue to be unconsciously rooted in memories of the sacred, in the stories and myths that inform religious belief.

Paul Tillich, in his *Theology of Culture*, also argues a position of the ultimate significance for religion in today's world. He denies that religion can be limited to one sphere, and in his analysis of modernity argues against the commonly accepted view of secularization as a necessary and inevitable outcome of an evolving society. He says that time is a qualitative construct rather than a methodical, cyclical form, and thereby rejects a concept of linear, evolutionary development in which religion is separated off and diminished in relation to the growth of technology. This idea, that time cannot be defined as a homogeneous measure in which events occur in a sequential order, is explored in Stephen Kern's thoughtful book *The Culture of Time and Space: 1800–1918*. He describes the essential heterogeneity of private time, a crucial dimension of religion, and its conflict with public or homogeneous time. Variously described as superficial, terrifying, and arbitrary, public time is unable "to order the diverse temporal experiences of life." [13] The calendar serves mainly as a way to express the rhythm of collective activities, not as a measure of change. "The theory that time is a flux and not a sum of discrete units is linked with the theory that human consciousness is a stream and not a conglomeration of separate faculties or ideas." [14] The view that religion is inevitably diminished in relation to modernity is a view that distorts the real experience of *durée* and denies the individual meanings that people attach to their inner, spiritual lives. Secularization is neither inevitable nor universal.

A more functionalist view has been presented by two sociologists, Peter Berger and Thomas Luckmann. Their analyses contain an implied denial of the inherent mystery of the sacred, giving the dominant role to society rather than to the individual. In his book *The Invisible Religion*, Luckmann explores the problem of religion in modern society. He suggests that rather than conclude that there has been a decline in religion as a result of increasing industrialization, we should be looking for a new form of religious expression that is less obvious than in the past. He sees the church becoming ambivalent with respect to its religious function as it enters into manifold relations with other secular institutions. Luckmann argues that religion is not so much increasingly separated off as it is seemingly secularized through its non-religious relationships, thereby becoming less visible. "The plausibility of the 'official' model of religion is potentially endangered by the 'secular' operations of the church." [15]

Acknowledging their debt to Marx, Weber, and Durkheim, Berger and Luckmann explore the "social construction of reality." They argue for the importance of symbolism and symbolic language as essential constituents of daily life. [16] There is a critical reflexivity in the relationship between religion and society. "It is just as possible to say that pluralism produces secularization as it is to say that secularization produces pluralism." [17] Berger's study of the religion-society relationship of today convinces him that religion "no longer legitimates 'the world'" and that increased acceptance of pluralistic possibilities has relativized choices. "The religious traditions have lost their character as overarching symbols for the society at large, which must find its integrating symbolism elsewhere."[18] Berger's definition of secularization – "the process by which sectors of society and culture are removed from the domination of religious institutions and symbols"[19] – is basic to his contention that it is more than simply a social-structural process. Secularization affects the totality of cultural life and incorporates a subjective, individual secularization of consciousness, a view in direct opposition to that of Eliade.

The only consensus seems to be that secularization does not imply a denial of religion, or its disappearance, but rather that religion's relationship to other areas of social life has changed. Discussing the dilemma of religion in the context of culture, Clifford Geertz argues that established forms of faith may be at odds – in conflict – with altered conditions of life. Out of that conflict, with resolution of that crisis, may come "modernization," the meaning of which must be seen both in spiritual terms and in such wordly terms as developments in the churches' connections with economic organizations, political parties, labour unions, youth groups, and other voluntary associations.[20]

In Quebec the contrasting histories, styles, and structures of the Protestant and Catholic churches make any sweeping generalizations about secularization impossible. In the past both Catholic and Protestant churches have functioned as legitimating and supporting institutions, affirming the values of their members and of the communities in which they served. With the Quiet Revolution of the early 1960s the relationships between religion and society in Quebec were fundamentally changed. I am suggesting that in Quebec the secularization process cannot be characterized with the same attributes as in other parts of the country or the world. The particular ways in which the religion-society relationship are being manifested among Quebec's anglophone church members are directly related to the social-political environment. As Wilson argues in his 1982 book, the meaning that people attach to their church attendance and to their financial support differs in different societies. The secularization process for Quebec anglophones is mediated by the particular social and political context within this historical period.

The concept of community incorporates many of the ideas touched upon in the foregoing discussion of religion-society relationships. It includes concepts such as "mechanical and organic" solidarity (Durkheim), communal and associational relationships (Weber), and societal transformation and alienation (Marx). Ultimately, however, community is an "untidy, confusing, and difficult term." [21] Regardless of its ambiguity, most people accept the validity and significance of community as a way of describing their daily relationships and existential life-worlds. For people in the church, their place of worship is a significant place: for prayer and meditation, for rites of passage, and for shared family and community relationships. Indeed, "it would be astonishing if religion was not deeply involved with local community and personal identity in that community." [22] Religion has incorporated the ideology of community. Religious symbolism has been relied upon to legitimate local life. Regardless of the ambiguity of the term "community", the parish church represents communities of belonging and meaning.

One characteristic linked to secularization relates to a specific change in social organization: from one that is communally based to one that is societally based. Studies suggest that the level of most consequence has shifted by stages from the little community, the town, to the big community, the nation, [23] and that as the wider society becomes more important as the locus of the individual's life, there is a concomitant diminution of the centrality of the church as a focus of community sharing. [24] Many observers regard modernization as the gradual undermining of the communal bonds linking individuals to locality. If one acknowledges the increasing importance of national and global communities, then one needs to look for new symbols by which people identify themselves. As the importance of the local church wanes, people no longer will have memorial plaques and family windows as symbols of their rootedness in a congregation. No longer will their roles as sidesmen or choirsters attest to their belonging to and participation in a community of historical meaning. For church members, religion can be interpreted as "a set of symbols which people assimilate and celebrate, and out of which they define their lives and create their world ... the world is personally and socially constructed in a process in which symbols play a constitutive part." [25] Religion is intimately tied to community, drawing its strength from the local, persisting relationships of the relatively stable group. The significance of community in relation to religious affiliation raises questions about the meanings that individuals attach to their locale and to their parish churches. Religion and spiritual experience are never wholly unrelated to the character of the places of our physical existence. [26] Community, "place" and identity are all important ideas, central to the religion-society relationship but also having profound implications for the individual. These concepts ground religion in the realm of the person.

The significance of symbols, community, and identity is graphically underlined in the following quotation:

Even sacrament becomes a badge and the members of the network wear the same badge with a difference. The result is an odd mixture of universal and particular. On the one side the sacred rite links the local congregation with the wider scope of the church at large. On the other side the quirks and quiddities give a special character to a local particular sentiment. People cling to the signs of their identity and their history.[27]

Today, the meanings, myths, symbols, and identity of society are being challenged. But it is questionable whether society could subsist on the basis of technical rationality alone. Religion has had a significant role in supporting the important traditions and symbols of our society. Among those who argue the opposite is Dominique Clift. In his book on Canadian identity he suggests that "whereas religion once provided the principal focus for group identity, language now seems to have taken over that function."[28] For anglophones in Quebec, however, a common language is not a unifying element, and the emerging multicultural context, for historical and political reasons, is precluding the continuance of any sense of an English (-speaking) community. Realistically one can refer only to an English-speaking group. Many anglophones in Quebec need a sense of group identity and belonging; since 1961 a secure basis of community has been severely limited for this part of the population. In his acclaimed book on the search for identity, Charles Taylor points out that a full definition of someone's identity usually involves some reference to the defining community and that "our modern notion of the self is just as much a historically local self-interpretation."[29]

The defining community for anglophones in Quebec has undergone transformation through the redefiniton of its status, the loss of its members, and, most important perhaps, the increasing irrelevance of the old stories, symbols, and myths that have historically affirmed belonging. Myths and stories are important in individual lives as the bases of identity formation, reflecting the ways in which individuals relate in terms of life-worlds, place, and their communities. The lack of consensus on a precise meaning for community has not lessened its importance as a concept incorporating people, shared stories, historical experience, and memories, all of which contribute to personal identity and belonging. As we shall see in the context of the parish churches, even physical proximity is not necessarily a valid criterion for determining community. On the other hand, there is evidence of a spatial dimension within people's understanding of their church communities. There is evidence of an evolving consensus about the meanings of community and social group that is directly associated with spatial proximity. Distinctive spatial patterns of church membership seem to relate to characteristics of the surrounding community and variations in people's existential life-worlds. These patterns are associated with different perspectives, historical traditions, and meanings attached to church membership and community.

As a community the church offers unique institutional support for shared experiences and the maintenance of significant myths and symbols; it also offers a rooted, material space to which symbols of continuity can be linked. Parish churches are both the existential focus of relationship and the experiential source of placed meaning (meanings that are rooted in a place). In times of dislocation, the tendency for religion to be separated off from language and culture is checked and the local community assumes greater importance. Communally based relationships and sacred places, through which local memories and stories affirm personal identity, become more important. A perception of place fulfils the individual's need for historically grounded meaning in the face of the collective society's structural impact in controlling daily experience. Attachment to a particular parish or church reflects personal meaning systems, and sacred landscapes may be important elements in understanding the centrality of the parish church as a focus of community.

Some changes in the Anglican Church, such as those that involve altering the shape of church interiors, the location of an organ or a baptismal font, and the arrangement of people during services, have become thorny issues for some parishioners in Montreal Diocese. Places are imbued with meanings that may or may not be consciously articulated, but that nevertheless play an integral part in one's commitment to a church. Under conditions of change, when life-histories are being challenged and social power eroded, the need for affirming identity will be more profound. The meaning of place will change because it is a fundamentally human product, inseparable from the transformation of society. Very little has been written about the processes by which perceptions of place become integrated into the individual's sense of identity. Part of the discussion in this book is directed at discerning how the local community and the church itself become integral parts of individual life-worlds. The importance of place coincides with the transmission of the symbolic qualities of an area, usually through the dominant social group.

One of the interesting and unexpected issues that emerged during the research concerned the competing perspectives among church members on the importance of place and tradition, and the role these competing views had in determining the outcome of specific topics of debate. Several episodes that I record in detail, relating to specific issues in the parishes, illustrate the ways in which place is intimately related to personal identity, as well as the processes through which the relationship a person has with a place evolves.

Meanings attached to community and place evolve imperceptibly but profoundly in the context of the social group. Meanings that confer belonging and identity come out of a *longue durée* that is historical, but more significantly, meanings are rooted in memory. "Remembering the past is crucial for our sense of identity."[30] "Memory," says Taylor, "is the soul's implicit knowledge of itself."[31] The problem is that memories of the past and current realities are no longer congruent for Quebec's anglophones. As their status changes in relation to the French-speaking population, they redefine themselves in terms of the significant places, symbols, and myths that have informed their past histories. Despite Clift's disclaimer about the role of religion in this context, the central theme of this book is that for one group of anglophone Quebecers, religion has had a role to play in maintaining a sense of rootedness and tradition, reinforcing a sense of community and belonging.

Insofar as the parish churches reflect community values, religion will incorporate the myths and stories that form a frame of meaning for people's existence and by which they define their life-worlds. Even as the local community seems threatened by the broad sweep of globalization, there is a need to affirm individual identity in the context of a social group that has shared experiences. While the level of interaction may change, people will search for ultimacy, described as a "whiff of the sacred." Individual meanings need to be placed in the context of people's communities and individual histories. "For the story of my life is always embedded in the story of those communities from which I derive my identity ... The possession of an historical identity and the possession of a social identity coincide."[32]

In Quebec, anglophones are struggling to redefine their identities in terms of both their larger societal context – Quebec – and their local community. For some, the church has become the one place they can retain a sense of rooted and historical meaning, where life-worlds reflect continuity and tradition. This study provides evidence that Anglican churches have served an important ideological function as communities of tradition; however, the parish churches have not become important centres that link their membership to the wider global community. Their potentially utopian role seems to have been submerged by the need to preserve identities perceived to be threatened by the ongoing changes in Quebec. As communities of shared values and historical experience, and as places having important meanings and symbolic roles, the churches are significant mediators of change. For individuals, the church has been a source of identity formation and affirmation, a place of shared stories and historical meaning, and a community in which social change can be mediated through old and new symbols of belonging.

The Anglican Church is presently involved in a series of changes that directly affect the way services are conducted: who may lead or participate in conducting the services; the words that are used; and even the spatial relations of the congregation at worship. All of these changes, proposed and adopted, are controversial. Their acceptance or rejection is not merely a matter of doctrine. The tensions generated by, on the one hand, the perceived need to "modernize" the liturgical language and form and, on the other, the argument for the retention of tradition, thus sustaining a unity of the world church, are themselves creating a dialogue.

In examining the ways the church in Quebec has responded to socio-political change, this book focuses on the meanings that people attach to all aspects of their church life: as spiritual worship; as an extension and celebration of their local community; as a building, a place with historical roots; as a symbol of the British tradition and cultural identity; and as a centre of shared personal experience. All of these meanings are intertwined with the local context, the social group, and the ongoing changes in church liturgy – that is, there are continuing interactive relationships between the individual, the institution, and their shared historical and structural frameworks.

In his articulate discussion of the contextuality of theology, Douglas Hall has said that the relationship between religion and society should not deny the importance of the rooted historical faith. The danger is, he said, that contextualism as it applies to time "will be too much influenced by the present and too little in touch with the past. Applied to place, it is the danger of being so thoroughly caught up in the life of one's own society (e.g. region, nation, language-world) that one tends to lose sight of the larger human community."[33] As this study reveals, some of the responses of Montreal Anglicans to the changing social and political milieu in Quebec indicate a reluctance to move into the present and seem to preclude participation in the global community.

2 Quebec and the Anglican Church: Changing Perspectives on Power, Identity, and Community

For the francophone middle class, neo-nationalism – with its francophone assertiveness and delegitimation of anglophone power in Montreal – would represent an important declaration of collective self-worth in response to a history of cultural stigmatization.

Marc V. Levine[9]

Any discussion of the history of anglophones in Quebec must incorporate an understanding of the questions of identity and social power that have been at the centre of all French-English relationships in Quebec since the eighteenth century. The world-views of these two main language groups have fundamentally different assumptions. The French see themselves as the majority group in a French-speaking province, but one under constant threat of extinction because of its minority status in North America; the English have the confidence inherent in being part of the majority in North America, but they are made painfully and more frequently aware of their minority position in the province. (Quebec anglophones today number fewer than 800,000, less than 10 per cent of the total population of Quebec.) The experience of both groups – similar and contrasting – is the ground upon which individual and collective identities have evolved. The fact is that relationships between the French-speaking and English-speaking communities are difficult because each community is experiencing, both separately and in relation to the other, an identity crisis. Historically, language has always been one essential element of group identity in Quebec. A second element has been religion. While the relevance of religion as a source of personal identity has been diminishing over the past thirty years, its cultural significance continues to be very different for the two founding collectivities, the French and the English. For anglophones, whose very sense of survival is threatened, the need to define a community of meaning is manifested in a continuing commitment to the church. The church for some, despite the diminished role of religion in personal meaning systems, continues to play an important role as a cultural and social institution protecting and promoting individual and collective identities.

An important element in the identities of anglophones has been their social power, through which they have traditionally been able to control their major institutions. But since the Quiet Revolution in the early 1960s, the balance of power has shifted dramatically. The overarching role in Quebec of the Roman Catholic Church in education, government, and all social relationships has now been largely superseded by a secular francophone elite. Concurrently, and with even more significant implications for English-speaking Quebecers, the balance of power between the two language groups has been reversed. By 1976, the year of the election of the separatist Parti Québécois, anglophones were faced with the reality that they were no longer able to behave as a majority and that their status was being redefined for them, as a minority in the province.

In addition to having to reinterpret what it means to be part of the "distinct society" of Quebec, anglophones must recognize that they do not constitute a homogeneous community that possesses a common story. Whereas francophones lay claim to a common heritage of historical experience, anglophones in Quebec are an increasingly diverse group, one without either the historical commonality of experience or the ethnic links that can foster a sense of community. Until 1941 anglophones were mainly from the British ethnic community, but with the immigration of Jews, Italians, and later Greeks and Portuguese, the majority of whom adopted the English language, the anglophone community became less British. By 1971 people of British heritage constituted only 61 per cent of Montreal's anglophone population.[2] Furthermore, as many commentators have pointed out, despite the formation of Alliance Quebec, which claimed to represent the interests of anglophone Quebecers, since the mid-1970s leadership within the anglophone community, which previously had come mainly from the anglo-business elite, has been sorely lacking. The demographic studies done by Gary Caldwell show two clear trends within the anglophone population. The first concerns spatial differentiation: Montreal has been claiming an in-

creasing proportion of the English-speaking people. The second involves the composition of the anglophone communities: there has
been an increasing heterogeneity of the group in Montreal, while in
rural and recreational areas to the north and south of the city the
dominant group continues to be of Anglo-Celtic origins. These two
trends have together led to the anglophones' increasing inability to
express themselves as a community. Finally, although as a percentage of the Quebec population the number of those whose mother
tongue is English has declined steadily since 1851, since 1976 there
has also been a decline in absolute numbers.

Table 1 (Appendix A) provides a summary of the significant time
periods and key events that had an impact upon the perceptions and
sense of security of Quebec anglophones. From the beginning of the
twentieth century, French Quebec has undergone a profound meta-
morphosis, from a rural to an urban society, and from an agrarian
to an industrial economy. Accompanying these changes has been an
increasing determination by francophones to correct the inherent
imbalance in the distribution of power. Gradually, all this has led to
profound changes at the ideological level, encompassing a move
away from the church, strong support for state involvement in the
economy, and the province's growing assertiveness in its dealings
with the federal government. A new neo-nationalism accompanied
the shifts from church to state power and from anglophone-
dominated business to a corporate sector controlled by French
Canadians through the political process. This nationalism only
became a prominent element in Quebec politics and social relations
in the 1960s. Since that time it has shaped Quebec's development
and "mediated the specific roles that dependence, cultural division of
labour, and relations among classes have played within this development."[3] As late as 1960 the sociologist Hubert Guindon commented
on the persistence of traditional elites in Quebec, even in the face of
sweeping economic change. He noted that the composition of the
power structure had not changed appreciably and that the clergy
continued to have a "decisive importance" in political and commercial spheres. One of the most significant changes, however, was the
growth of a "structurally significant group" of salaried, white-collar
workers.[4]

Guindon argues that a major reason for the apparently successful
ethnic accommodation in Quebec until after the Second World War
was the mutually agreed upon separation of institutions, in education, religion, welfare, and leisure. In addition, spatial segregation
allowed anglophones to live entirely in English, virtually ignoring
French life around them. Anglophone domination of the economy,

both national and provincial, gave English status as the language of power and upward mobility, a fact not lost upon the new immigrants, attracting them to the anglophone sphere. Language began to assume increased importance in the changing perspectives of the two founding collectivities.

In his discussion of the symbiotic relationship that had developed between anglophone businesspeople and francophone politicians prior to 1960, Levine describes the mutual non-aggression between the two groups: the business leaders donated handsomely to political coffers and Quebec politicians offered non-interference in anglophone business affairs in exchange. Furthermore, even in the question of schooling there was "deference toward English and an acceptance of Montreal as a bilingual city in which French was a subordinate language."[5] This deference was rooted in an ideology that saw cultural survival in church control over education and social and health services. Neither group was interested in encouraging state involvement in language and educational issues. But the Quiet Revolution, inaugurated soon after the death in August 1959 of Premier Maurice Duplessis, changed all of these relationships completely and forever. By the end of the decade "the deferential attitude of francophones to English vanished, as did the serene sense on the part of anglophones that living in Montreal was no different from living in Toronto or Boston."[6]

Not only did the Quiet Revolution represent a modernization of industrial structures and educational institutions, it was fundamentally an emancipatory movement. Premier Jean Lesage's call to liberation, to be "maître chez nous," was a symbolic torch of freedom. Encouraged by their pride in successful hydroelectric developments, French Quebecers began to demand a full decision-making role in the development of their province. They set out to redress the imbalance of two hundred years. "The disappearance of 'la foi' and 'la race' and the myth of the land as distinguishing characteristics left language as the last expression of national identity for French society in Quebec ... For the English and French in Montreal, language had become not only the principal point of difference but also the principal point of rivalry."[7]

Analysis of the period of the early 1960s reveals a multitude of factors and trends, the most significant being the politicization of a new middle class. The Quiet Revolution was a process of "liberation from a long-dominant ideology ... [it was] the long avoided reconciliation with social and economic development."[8] It has been interpreted not merely as a utilitarian response to industrialization, but more importantly as an issue of identity that necessitated the affirmation of the French Canadian collectivity. Francophones were no longer willing to exchange cultural survival for a higher standard of living. Both could be achieved by replacing the formerly dominant church by a new and more powerful state. The central theme of the Quiet Revolution, "maître chez nous," politicized language issues and thereby destroyed the linguistic entente that had existed since Confederation. Nevertheless, through the 1960s English remained the language of the economy. As late as 1971, while 75 per cent of the Quebec labour force was French speaking, only 28 per cent of the top management jobs were held by francophones.[9] Even as the structures of Quebec's political, educational, and health institutions were changing, English-speaking Quebecers remained dominant in the economy. As a result, the significance of what was happening was not immediately apparent to most anglophones.

Initially, in the drive for separation of church and state, for economic growth and educational improvements, it seemed as though their francophone neighbours were being converted to English goals and values. "It was assumed that this ideological convergence would support a stronger Canadian unity, a unity that was impossible as long as French Canadians had subscribed to traditional values."[10] For French Canadians, on the other hand, the change in ideology touched every corner of social and political life. They were transforming their self-perceptions and affirming their own capabilities. They also redefined their boundaries, basing their nationalism on a territorial identification, which by the time of the 1980 referendum had "reinforced the boundary around Quebec, rendering the ethnic and collective space much more secure."[11]

The creation and expansion of state enterprises in the 1960s, such as Hydro-Québec, the Société générale de financement (SGF), and the Caisse de dépôt, resulted in a major new francophone presence in the economy. The cooperative movement and more aggressive ventures into banking, such as the *caisses populaires* and the Banque canadienne nationale, solidified their positions. At the same time, however, Montreal was declining as a national economic centre, a trend that undermined an important structural support to anglophone power. Inevitably, French opinion leaders began to question the role of English-speaking businesspeople in the provincial economy.[12] With francophones demanding more equitable representation at managerial levels, and with a language of work reflecting the provincial demographic structure, anglophones began to feel that their own economic opportunities were threatened. The separation of economic worlds was being challenged.

When the government began its systematic overhaul of the educational system, removing church control, anglophones at first supported the changes. But when attention focused on language and when legislation restricting entry to English-language schools was proposed, anglophones began to express their uneasiness and finally their strong opposition to the legislation. One response was for the Protestant school boards to open French schools, thereby allowing immigrants legally to enrol in their system and at the same time enabling the boards to retain their administrative structures. The irony, of course, is that this move paved the way for French-speaking school commissioners to be elected to the Protestant boards. As is now becoming increasingly apparent to anglophones, the creation of French schools, designed to protect their administrative control of education, is now threatening to have the opposite effect, with a greater number of francophone commissioners elected to the Protestant boards. The announcement in 1993 of renewed commitment on the part of the government to reorganize the educational system along linguistic lines proposes to institutionalize the separation of French and English language education. The result will be that traditionally large English-dominated Protestant boards will disappear, leaving smaller, nucleated English boards whose effective power will be considerably reduced. The result is an awareness by anglophones that even in the field of education there is an erosion of the control they had retained even after the Quiet Revolution of the 1960s.

Similar concerns are expressed about the loss of power over hospitals and other social welfare institutions. Even municipal jurisdictions are affected, with laws basing the bilingual status of a town on the demographic structure of the population. "This new political dependency of institutional managers on the state [has] had the added effect, in the case of the anglophone institutional elite, of tranforming them into a minority dependent on majority decisions, or, what is more to the point, on the majority's definition of the rules of the game."[13]

Slow to recognize the import of the social changes around them, anglophones have also had difficulty adjusting to the reality that their status has been redefined for them. Clift and Arnopolous argue that this is because the English population in Montreal has traditionally been sheltered from the cultural and ideological experiences of other business elites: "They have treated nationalism as a movement which could be turned back with economic arguments."[14] And as Christian Dufour notes, "In the 1960's, there was a transfer from religion to politics then, in the 1980's, a transfer from politics to economics."[15]

The Quiet Revolution was fundamentally associated with ideological and structural change. By the 1970s the new ideology was implemented and firmly entrenched through legislation affecting education and the language of signs, the most important of which was Bill 101. Its impact upon the perceptions of anglophones with respect to their status in the province cannot be overstated. While the regulations for the most part have been mere irritants in terms of their concrete effect on daily lives, their symbolic meaning has generated profound tensions. The adoption in December 1988 of Bill 178, prohibiting the use of any language except French on outdoor signs, represented for many anglophones the final denial of their individual rights and the ultimate rejection of them as a legitimate part of Quebec society. "There is a price for a new political consensus in Canada. And certain groups will have to pay this price. Those two unfortunate groups are the French outside Quebec and the English in Quebec."[16]

ONE RESPONSE: OUT-MIGRATION

The election of the separatist Parti Québécois in November 1976 provoked an immediate and dramatic response among anglophones. In substantial numbers, they began to migrate out of the province. The net out-migration of anglophones from Quebec has been a major factor in the decreasing Anglican membership in Montreal. While the departure of English-speaking people had been going on for many years, the rate increased significantly after 1975. The figures show that out-migration more than doubled after that year, peaking in the 1977–79 period. (See Table 2 in Appendix A.) It is important to recognize both components of the net figure. Not only did Quebec experience high out-migration, but there were also fewer people moving into the province, one-third fewer in the late 1970s than in the first half of the decade.

The migration data show a dominance of anglophones in the migration totals, accounting for about two-thirds of the exits in the 1976–81 period. Moreover, while there was an increase of 40 per cent in the numbers leaving the province between 1976 and 1981 over the previous five years, there was an equivalent 40 per cent decrease in the number of English-speaking people coming into Quebec. The combination of higher numbers leaving the province and fewer English speakers entering meant that the net out-migration of English mother-tongue migrants doubled in the late 1970s. Between 1974 and 1976 an average of 16,000 anglophones left the province each year, whereas in 1977, 25,000 anglophones left, an increase of 50 per cent.

The characteristics of the anglophones who were leaving were highly specific. The net loss of anglophones between 1976 and 1981 was 106,300 people, of whom more than half were between the ages of 20 and 44. Furthermore, one-fifth of the English speakers leaving the province held university degrees.[17] Between 1966 and 1981, not only did 15 per cent of the English-speaking ("mother tongue") community leave, but also those who migrated represented the younger, more highly educated segments of the community. Of those in the English-speaking community who had a degree, one-third left; and of those who were English and between the ages of 20 and 29, one-quarter left the province.[18] In the period 1971–81, according to the census, there was an 11 per cent decrease in that part of Quebec's population whose mother tongue was English. Moreover, and significantly for Montreal's Anglican Church, those of British ethnic heritage showed an even higher rate of decrease, over 16 per cent in that decade alone.

Therefore, even with the possibility that new members from the existing local community might join, the churches experienced two significant trends whose effects were additive: a loss of members directly attributable to out-migration and a lower rate of new members joining. In addition, the selective migration meant that fewer young families joined Quebec churches and that older, more conservative congregations had to adjust to the turmoil of Quebec society. At the same time, Anglicans were confronted with the possibility of changes within the church itself. Those who stayed, forming an increasing proportion of the congregrations, are people who have had a long history in their individual churches. They have a strong sense of tradition and commitment.

In addition to concern about the separatist party in power, there was increased apprehension with the passing of Bill 101, limiting access to English schools and restricting choice in the language of signs. Despite the feeling among demographers that the impact of Bill 101 on the decision to leave or to enter the province would be temporary,[19] the number of English-speaking people coming into the province continues to be lower than the number of those who leave, with the result that net migration is still negative. The recovery between the 1977–78 period, when the net loss of population was 46,429, and the 1985–86 period, when the net loss was only 3,415, is significant.[20] Nevertheless, when these trends are combined with a birth rate that is below replacement, the implications for the anglophone community in Quebec are obvious. The absolute numbers are declining, and the age groups most affected are the economically productive, family-forming groups. The average age of anglophones in Quebec is rising, and the number of children is falling. Furthermore, even after the 1980 referendum, which affirmed Quebec's desire to stay in Canada, as many as 73,887 English speakers left the province between 1981 and 1985.[21]

In his 1984 study on the demographic trends in Quebec, Jacques Henripin did not foresee any change in the direction of these patterns. Examining birth rates, mortality rates, migration patterns, and linguistic transfers, he concluded that the number of anglophones in the province, in both absolute and relative terms, would continue to decline. He included economic and social considerations, incorporating four different socio-economic scenarios to arrive at his projections. Using the scenario of "mediocre socio-economic conditions and great improvement in the situation regarding French," he predicted a decline of 12 per cent in the numbers of "mother tongue" English speakers and a decline of 20 per cent in English "home language" by 2001.[22] His "low" predictions were between 3 per cent and 7 per cent for the two categories of English speakers. Just as important are his predictions for the age groups, which suggest a major increase in the proportion of the older groups and a decrease in young people ages 0–19 years. In addition to an older and declining English-speaking population, the churches are now faced with the possibility of a second wave of out-migration. Based mainly on anecdotal evidence but referring to a May 1990 Sorecom poll, a column in the *Montreal Gazette* in June 1990, under the headline "Anglo exodus has an echo," discussed the possibility that older people would begin to follow their children, partly as "a form of battle fatigue." The secondary exodus would also be linked to an understandable desire to be closer to grandchildren. The poll indicated that 10 per cent of anglophones were making plans to leave within two years, while 24 per cent said leaving was a possibility. Those most likely to go, nevertheless, are in the 18–24 age group (46 per cent) and the 25–34 group (42 per cent). The community feels threatened.

A 1984 report by Alliance Quebec made the following comment on the Henripin projections:

The English-speaking community feels no less threatened today than the French-speaking community did in the seventies. The demographic predictions for our community offer serious cause for concern. The shrinking numbers threaten our ability to maintain the institutions which support our community. This infrastructure of schools, cultural institutions, health and social service institutions is the tangible symbol of a society.[23]

Absolute numbers are important; loss of social power is important; and also important is the experience of day-to-day living with these new relationships, which seem to offer fewer opportunities, less control, and fewer choices. A telling article in the *Montreal Gazette* in March 1991 reported on the increase in calls to Tele-Aide by elderly anglophones who "don't know what to do with their homes. Their families are all moving. They have no contacts left."

The one major anglophone institution that has not been directly threatened by the new laws and political ideology has been the church. In contrast to the changed relationships the French Catholic Church experienced in the 1960s with regard to every other institutional sphere, the Protestant churches have not been directly threatened by new rules and administrations. Religion provides a way to protect ethnic and cultural identity at the level of the local community. For many people it also represents tradition, roots, shared experiences, and memories. People relate to it at both the individual and the collective levels. The church offers both local community relationships, with particular histories and myths, and, through the institutional structures, a link to traditions affirming cultural identity and rooted meaning systems.

A CHURCH IN TRANSITION

Even as Quebec Anglicans were struggling to adapt to the sociopolitical changes in the province, their church was in the midst of making changes that would affect a wide spectrum of church practice. Starting in the 1960s, Christian churches around the world began to reflect upon their role in society, on their relevance and contribution to issues of justice and public policy. Anglicans were slow to follow the lead of the Catholic Church in this movement.[24] The churches sought to become more relevant, to determine appropriate responses in an increasingly secular society. The "kiss of Peace" was revived, and as John W. Grant describes, many other innovative practices were introduced.

Celebration replaced reverence as the ideal of liturgical reformers, introducing displays of banners, flourishes of trumpets, and a revival of liturgical dance. A splendid red hymn book published by the Anglican and United churches in 1972, along with other new denominational collections, had to contend from the outset with stiff competition from contemporary compositions that made free use of folk rhythms. Some experimenters brought into play current techniques of group dynamics and sensitivity training.[25]

A 1969 study commissioned by the Anglican Church on the relationship of the church to Native peoples also contributed to a new, uncomfortable turbulence, leading to a process of self-examination. Adding to the turmoil during these years was the emergence of increasingly pronounced divergent paths within individual churches.

New cults and sects were one part of this trend. But within the mainstream churches, charismatics, evangelicals, "Catholic" Anglicans, and traditionalists became increasingly polarized, generating tensions and resentments down to the parish level. Furthermore, the ecumenism of the late 1960s had begun to wane by the early 1970s, and by 1975 the movement was in retreat. Efforts at formal ecumenical advance ceased in 1985.

An increase in plural options, even within a single denomination, has been described as one inevitable aspect of secularization, incorporating a so-called marketing approach to religion, which Reginald Bibby describes as "fragmentation."[26] Religion is expected to provide "satisfaction." Commitment, without a social milieu that supports and demands adherence, rather than being an obligation or a duty as in times past is now tied to personal fulfilment. The drop-off in church attendance is seen as a symptom of the tendency to "consume" religion selectively, and the decreasing numbers of Canadians attending services every week suggests that many feel weekly attendance is unnecessary for religious commitment.[27] Grant describes these changes with particular reference to discernible ideologies within the church.

Grant sees a tendency for selectivity and increasing distinctiveness between congregations. Evangelism has become almost synonymous with conservatism, and social action with doctrinal novelty. "What seems most lacking is a sense of historical continuity that allows for movement with the times while retaining a sense of direction from the past."[28]

This analysis reveals the divergent threads of secularization, threads that express a variety of needs and expectations among the faithful as well as various responses of the churches themselves. Across the country, fragmentation – a movement "from commitment to consumption" – seems to be a common pattern.[29] The relative proportions of people attending church had begun to decline soon after the Second World War, although absolute numbers of church members continued to grow until 1965. In Canada in 1946, 60 per cent of Protestants claimed to have attended a Sunday church service that week, a figure that dropped to 45 per cent in the mid-1950s and to less than 30 per cent by the mid-1960s. At present (1993) it is about 25 per cent.[30] In the period 1961–91, Canadian membership in the Anglican Church fell by 41 per cent, while membership in Montreal's Anglican Church decreased by almost three-quarters.

Despite these common patterns of declining membership and religious selectivity across the country, there are significant regional variations in specific aspects of religious faith. Everywhere in Canada a majority of people claim to believe in God, but as Bibby's surveys have shown, in the "practice, experience, and knowledge" of Judeo-Christian faith, there is a persistent pattern of "Atlantic High, Pacific Low."[31] The Atlantic provinces and British Columbia are at opposite ends of the spectrum in terms of commitment to religious faith as measured by regular attendance at Sunday services. Quebec shows a somewhat mixed pattern, but it approximates the Canadian average on most measures, except membership and baptisms. One difficulty in the interpretation of the 312 Quebec survey responses received by Bibby is the absence of information with respect to the proportions of French Canadians and English Canadians who responded. In his examination of data that might establish a relationship between fragmentation (different beliefs and levels of participation) and characteristics such as sex, education, and income, Bibby reached conclusions similar to those of American studies: only modest relationships could be seen. The only demographic characteristic having any importance was year of birth, or the average age of respondents, although age in itself was not shown to be an explanatory variable. "To the extent that there is a change in the commitment and participation styles of Canadians, the era in which one was born and subsequent socialization experiences have played a far more important role than formal education. Cultural and historical experience, rather than rational choice, seems to be the more important determinant of the style of religion Canadians adopt."[32]

Another study, released as the "National Long Range Planning Report" for the Canadian Anglican Church in 1986, supports these findings. The patterns of membership and participation in the Canadian Anglican Church are similar to those for all denominations. In Canada, while about 10 per cent of the population is Anglican, fewer than 10 per cent of census Anglicans worship in churches on a weekly basis, and only 20 per cent of members who are on church rolls worship on a weekly basis. The study also confirms the trends of an east-west pattern of decreasing conservatism and adherence to traditional religious participatory patterns. Some of the more prominent patterns described by the data include: (1) a variation in the ratio of confirmed Anglicans to census Anglicans, from 41 per cent in the ecclesiastical Province of Canada (Atlantic and Quebec) to 13 per cent in the Province of British Columbia; (2) a decline in average Sunday attendance by census Anglicans, from 12 per cent in the East to 6 per cent in British Columbia; (3) a declining proportion of census Anglicans who are identifiable givers, from 18 per cent in the East to 5 per cent in the West; (4) a marked decrease in the ratio of membership on parish rolls to census Anglicans, from two out of three members in the East (Province of Canada) to only one in five census Anglicans who are on a parish roll in British Columbia.[33]

When the first settlers brought the Anglican Church to Canada from Britain, the church was known as the Church of England, a name that did not change in this country until 1955. It had a central role in the maintenance of order and morality, and it was taken for granted that the church "was as necessary for civilization as language and political institutions."[34] As time went on, it became a church associated with wealth and privilege, many of its members being leaders in the Canadian corporate world. During the period of massive immigration in the first two decades of the twentieth century, the church was seen as the protector of that aspect of Canada's identity incorporated in the notion that the Dominion of Canada would reflect the "Dominion of our Lord."[35] This could be accomplished, it was thought, through the preferential encouragement of British immigrants and those of "our stock" from western and northern Europe.

The close ties of the Anglican Church to culture, class, and hierarchy were extended to the family unit, with strict rules regarding divorce, not relaxed until 1968. It has been argued that despite a tenuous correspondence between Anglicanism and the English culture, the Anglican Church has perceived itself as an important protector of English culture, incorporating symbolic gestures such as prayers on behalf of the royal family and displaying the Union Jack in their churches. In emphasizing the cultural ties to England, Anglicans have continued to present a non-welcoming face to other nationalities, apparently separating themselves as a ruling aristocracy aloof from the rank and file. "In contrast to other ethnic groups, it could afford the relaxed posture of those to whom others adjust rather than those who have to do the adapting."[36] Related to this posture, and to the Anglican Church's continuing links with the church in England is the fact that a significant number of bishops born in Britain have become leaders in the Canadian church. In 1952 only ten out of the twenty-six bishops were of Canadian birth.[37] Taking a broader definition of Canadian roots – that is, considering those who were priested in Canada – 93 per cent of the bishops between 1962 and 1976 were indigenous.

In comparison to the Canadian population as a whole, which is 68 per cent English speaking and 40 per cent British, 98 per cent of Anglican Church members are English speaking and 80.3 per cent are British. A higher than average proportion of older people and an underrepresentation of the younger age groups are tendencies in the Anglican Church. Compared to the Canadian average of 23 per cent in the over aged 50 category, 29 per cent of Anglicans are in this age group. In contrast, the aged 0–14 group accounts for 23 per cent of the general population, while this age group accounts for 20 per cent of Anglicans.[38]

When we examine the figures describing Montreal Anglicans, we see that some of these characteristics are even more pronounced in that city. An older and less mobile population is more descriptive of Anglicans in Montreal and Quebec dioceses than of Anglican populations in Toronto and Canada as a whole.[39] Nevertheless, in Montreal the average household income of Anglicans is 16 per cent higher than the Canadian average. The high proportion of older Anglicans has important implications in terms of the potential impact upon individual churches. Congregational acceptance of change, level of contributions, and the types of activities in the church will all be affected by the average age and stage in the life cycle. There are also important implications for the extent to which family histories tend to dominate the mythology and organizational norms of the churches. A combination of high average age and lower percentages of in-migrants in Quebec churches suggests a church population firmly rooted in "the way things have always been done."

The part of the "Long Range" study relating to levels of involvement provided some interesting observations. The statistics on membership, attendance, confirmation, and numbers of identifiable givers all showed strong patterns of decreasing levels of participation and involvement from east to west across Canada. For example, while nationally only one-quarter of the census Anglicans have been confirmed, the percentages vary across the country from 41 per cent in the ecclesiastical Province of Canada to 13 per cent in British Columbia (see Table 7, Appendix A). Montreal Diocese, however, shows patterns quite distinct from the rest of the ecclesiastical province. Here we find rates of participation consistently lower than the rest of eastern Canada, but consistently higher than the rest of country. With respect to percentages of census Anglicans, Montreal Diocese in 1981 had more members on parish rolls, proportionately more confirmed Anglicans, and a greater percentage of people who attended services and supported the church financially than anywhere else in Canada except the Maritime provinces. Interestingly, Quebec Diocese shows even higher rates of participation. Although it was not possible to investigate Quebec Diocese further, the data certainly suggest a process of cultural identification similar to what is being argued for Montreal. In this numerically small but territorially large diocese, extending from the Eastern Townships north to the Gaspé, the importance of the church as a community focus and as an affirmation of cultural values seems to be even more pronounced than in Montreal. This was reflected in the special 150th anniversary celebrations in July 1992 for the small church at Brookfield near Bury, attended by the bishop and the primate of Canada.

In comparisons of participation rates of various dioceses, it is recognized that Montreal has metropolitan characteristics similar to Toronto's. A comparison with Toronto Diocese shows Montreal still with higher participation rates, higher by over 50 per cent on all measures. The figures for membership confirm similar patterns. Although the definition of membership in one sense is very simple, it does present some difficulties, which are discussed in Appendix D. Simply put, membership is defined by the number of parishioners on parish lists.

While there has been a general decrease in membership across the country, the distinctive east-west regional pattern is also reflected in the membership figures. There are generally lower rates of decrease in membership on parish rolls in eastern Canada. The years of greatest decline everywhere in Canada were in the late 1960s, although the size of the relative change varied markedly, from −6 per cent (1966–71) in the Maritimes and Quebec (the ecclesiastical "Province of Canada") to −25 per cent in British Columbia. Montreal Diocese should be considered separately, since its trends are at odds with other dioceses in eastern Canada. The small rate of decline in the Province of Canada would be negligible were it not for the very sharp decrease in Montreal Diocese. The effect of Montreal on this ecclesiastical province is pronounced, especially because of the decline in Montreal's share of Anglican members, from 26 per cent in 1961 to only 10 per cent in 1986 and less than 9 per cent in 1991.

The membership in the Province of Canada, excluding Montreal, was 273,763 in 1961 and 265,631 in 1991, a small decrease of only 3 per cent. This compares to a decrease of 75 per cent for Montreal Diocese and over 41 per cent for Canada as a whole. In the 1976–81 period alone, Montreal's decline in absolute membership was double that for the rest of the ecclesiastical province combined: 6,497 for the rest of the province and 13,391 for Montreal Diocese. The sharp decrease in the number of Montreal Anglicans is, of course, directly related to the high net out-migration of anglophones described earlier.

Whereas the sharp decline in membership in Montreal is uncharacteristic of the rest of eastern Canada, the Montreal trends do have some parallels with the Toronto experience. Figure 1 in Appendix B shows the significant decrease in membership for Canada, Montreal, and Toronto, with Montreal having the sharpest rate of decrease (indicated by the steepness of the line). In the period from 1961 to 1991, Montreal Diocese experienced a decline of more than 70,000 from its parish rolls, representing almost three-quarters of its membership. In the same period there was a decrease of 41 per cent in Canadian membership and a decrease of 54 per cent in the numbers on parish rolls in Toronto Diocese. Membership across Canada experienced a precipitous decline in the period after 1966. The peak year for membership in Canada was 1964, and the greatest rate of decrease occurred in 1966–67, when in a single year there was a drop of almost 6 per cent in membership. Toronto and Montreal experienced sharper rates of decline in membership compared to the Canadian average until the 1980s, when Toronto's decrease levelled off. In the years 1966–76 Montreal and Toronto suffered similar rates of decrease. This period is bracketed by two five-year periods when Montreal experienced a percentage decline in membership twice that of Toronto and triple that of Canada. Especially notable is the decline of 26 per cent in membership in Montreal Diocese in the period 1976–81, the years during which there was the highest rate of net out-migration.

Some of the controversial issues in recent years have been the ordination of women, permitted in Montreal Diocese since 1978; admittance of young children to communion before confirmation; acceptance of an ecumenical lectionary (which stipulates the calendar of biblical readings); involvement in social issues, such as refugees; and, the most divisive issue of all, the proposal to adopt a new, "modern language" prayer book. The traditional prayer book is referred to as "the red book," the Book of Common Prayer, or the "BCP." The new prayer book, known as the "BAS," or the Book of Alternative Services, was introduced as a provisional book, approved by the National Synod in 1983 and published for distribution in 1985. It uses modern English and was introduced for a ten-year trial. Its use in individual parishes was to be at the discretion of the parish priest in consultation with the congregation. Following the trial period there would be a decision taken as to the precise nature of a new prayer book. Many debates have focused on this point alone: whether or not the church will continue with two books, whether the BAS is a "devious" introduction to an entirely new book, or whether some of the traditional BCP will be retained in one book together with sections of the modern version. At the June 1991 Montreal Synod meeting, a motion was presented asking that the national church officially recognize and approve two prayer books. Of all motions presented at that meeting, this one provoked the most vigorous discussion. In the end, with the compliance of the new diocesan bishop, the motion was tabled. To date no consensus seems imminent.

The modern English of the BAS and the various liturgical options it includes are only two of the controversial issues surrounding its introduction. There are also questions about whether doctrine is being altered and the form of the service changed in the new book. The antagonism and dissatisfaction directed towards the BAS and those who have taken strong positions in its favour reflect deep feelings that are not easily explained. As I shall suggest in the following chapters, with respect to the Montreal churches there seems to be a link to the Quebec context. Another factor is unquestionably the historical role this book has had in the church. "Public prayer in Anglicanism has, from the mid-sixteenth century, been shaped by one remarkable book. All churches are made what they are, in great measure, by their distinctive ways of worship. But the Anglican ethos is peculiar in that so little else shares the central, formative, traditional place that is occupied by the Book of Common Prayer."[40] Even in the face of differing theological emphases and outlooks, the prayer book has been the source and inspiration for the corporate expression of Anglican spirituality. It is a book that has insisted neither upon a specific shape to ministry, nor particular methods in prayer, nor even how to use the scriptures.

The earliest Church of England prayer book was basically a version of the Catholic missal and breviary. Protestant elements were gradually introduced into subsequent editions and eventually incorporated into the version of the Book of Common Prayer that was finally adopted in 1662. Their inclusion was seen to be a guarantee of the church's Protestant nature. The ongoing debate about the essential nature of Anglican faith has been reflected in parliamentary measures introduced in order to ensure the integrity of the Book of Common Prayer. The prayer book is the pragmatic focus for Anglicans, the crux of their faith. Therefore, any changes to it that seem to undermine its historical and traditional roots will inevitably be challenged. As one might expect, much of the antagonism to the BAS has come from older members of congregations, while younger people tend to be more accommodating. In the following chapters we shall look more closely at the ways in which older and younger parish members with different perceptions of community have responded to these issues.

Parish members in Montreal Diocese said goodbye to many friends, relatives, and neighbours throughout the 1970s; they experienced decreased congregations at their regular Sunday services; new laws introduced by the Quebec government underlined their minority status and restricted their freedoms in education, their public visibility, and the language of communication in their daily lives; and their national church was proposing changes that would alter the ways in which they could experience worship. There was a sense that the entire foundation of their identity and experiential life-world was being threatened. It would be surprising if there were not discernible and clearly specific ways in which Montreal Anglicans responded.

3 Response and Commitment in Montreal

The secularization of Canadian society and the socio-political pressures within Quebec were powerful forces acting upon the Anglican Church and provoking distinctive responses among the parish members. Concurrently, the church was asking parishioners to consider adopting a new prayer book, to accept female clergy leadership, and to increase their contributions to mission outreach. For many people it all seemed too much. Members began to resist both passively and in active confrontations with the church leadership. As the following pages describe, there were a variety of responses. The interesting patterns that emerged were related in part to a distinctive Quebec environment of social and political change and in part to differing meanings and perspectives of community. This chapter focuses on the evidence for a distinctive diocesan response to the Quebec milieu. After a brief examination of participation in terms of attendance at regular and festival services, we shall explore the relationships of the Montreal church to its Quebec environment as depicted in journal articles, Synod *Proceedings,* and the pronouncements of the leadership. While the Canadian trend of declining attendance is apparent, there are other significant elements of the church-society relationship that can be traced directly to the unique situation in Quebec.

ATTENDANCE

One obvious measure of religious involvement is attendance at both regular services and special festivals. Unfortunately, average attendance figures, which are reported for most dioceses in Canada, are available for Montreal only for the years 1973–77. With regard to attendance as a percentage of total membership, Montreal is shown to have a very low participation of about 17 per cent in the years 1973–77, compared to 21 per cent for Toronto and Ottawa dioceses. Although there is a slight increase in average attendance in Montreal over these years, it is not possible to draw any firm conclusions on the basis of such a brief span of time. In the case of the other dioceses, however, the availability of data over a longer time allow us to conclude that there seems to have been a steady increase in the rate of participation as measured by average attendance compared to membership. A variety of factors may explain this. Mobility patterns, for example, can affect participation rates measured in this way, insofar as new members who have recently moved into an area are more likely to attend than those whose names have been on a list for many years despite infrequent attendance. On the other hand, average attendance would rise if church corporations were to eliminate non-attenders from the rolls, thereby making the roll more reflective of actual religious commitment. Average attendance would also increase, of course, with a real increase in the attendance. One can accurately assess the meaning of these data only by referring to statistics for individual churches and by considering the role of the resident minister, who can be an important factor in the level of active participation and the size of a congregation. The variations seen in individual parishes are the subject of another chapter.

In Montreal, despite high numbers moving out of Quebec, many departing church members choose to retain an affiliation with their family church, requesting that their names remain on the parish lists. Montreal's lower average attendance as a proportion of membership may also indicate a high number of people on the fringe who claim membership but attend only once or twice a year, typically the special festivals.

The special festivals of Christmas and Easter suggest another way in which the question of active participation in the worship services may be approached. For many members, regardless of their lack of participation at any other time, attendance at these festivals is important. The commitment to faith and to the community together with the symbolic affirmation of social and community values expressed through the Easter and Christmas services draw large numbers to special festivals, and among these are many people associated with the fringe group of church members. Because it is the Easter service that is most important for Anglicans and because Christmas attendance is significantly affected by both the weather and the day of the week on which Christmas falls, the Easter attendance figures have been used. They are compared to average attendance and membership so that we might better understand the way in which people participate in their churches.

The trends in Easter communicants for Montreal and Canada are shown in Figure 5 (Appendix B), plotted on a semi-logrithmic scale. There was a steady decrease in Canada between 1963 and 1972, but since 1972 there was a slight increase in the numbers. For Montreal, however, with the exception of what might have been a significant stable period from 1972 to 1977, there has been a steady decline in the numbers of Easter communicants, probably related to the very high loss in membership associated with out-migration. What is especially interesting is the derivation of a membership to Easter communicants ratio, shown in Figure 4 (Appendix B), which indicates the extent to which membership actually reflects a degree of religious adherence. Several generalizations can be made about church participation based on these ratios (shown in Table 20 in Appendix A).

The ratios shown in Table 20 will be larger when there are relatively fewer people attending the Easter service compared to membership. To express this another way, the higher ratios indicate a larger membership in relation to the numbers of people who participate in the festival services, apparently reflecting a larger fringe group of church adherents. The data show a consistent pattern of declining ratios for Canada, indicating that of those who retain membership a larger proportion are attending at least once a year. Secondly, compared to the rest of Canada, Montreal has generally high ratios, with lower ratios than both Toronto and Canada in only one period, the four years 1961–65. The Montreal Diocese ratio is lower than the Canadian average during only one other period, from 1970 to 1976. It is possible that the lower ratios in five of these seven years reflect higher rates of participation at the beginning of the 1970s, when political tensions were rising. However, the evidence in support of this contention, based on such a short time frame, must be taken as tenuous at best.

It would appear that Montreal has in fact maintained a larger group of occasional church attenders, a fringe group, than other parts of the country, with ratios consistently higher than both Canada and Toronto since 1977. The average ratio for Montreal in this last time period is 2.48, compared to 2.32 for Canada and 1.92 for Toronto. As suggested earlier, there is also the caveat that inflated parish rolls may contribute to the higher ratios by the inclusion of non-resident members.

Whereas the mood of laity and clergy alike in Montreal's churches is frequently pessimistic and deprecating with regard to participation, in fact the evidence for involvement cannot be interpreted easily. As noted in the previous chapter, in terms of census Anglicans Montreal shows higher rates of commitment, and as we see here, the diocese has retained a larger group of occasional attenders. The challenge to the church would seem to be to increase the level of active participation.

THE "WINDS OF CHANGE" AND MUTUAL RESPONSIBILITY

The mixed messages shown in the participation figures also characterize the responses reflected in the documentary evidence. "Institutions which function on the basis of personal relationships and are sacred in character find it more difficult to compromise with an incoming group than those which are concerned with impersonal relationships and perform more secular functions."[1] In a 1954 article, Aileen Ross discussed the increasing hostility of the English-speaking population, which perceived that it was pushed out of the Eastern Townships in the 1950s. She described the gradual merging of French and English populations in economic and political institutions, but found that linguistic tensions were more apparent in the educational and religious institutions. What is particularly interesting is her observation that because of their denominational distinctions, the English-speaking Protestant churches were unable to function as rallying points for community activities and support. The religious divisions of the people were reflected in their social life. Furthermore, Protestants and Catholics were so far apart that the Protestants would do without religious services rather than attend Catholic churches when their own churches had closed.

The patterns that Ross discerned in this early period of anglophone decline in the Townships can still be seen in Montreal Diocese; they are reflected in the articles published in the Anglican newspaper and in the words of the bishop's annual addresses. This documentary evidence showing how Quebec Anglicans have responded to socio-political changes suggests that the patterns described by Ross are in fact deeply entrenched.

Until the 1950s the Protestant churches had performed a significant role in affirming Canadian identity, providing a sacralized image of Canadians as part of a homogeneous population sharing a heritage of political democracy and evangelical Christianity.[2] In the 1950s the churches lost this central role of legitimation and affirmation. Documents such as the *Montreal Churchman*[3] and the *Proceedings* of annual Synod meetings indicate a certain detachment of the Anglican Church in Quebec from its social milieu. In the socio-political ferment of the late 1960s and early 1970s, however, changes were forced upon the consciousness of church members, and the Anglican Church responded in two important ways. First, in recognizing the importance of participation in the decision-making process, the church became more actively involved in the society around it. Second, individuals began relying upon the church for affirmation and reassurance of identity and belonging. This double-edged response has carried with it both participatory and defensive attitudes. While the church is now reaching out to the wider community, its members are protecting a core of tradition. There is evidence of institutional outreach in the stated policies and directives of the leadership, but as described later, for individuals adjustment to change has been more ambivalent. In the parish churches resistance and even confrontation indicate a focus on tradition and a need for stability.

During the pivotal 1950s, the decade of transition for the church in Canada, the Synod *Proceedings* for Montreal Diocese reveal an ideology that had four main characteristics. The first was a concern for global patterns of social change and conflict, without specific acknowledgment of Quebec. The second was the desire to preserve the status quo, implied in the lack of any radical motions or discussion of new initiatives. The third was a preoccupation with administrative issues such as pensions. Finally, the rapid pace of suburbanization focused attention on a need for new churches and for the training of more priests. Not only is there no evidence that the church was actively involved in the society around it, the Synod *Proceedings* through the 1950s do not record either an awareness of or interest in Quebec society. Even the death of the formidable Premier Maurice Duplessis in 1959 did not provoke any comment in the published proceedings. References to government were invariably to the federal level and were usually commendations. In 1962, the final year of his tenure, Bishop Dixon acknowledged the outside world in his address to the annual Synod meeting: "The winds of change in the world field of the Christian bodies are forcing themselves upon our attention."[4]

In the 1960s throughout Canada, following an absolute peak in church membership in 1964, declining church attendance began to have an increasing impact upon congregations. The initial response by all denominations was in the form of studies and reports. All churches began to examine their role in society and to question the ways in which their message was being communicated. In 1964 the Anglican Church of Canada endorsed a major initiative aimed at increasing its involvement in mission through acceptance of a statement entitled *Mutual Responsibility and Interdependence*. In 1965 the United Church published its study *The Changing Church in Canada,* and in 1969 there was a study called *Ministry of the Presbyterian Church in Canada*. The Catholic Church's 1971 *Dumont Report* represented a significant attempt to increase lay involvement in the church and to work towards social justice. These studies reflected a consensus among church leaders on the need for greater participation in society and an acknowledgment that secularization seriously threatened the role of religion in society.

Indications of social awareness by Montreal's Anglican Church emerged slowly and in limited ways. During his first address to Synod in 1963, the new bishop announced the inauguration of French language training courses for priests. This was the first explicit acknowledgment of a need to integrate into Quebec life. The following year he described the church, not as a "luxury liner," but rather "as a life-boat with a mission." In the *Montreal Churchman* that year, in a front-page article reporting on the consultation on the Mutual Responsibility document, one commentator suggested, "It is easy for a minority church, as we are here .... to become a sort of club." [5] In another issue of the *Churchman*, it was pointed out that "our communion is now no longer exclusively Anglo-Saxon nor exclusively English-speaking." [6] During the next few years new committees and study groups were formed on religion and labour, foster homes, and the Protestant school system. These moves testified to a broadening commitment to participation and community responsibility. In May 1965 women for the first time were permitted to attend Synod as voting delegates. In his annual Synod address of 1967, the bishop mentioned political events at the national level for the first time when he mourned the death of Governor General Vanier and called for peace in Vietnam. Later that year a conference on poverty in Quebec specifically addressed the need for the Anglican Church to define a new role for itself as an "ally of the powerless." One participant complained that the church "is just another bastion of the Establishment and Privilege" and that it does nothing at all except "ambulance work".[7] The published evidence suggests that by the end of the 1960s the Anglican Church in Montreal was beginning to be aware of its socio-political context and to speak out on such broad social issues as women's roles and poverty. Despite this, the sources do not yet show an acknowledgment of the nationalist movement gathering momentum around it. Except for the French courses, neither the Synod *Proceedings* nor the *Churchman* gives any hint of the socio-political ferment in French Canadian society.

On the other hand, there is some evidence of official church response to public policies in the form of briefs prepared by Montreal Diocese concerning proposed legislation. In a brief written in reaction to Bill 62 (tabled in October 1969), which sought to unify the school boards under a linguistic rather than confessional administration, the diocese accepted the concept of linguistic boards as long as they stayed within the framework of confessional guarantees and freedom of choice of the language of education. There was explicit acceptance of bilingualism and recognition of an increasingly pluralistic society. One analyst, John Lee, suggests that this acceptance was rooted in an underlying attitude of self-interest. The church may be "open to the charge that immigrants were being used as a screen for English self-interest."[8] Interpretation of the motives behind the Anglican response is difficult. But whether or not it was essentially self-interest, as Lee suggests, it seems that the church leadership recognized the inevitability of an increasingly multicultural context for Quebec. It also sought a moral position affirming the need for greater equality for all. Indeed, the Anglican brief explicitly accepts responsibility for the "two solitudes" and acknowledges "our slowness to promote equality of economic opportunity."[9]

A few months later further concrete expression of concern came in the bishop's address to the annual Synod meeting in May 1970, just months before the October FLQ crisis. Bishop Maguire said that "some English-speaking Quebecers feel threatened and wonder about their future here ... [we must appreciate] the very real threat our French-speaking brothers see to their language and culture in this vast North American continent."[10] The following year he asked that the church "aim at authenticity in our role in the new developing Quebec ... In the society of our day we must be prepared to bless new forms of life, living experiences, social and economic ordering."[11] In 1972 the bishop opened his review with comments on three bills being presented in the Quebec legislature. These bills were aimed at the reorganization of the ministries of Health and Welfare and Education, and at changes in the rules for real estate assessment. This was far different from twelve years earlier, when even the death of Premier Duplessis provoked no comment. This was the first time the church had openly commented on the political process in Quebec. Within the next couple of years bilingualism had become "not simply an advantage but a necessity,"[12] and the new bishop, Reginald Hollis, in his address in 1976 commented on the political confrontation between teachers and the Quebec government. The position of the bishop's letter as set forth on the front page of the December 1976 issue of the *Churchman* reflects the importance the church now attached to the political process in Quebec. This letter focused on the results of the November 15 provincial election in which the separatist Parti Québécois won a majority of the seats in the legislature. Bishop Hollis asked the question, "Is there room for us?" Then he continued:

Whatever happens in the political field I see our church continuing to have a role here. The English "minority" is not the tiny fragment that some people imagine that it is ... Increasingly we shall try also to reach out to the French community ... Let's not forget that our Anglican Church is not just an English Church ... However, it would be foolish to deny that we are at a crossroads, a very significant point in our nation's history. [13]

In the United Church, within a year of the election of the Parti Québécois, a report of the General Council acknowledged that conflict was inevitable but saw it "as an opportunity for growth and participation and not as a tragedy or reason for avoidance." [14] A significant change in attitude was evident in the issues of the Anglican newspaper that followed all through 1977 and 1978. In the February 1977 issue there was a report on a national television broadcast by Radio Canada of a French Eucharist service at Christ Church Cathedral in Montreal. This event provoked the following slightly ambiguous poem by Keith Stowell:

En français the Anglos pray....
Who'd have thought to see the day!
Let's hope tomorrow in La Presse
The Francos don't say "What a messe!" [15]

In the same issue and on the front page, a headline proclaimed the upcoming "Silver Jubilee of Queen service at St. Matthias," commemorating the accession of Queen Elizabeth. The event had been initiated by the Monarchist League of Canada and was to be televised nationally. Perhaps the placement of the two stories, monarchy on page one and French service on page two, is indicative of the real importance attached to each initiative. Another article in this issue reported that the primate had appointed an adviser on English-French relations and referred to the establishment a few months earlier of an ecumenical consultation on the problems of Quebec. Describing the outcome of the meetings, the article noted that there was surprise among the thirteen Anglicans who participated in the consultation at "the depth of socialist feeling" expressed by the French-speaking participants. Suggestive of the extent to which Anglicans had remained detached from the evolving ideologies of French Quebec, the article reflected some apprehension about a new direction for Quebec towards a left-leaning agenda.

By the spring of 1977 the provincial government, through its White Paper, was already proposing changes to the language of education. Again the bishop responded with a front-page letter to the church members:

One of the big debates of the present is whether to speak out or to keep silence ... The government wants all areas of life to reflect the Frenchness which it equates with Quebec ... It is not surprising that in this call to "nationhood" there should be emotion ... we must speak for freedom of access for all citizens of this country to English and French education. We must protest education being controlled for political ends.[16]

A few weeks later, at the annual Synod meeting, there was vigorous debate over Quebec nationalism. In his charge (address) that opened the meeting, the bishop made strong political comments that were subsequently emphasized in the television reports. After summarizing the "good news" of diocesan life, Bishop Hollis, responding to charges that he "had his head in the sand," denied his avoidance of political realities, arguing that "the political future is not inevitably set. We have a part to play in it." He went on to point out that the church must respond to the White Paper and Language Charter (Bill 1) because of their important implications. "The use of education," he said, "to attain political ends is deplorable."

Quebec is not just a French province. How can it be a French province when there are more Anglophones here than in six of the other provinces that make up this country? I am not speaking of just the English language, but of an Anglo culture that has contributed to this province ... The English minority is not a colony of newcomers, nor are we of insignificant numbers. We belong in Quebec, we still have a contribution to make to Quebec.[17]

He gave the example of the French ministry in the diocese, noting that in past times the French Canadian community had been a tightly knit community identified with the Roman Catholic Church, but that the changing times offered new opportunities. While there seem to be overtones of defensiveness and self-justification in the message, many of the clergy for whom it was intended saw it as optimistic. The *Montreal Churchman* commented on the clergy's generally positive reactions to the address, although there were those who felt it was politically naive.

During the next two days of Synod there was heated debate about the wording of a motion to be communicated to Premier René Lévesque. The final form was as follows: "This Synod expresses its support for any Governmental legislation based on justice and equity for all and which will enhance the multi-facets of Quebec society. And be it further resolved that this Synod opposes any encroachment or infringement on civil liberties within this province."[18] As part of the letter to Premier Lévesque, the motion was published in the June 1977 issue of the *Churchman*. In the letter the bishop described the association of the Anglican Church with the English community as the "result of historical pressures and the strong identification of the French community with the Roman Catholic church." He added that there was no desire "to be an ethnic church, and many of our younger clergy are fluently bilingual."[19]

For the first time the church was being openly responsive to political events and was even attempting to enter into a dialogue with political leaders. Regardless of the fears and self-interest underlying these efforts, there can be no dispute about the fact that the church had recognized and acknowledged the significance of the changing social and political milieu. At the same time, the struggle to come to terms with the new realities was manifested in the differing points of view and debates within the church. The original motion dealing with Bill 1 was very different from the one described above, which the church eventually passed. The original motion asked that Synod support the guiding principles of Bill 1, recognizing "the legitimate concern of the Quebec government to preserve and protect French language and culture in the midst of an anglophone continent," noting anglophone worries about the infringement "upon equally vital concerns of minority groups in the province," and urging the government to "use its power to ensure the continuing vitality and strength of both anglophone and francophone communities." It is difficult today to understand objections to this statement, but at the time it initiated a vigorous, and at times hostile, debate, which ended with a complete rewording of the motion. Although several people opposed the new motion, pleading for a greater degree of trust in the government, the amended version passed with a large majority and a standing ovation for its mover.[20]

In the following issue of the *Churchman*, in September 1977, the front-page headline read, "Bishops' brief not presented." A brief prepared by six Anglican bishops had not been allowed to be presented at the government hearings. In fact, all presentations from the religious community, all of which were anglophone, had been rejected. There can be no question that the leadership in the Anglican Church felt threatened by the new legislation as well as frustrated in their inability to make themselves heard. The church began to examine its status and role in society. Three months later the newspaper reported on an "encouraging" statistical study of Montreal Diocese:

To see if the prophets of doom had any credence in their predictions that the Anglican community in this Diocese was shrinking fast due to socio-political developments, statistics have been produced covering attendance, and finances for the past 35 years. It must be granted that many experts have stated that "statistics can be made to prove anything or nothing." Whether one wishes to give a positive interpretation to such data will depend a lot on the level of one's faith. [21]

The difficulty, of course, is interpretation. The study showed a drop in average attendance of almost 7 per cent throughout the diocese, but in the same paragraph singled out two West Island deaneries where the English population had been increasing; the conclusion was drawn that "there appears to be not too much to worry about when the difference over five years [1972–77] in the case of these deaneries is a little over 4 per cent." What is particularly interesting was the comparison between the attendance and the membership figures. While attendance had dropped by 7 per cent, membership declined by 10 per cent. Membership was directly affected by out-migration, while attendance is a function of motivation. One priest who examined the statistical results of the study suggested, "The church seems strongest when facing challenge." Another priest opined, "Certainly, when one looks at the involvement of church members today and the level of their support, there's no cause for worry." The figures I have examined relating to attendance are ambiguous, but certainly those for financial commitment seem to support the notion that the level of support continued to be high. The decrease in membership stands in contrast to an increase in the number of identifiable givers, from 13,611 in 1972 to 13,740 in 1977. Those who studied the survey concluded that "although the numbers have declined the interest of the average parishioner has increased." [22]

Church leaders were concerned that social and political turmoil in Quebec would cause a loss of membership through out-migration, which would mean the gradual absolute decline of the Anglican Church in Quebec. Church leaders were publicly predicting a smaller church, but a more committed one. The bishop, in his monthly letter, noted that the statistics showed the church losing ground, and expressed the view that Anglicans should therefore "give all our powers to make our mission more effective in reaching people." [23]

Two months later his letter expressed a growing concern:

My dear people,

I'm writing a couple of days after the announcement by the Sun Life that they intend to seek approval for a move to Toronto. That really is a blow. We'd survived 1977 without the disastrous move of the anglophone population that had been predicted by some, but Sun Life's action raises speculation again about the possibility of more wholesale moves.

As a church, though, we cannot afford to live with a defeatist mentality. Instead we're going to take the initiative. By invitation of the Diocesan Council, Bishop Festo Kivengere is going to lead us in a diocesan mission next September. The mission has two purposes. One is to get [people] into church ... and the other purpose is to try and present the Christian faith in a way that can be understood by those outside the church. [24]

This initiative represented the first of several prayer and renewal conferences that marked the sixteen-year tenure of Bishop Hollis, from 1975 to 1990. While it is always difficult to separate trends in the church from the individual styles and priorities of its leaders, there is no question that Bishop Hollis was instrumental in developing a particular type of diocesan ministry that focused on prayer and renewal conferences, reflecting his personal faith. As one priest said to me, "As the bishop goes, so goes the diocese." Priests who identified more strongly with social justice issues and who tended to become involved politically, found themselves marginalized to a certain degree. As in other parts of the country, Montreal Diocese experienced increasingly distinctive streams within the church, a trend noted in a 1978 article describing the outcome of a day-long workshop: "Three different religions? If someone had not known the nature of the meeting, they might have been excused for thinking just that. But the panelists were all members of one church." [25] Even as "Anglicanism" became a more significant cultural institution within the context of Quebec's anglophone experience, there was clear evidence of distinctive Anglo-Catholic, charismatic, and fundamentalist streams within the church.

In their attention to legislation affecting education, Anglicans were expressing their apprehension about the long-term effects that restricting school enrolments would have on the English-language system. There was another controversial aspect to education, one perceived as having an impact upon the English-speaking community and, of course, upon Anglicans. This was the issue of the basis of school board organization. Beginning in the 1960s, various governmental committees had tried to change school board organization from a confessional to a linguistic definition. Apart from the constitutional guarantees provided for confessional school boards, there was also the question of control. As long as some boards retained their Protestant identity, the Anglican Church was able to claim at least a symbolic, if not a practical, responsibility for education and, by extension, for the dissemination of cultural values.

It is no coincidence that in February 1978 a major article appeared in the *Churchman* describing and commenting upon the role of religion in Quebec schools. Referring to the mandate of the Protestant Committee of the Superior Council of Education of Quebec, the article explained the role of the Protestant Committee in protecting and advancing the religious and moral values particular to Protestantism. A Protestant school, the article said, "is an institution which in its administration, pedagogical approach, and discipline, maintains those values which have been integral to the Protestant community of Quebec." The article addressed the question of the validity and desirability of having confessional boards by quoting the Protestant Committee's argument:

In short we hold to the position that the moral elevation of society does not come by abandoning one's principles to the lowest common denominator of the common school: nor is cultural survival made more likely by definitions framed in terms of the superficialities of language. Rather, moral elevation and cultural survival will come by holding fast to principles and by embodying those principles in the school system.[26]

To the charge that support of the confessional system really reflects a desire to protect English rights and privileges, the article pointed out that there were nearly 100,000 French Protestants in the province and that the number was growing. It appears that the engagement of the Anglican Church in this issue was related to its desire to retain a measure of symbolic power in the context of the institutional framework, as well as to its awareness that it should become more publicly and politically involved. The church understood the significant links between education and culture, and its own contribution to this relationship seemed to demand continuation of the confessional system. In addition to their place within the broad cultural context, schools have a multifaceted role within their communities, to encourage and support community-building relationships in a wide social context, with regard to which the Anglican Church would need to retain institutionalized links. In other words, not only was the Anglican support for confessional boards based upon broad cultural considerations, but it was linked to an understanding of the individual social experience.

From 1969 to 1978 the church became increasingly involved in the socio-political environment in which it was situated. In the spring of 1978 its efforts to come to terms with change were evident in the *Churchman*'s front-page story headlined "Premier Lévesque lectures Canadian Club," which included a photo of the bishop talking to the Quebec premier. The lead paragraph described a head table of business leaders, including "prominent Anglicans," the chancellor of McGill University, and the president of the Montreal Board of Trade. By implication rather than words, the article underlined the church's need to redefine and strengthen its role in Quebec society, both in terms of its members as business and educational leaders and in terms of its commentary on the political process. There are hints of ambivalence in the reporting. The article did not say that the premier had pointed out that business investment in Quebec had increased under the Parti Québécois, but rather that the premier had "claimed" that "investment is up in Quebec." The final quotation used in the article a statement by Lévesque: "It must be understood that free choice is out in matters of education." There was clearly a struggle in the church's adjustment to change – perceptibly that of an outsider seeking to ensure not only that it would be heard, but also that it would be responded to. The bishop's letter in the same issue of the *Churchman* expressed the uncomfortable status of Anglicans: "I do hope you will seriously pray for Mr. Lévesque as well as for our other political leaders. Prayer is a very real way in which we can make a contribution on the political front. But remember that prayer often leads us into action. If it is serious prayer it may push us into all kinds of other involvement."[27]

Not only was the church responding to society, but it was beginning to take the initiative in integrating itself through the development of a French-language ministry. A conference held in May 1978 under the theme "What it means to be a Francophone Anglican" looked at the relationship of Anglicanism to culture, at obstacles and trends in French-language ministry, and at relationships with other Christians. It seemed clear to the forty participants that "the greatest perceived need was for ways to communicate the nature of our communion in the French milieu ... The association of our church over the years with British culture has made it very difficult for us to be truly and honestly French."[28]

Another meeting of significance occurred that summer when Anglican and Roman Catholic bishops met to exchange views on political events in Quebec, the positions of majorities and minorities, evangelism, and the possibilities for improved cooperation between the churches. The following day a meeting of the Anglican leadership focused on a French-language ministry and administrative changes such as bilingual information pamphlets, prayer book, and statistical forms, none of which had ever been available in Quebec.

In his opening address to Synod that year, the bishop concluded that the impact on the church of anglophones emigrating had not been "to any considerable degree at this point." He noted the loss of "valuable lay leadership" but also remarked that the clergy had not left "seeking greener pastures." He also pointed out that the financial picture was not as bleak as some had predicted. Despite these notes of optimism, later in the Synod meetings there was lengthy discussion about a proposal to cut back the amount of money sent to the national office. Even as the per capita contributions were rising, the awareness of declining membership was causing Montreal Diocese to hold back on contributions outside its borders.

The church in Quebec was also being buffeted by changes in the national church, specifically by the controversies around Christian initiation (baptism) and the ordination of women, which had been approved by the National Synod in 1975. In 1978 Montreal Diocese accepted the ordination of women, and in October of that year the first woman priest was ordained in Montreal, despite protest by a small but articulate group of clergy and lay members.

The beginning of 1979 seemed to offer a greater degree of stability even though political uncertainty continued to preoccupy the church. The bishop acknowledged that 1978 had seen a 25 per cent turnover in clergy – "unusually high for us" [29] – but he continued to call for an optimistic perspective, seeing the new year as one of "opportunity and challenges." [30] In fact, an awareness of these challenges was reflected in the financial commitment of parishioners. As will be discussed in chapter 4, growing insecurity was apparent in the responses of the parishes to the National Synod's request for increased financial contributions. On the one hand, delegates to Synod balked at increasing their "apportionment," which would support initiatives of the national church, while on the other, parishioners gave more to their local churches.

Coming into the 1980s in Montreal, the Anglican Church was a changed institution. The struggle to retain a strong sense of purpose and identity continued as the church engaged in the debates leading up to the referendum of 21 May 1980, which asked Quebecers to decide whether they wished to proceed to negotiations on sovereignty-association. During the months leading up to the referendum, articles in the *Churchman* referred to discussions among the bishops of both the Roman Catholic and Anglican churches. In his monthly letters published in the *Montreal Churchman*, Bishop Hollis called for church members to become politically involved; an editorial even suggested a Lenten study program that would focus on the theological implications of sovereignty. The editorial pointed to adjustments the Anglicans had made: "We have to come to grips with being a minority within a minority." In May a communiqué was signed by ten Anglican bishops urging the laity to "play as full a part as possible in the development of political structures." A summary of the Synod *Proceedings* prepared for the June issue of the *Churchman* provides a telling glimpse of the ways in which people in the church were responding. Father Bradley described the opening Eucharist service as one expressing the "desire to hold onto the traditions we have." He continued: "The opening Eucharist was a return to the older pattern of clergy vested and sitting separately, which gave a chance for a lot of colour. Banners and crosses seemed to abound as three bishops, archdeacons and canons were appropriately attended and distinctively seated in places of honour."[31]

The bishop's charge that year included a paragraph in French, and fully one-half of it addressed the question of Quebec and the changing socio-political environment. The bishop wrote: "Whatever the vote in the referendum, we have a contribution to make to life in Quebec. As a church we have been here for 220 years, and that cannot be lightly abandoned. Indeed, our hope is to widen our contribution to Quebec."[32] When one contrasts this address with those presented in the 1960s, one can see a dramatic change. The bishop went on to acknowledge "with regret" that nothing had been done to advance French-language evangelism. Nevertheless, the front page of the April issue of the *Churchman* announced the "première ordination en français à Montréal" of a deacon from Zaire. The rejection of a "yes" vote in the referendum gave the church an opportunity to address other concerns. That there was a sense of relief following the referendum result is evident in the fact that subsequent news stories contained fewer specific references to the Quebec political situation.

By September 1980 the *Churchman* included more articles on issues such as the new prayer book, Third World involvement, and refugees, as well as on administrative concerns, such as the renovation of the Christ Church Cathedral in downtown Montreal. The bishop's letter referred to the cathedral renovation as a sign that the church was not "fading away." The increase in adult confirmations, he said, did not point to "a dying church" and the six churches achieving rectory status did not reflect a church that was "closing up shop." He also reported on the creation of a task force that would consider the future "deployment of ordained personnel." While there were many signs of strength, the bishop's need to point to them is indicative of the existence of ongoing concern for the future of the church.

In his address opening Synod in 1981, Bishop Hollis commented on the changing demographics of the Anglican Church, characterized by "less Anglo-Saxon and more the Canadian cultural mix." He affirmed the "need to be involved in political processes that shape our society." Later that year he "deplored" the use of emotional levers by politicians in their attempts to guide the constitutional debate. He urged fellow Anglicans to "express our disquiet" over the rhetoric being used. While Quebec Anglicans continued to feel "the pressures of living in our province under what at times appear to be discriminatory measures,"[33] they also were more receptive to the idea of "mission." "Wardens enthusiastically support mission" headlined a story about parish budget commitments in 1981. Individual parishes had pledged an increase of 10 per cent in their mission allotments, money that would be used outside their parishes. Other indications of an opening up to global responsibilities came with the publication of the church's social service report in 1982. "In the decade preceding this report, the Diocese of Montreal has indicated clearly a renewed interest and intent to pursue more actively broad areas of social concern."[34] The report noted the support given to Vietnamese refugees, the increasing involvement of Anglicans in school chaplaincy work, and Anglican contributions to the debate over the government's proposal to deconfessionalize school boards.

At the same time as the church was actively responding to the social and political context around it, there was evidence of increased commitment in another area. Some Anglicans sought to protect their church by increasing their financial contributions. The bishop's letter in March 1982 noted conflicting responses to Quebec's unstable environment:

I'm faced with two pictures. The first is a depressing one, but the second is in stark contrast to the first and gives me encouragement. A recent poll shows the possibility of a significant decrease in the Anglophone population within five years. There is a growing frustration that Anglophone opinion carries no weight with the government. Our school system is threatened ... The second picture is from some personal returns that the clergy prepared for me ... the financial picture across the diocese was very encouraging for 1981. The reality is that church members want our church to stay and to bear witness.[35]

Accompanying concerns over the financial stability of the church and declining membership were apprehensions about changes being proposed and adopted within the church itself. Montreal Anglicans were confronted with significant changes in liturgy, the form and language of worship, and women's ordination, and with the question of pre-confirmation children receiving communion. Together with these liturgical issues social issues regained prominence in the wake of Quebec's socio-political storm. Stories in the *Churchman* focused on women's issues (for example, the establishment of the Ecumenical Women's Centre), homosexuality, AIDS, and abortion.

Summarizing the many changes in his tenure of sixteen years as bishop, Hollis pointed out the following:

Our social service ministry has expanded, with St. Michael's Mission being firmly established for the transient at the Church of St. John the Evangelist, with the opening of Auberge Madelaine for transient women, with the formation of the Montreal Pastoral Institute as an ecumenical centre for counselling, and with an active programme to aid refugees at Tyndale–St. George

... We still have a long way to go in the area of French ministry, but the diocese is now much more related to the French fact than it was when I became bishop.[36]

A more public and politically engaged ideology was accompanied by resistance and defensive behaviour in relation to the initiatives for change proposed by the national church. On the one hand, there was recognition of the need to be involved in society, locally and globally; on the other hand, the members were painfully aware of the threat to their daily life-worlds of experience through which they assumed their identities. Parishes feared for their survival and through individual members expressed a need to retain traditional forms.

THE PRAYER BOOK AND CONFLICT IN THE CHURCH

Individuals behave in distinctive ways when they feel cut off from the flow of time, excessively attached to the past, isolated in the present, without a future, or rushing toward one.[37]

As Montreal Anglicans struggled to adjust to the social and political changes around them, feeling cut off from the mainstream of events and powerless to influence them, they were also faced with changes within the church itself. For some this challenge has created enormous difficulties. One of the most traumatic changes in the church has been the introduction of a new prayer book. The first part of this section will describe the various responses to the new prayer book, as reflected in the monthly newspaper, parish newsletters, interviews, and the results of a survey I conducted in 1988. A national survey on the level of acceptance of the new Book of Alternative Services was conducted a few months earlier, so there is a basis for comparison. I shall be arguing that the strong opposition to the proposed new prayer book (a book of "alternative" services) in Montreal is related, in part at least, to the insecurities caused by the unstable social and political milieu. While the strength of opposition is difficult to measure, Montreal Diocese appears to have been particularly resistant to adopting the new BAS prayer book. The following story appeared in a parish newsletter in 1987:

For all of us Christmas Present is enhanced by memories of Christmas Past. On Christmas Eve we drive ... somehow always through a gentle fall of snow ... to where the lights of the church gleam yellow through the night, the aromas of evergreen and hot wax greet us, and the old familiar carols which we have sung since grade school once again shake the rafters. And, though in our peripatetic lives the voices in the chancel may change, the words of the service echo down through the years. This is Peace, and Joy, and Home. What if. What if after the turkey has been pummeled about, after the grandchildren have been put to bed with the same rituals their parents expected, we drive to our church and find a "For Sale" sign? With a "Sold" sticker superimposed. Sound like nightmare country? Look around ... it's happening.[38]

Written by a 68-year-old woman, the story shows her own fears for survival. She describes her own journey back to her roots in a small Townships village. Finding the little church converted to offices was a "considerable shock," and in the cemetery where her parents were buried, "the grass was very long, one of the tall tombstones had toppled over and there was a sinister looking subsidence in one corner." Turning from her past, she looked at her own parish today, a few miles from downtown Montreal, and wondered about the future. She was expressing her need to preserve the landscapes, traditions, and language of her Anglican Church. She was threatened by the changes around her – some changes only vaguely understood and others challenging her sense of rootedness. For her, the words in the new prayer book do not "echo down through the years."

Following its publication in the fall of 1985, the Book of Alternative Services was introduced into Montreal Diocese in the spring of 1986 on the understanding that it was to be on a trial basis. While there have been some reasoned arguments of a theological nature put forward against specific changes incorporated into the BAS, much of the debate has focused on the modern language. The debate has for the most part been local and emotional, and it has had a profound impact on the individual church member. It has often been conducted surreptitiously rather than in open forum. In Montreal, parishes have been divided, people have left the church, and ministers have been personally attacked and blamed. Contentious issues include changes in the order of service, the emphasis on the Holy Spirit being called down upon inanimate objects, the introduction of the "exchange of the Peace," and the very language of worship. While congregations have not been especially concerned about the first two matters, the dissension generated by the new language and the exchange of the Peace has been profound.

In its editorial in March 1988, the *Montreal Churchman* commented, "No gain without pain." Church leaders, it stated, would do well to apply the words of the hymn "Only he who bears the cross may hope to wear the glorious crown" as they attempt to resolve the "portentous issues presently occupying much of our attention and energy." The editorialist described the situation in his own parish:

There is deep feeling, both for and against. We are using both books, and three forms of the Eucharist. Not everyone is happy; some are disgusted. Some will not budge to exchange the Peace; others leap into action, beaming bright like the Star of Bethlehem in orbit for a dubious birth. But the Sacrament is unchanged ... Grace is invalidated only when we refuse to accept it: not by strange words, or actions that invade our privacy, or female priests. [39]

The bishop's support of the new prayer book, as reflected in his annual addresses to Synod, was consistently cautious. While acknowledging that the Anglican Book Centre could be "justly proud" of the BAS's format, he also pointed out that the Book of Common Prayer published in 1959 was still the official book of the church, and he left the decision as to the use of the new prayer book up to the individual parishes. In his 1987 address, Bishop Hollis noted that the introduction of the BAS had been difficult in some parishes, and he stated that its use at the opening Eucharist at Synod that year signalled the beginning of its use in alternate years. He underlined the need for parishes to give the book a "healthy trial" so that they might provide useful feedback to the national liturgical commission. And in 1988 he again asked that "the voice of the wider church be heard" in order to ensure an effective process of revision.

His words did not hint at the storms gathering strength in many parishes. Because the bishop left the timing and method of introduction of the BAS to individual clergy, its successful introduction depended to a large extent upon the diplomacy, personality, and communication skills of the local priest as well as upon the relationship between the rector and the congregation. One priest said to me (not entirely in jest), "Whatever I tell them, they'll do." But there has never been a BAS service at his church because its introduction would finally drive away the last of the elderly congregation. At churches where the BAS is used once a month on a regular basis, certain parishioners do not attend those services. Many churches have two congregations: those who attend only BCP services and those who attend regardless of which prayer book is used. At an annual vestry meeting in 1988 there was vigorous discussion about a proposal to increase the number of BAS services per month from one to two. The matter was put to a vote, and the result was a tie (13 to 13). The priest opted for the status quo.[40] At another church, where there has been almost no use of the BAS, the congregation was so opposed to it that the clergy scarcely mentioned the possibility of its introduction. I asked one member of this church for her opinion of the new prayer book. Her response was unequivocal:

I love the traditional hymns and the choir. I don't like the kissing and shaking hands in the Peace. That's an invasion of my private space. I want the service to just kind of roll over me. I don't want to think about the words. I've said the traditional service for all my life; I don't even need the prayer book. I used to go to church six days a week when I was growing up. Dad would never miss church on Sundays in Toronto, and the other five days was when I was at school [a private girls' school]. That is all part of me.[41]

When I asked her what she would do were the BAS to be used at the regular eleven o'clock service, she replied that she doesn't want it forced on them, and if it were she would simply leave. "No fuss. I'd just kind of quietly slide out." Another parishioner at the same church described the process by which the rector had introduced the new prayer book. When, after three special meetings called to "explain" the BAS, it became obvious that the congregation would not accept it, the solution adopted was to have a third service on Sunday mornings for those who wanted to use the new, modern-language book. The result was a service that attracted five to ten people and was discontinued after about eighteen months. The man describing this process to me said that when he had informed a meeting of the advisory board of the book's general acceptance across Canada, "it was like closing an iron door; the faces turned to stone. One person said that sociability was for outside the church."[42] The parishioner had told the meeting that at a California church he had found the exchange of the Peace a joyful experience and he wondered whether it was not "sad" that they seemed so morose about their faith. At that point someone had jumped up and "sternly, with great emotion, said 'How can you make jest with what we take very seriously indeed?'"

In those churches in the diocese where the BAS has general acceptance, two factors seem to be important: the attitude and communication skills of the rector and the characteristics of the congregation. The relationship between these factors is both dialectical and in a very delicate balance. While the characteristics of the social group and community of the church seem to be the dominant factor, the role of the rector can be decisive. At a suburban church with a mobile population and an active Sunday school, introduction of the BAS was achieved relatively comfortably. By a general consensus of the monthly advisory board, not by a formal vote at the annual vestry, the congregation agreed to use the BAS at about half of the regular services. It was gradually used more and more. At one meeting someone mentioned this, with the mild complaint that he always seemed to be "flipping back and forth" (from section to section). The response from one of the wardens was: "I'm older than you and I manage!", at which everyone laughed.

These two very different congregations clearly had very different reactions to the new prayer book. The two congregations were experiencing themselves as community in fundamentally different ways. In the older church, built in the nineteenth century, the central importance of tradition was a defining characteristic of the group identity; the need to protect and promote the status quo was a dominant element permeating every element of church life. In the newer suburban church, on the other hand, the community was characterized by high mobility and a high proportion of young families. Shared activities rather than "memory" defined the meanings and commitment for members.

One public manifestation of opposition to the new book was the organization of the Prayer Book Society, first formed in Toronto in 1986 soon after the publication of the BAS. In October 1988 an inaugural meeting for the establishment of a Montreal branch was held at St Matthias Church. Disclaiming any ideological connection with the organization, the rector of St Matthias assured me that "they" were simply renting the facilities. Despite the disclaimer, it is likely no coincidence that the meeting site selected was a church where the BAS was not used. With about 150 people attending, the large hall was almost full. In the audience were both Montreal bishops (Bishop Hollis and his adjutant, Bishop MacLean), ten clergy, and laity from about ten different churches. Men outnumbered the women. The theme announced for this meeting was "The Prayer Book and the Church in Crisis," and one of the handouts was a quotation from a letter to the *Daily Telegraph* (January 1987), written by Terry Waite just before he disappeared on his ill-fated mission to Beirut: "Over the years, in very many ways, we have removed ourselves from our history and our heritage ... the secular spirit devours everything within its path ... We need to be restored to our past so that we can continue confidently into the future. Oh for leaders who know the language of symbol ... who realize that bread alone does not satisfy."[43]

In his opening remarks to the meeting, the chairman said, "We are members of this organization because we're deeply concerned to keep the prayer book central to the Anglican faith." The speaker, Dr Robert Crouse, defined liberal and conservative factions in the church, the first being those for whom truth is related to personal experience and the second being those who believe that "truth is tied definitely to scripture." He went on to say that "the task of a conservative with his [sic] belief is obedience and understanding," and suggested that the issue of the prayer book is "not an isolated phenomenon" but rather only the beginning of a significant "reformation." The prayer book, he pointed out, "has shaped our spirituality; our self-definition as Anglicans." He expressed concern that with the ongoing liturgical chaos there might be no decision taken on a new book for at least ten years. "The American church should serve as an object lesson for us, where the use of the traditional book has been declared illegal."[44]

During the question period someone asked whether the BAS was a deviation from sound doctrine. Admitting it was a difficult question, Dr Crouse replied, "The short answer would be 'yes.'" Many of the clergy at the meeting seemed intent on expressing their support for the new book. One priest pointedly exposed the many-faceted traditions of the Book of Common Prayer when he asked which version of the book Dr Crouse considered to be "the tradition." Another priest expressed concern that the speaker had made an inappropriate connection between the BAS (as cause) and the fact that the Anglican Church now remarries divorced people. Dr Crouse denied the causal relationship but did suggest that indeed the BAS "recognizes and, in a sense, sanctifies certain changes ongoing in society."

During the entire discussion only three or four people asked questions that indicated support for the speaker, and neither of the bishops said anything at all. While most of the people at the meeting appeared to support the views of the Prayer Book Society, most of the priests in attendance spoke in defence of the BAS.

Six months later another meeting was held, attended by only about fifty people. A petition was distributed, to be signed and sent to the bishop, requesting that "the starting point of any future revision of the Anglican liturgies be the Book of Common Prayer." In his address to Synod later that week, Bishop Hollis expressed support for the ongoing revisionary work of the national liturgical commission; he asked for mutual understanding, as "we are not all helped to worship by the same forms" and the acceptance of divergent forms "might save our church from losing numbers." Despite the Prayer Book Society, there seems to have been only limited interest in active participatory opposition to the BAS. Nevertheless, the results of the surveys show a strong core of opposition in Montreal, more pervasive than in other parts of the country.

The national survey took place at the end of 1987, and by May 1988, 40.5 per cent of congregations who received the questionnaire had replied. My own Montreal survey was mailed in March 1988, with final returns of 73 per cent received by August. In both surveys, questions were asked about the extent of use of the Book of Alternative Services and about whether or not the churches own copies of the book. The major difficulty in interpreting the results derives from the use of the word "regularly," since it can be interpreted to mean either once a month or once a week.

At the national level, 70 per cent of congregations use primarily the BAS for Eucharist services, and 20 per cent of congregations do not use the BAS regularly. The most conservative of the dioceses is Fredericton, where only one-third of parishes use it for Eucharist services. After (in order) Fredericton, Quebec, and Nova Scotia, Montreal is the most conservative diocese in the country. This pattern corresponds precisely to an east-west conservatism described by Bibby and geographer David Ley.[45] On the other hand, because Montreal is a metropolitan diocese, one would anticipate certain similarities to the experience of Toronto. Comparing the nation's two metropolitan dioceses, one sees a marked contrast: in Toronto only one in six congregations do not use the BAS regularly, whereas in Montreal almost four in ten are in this category. Using another measure, in Montreal only half the parishes use primarily the BAS for the Eucharist, whereas in Toronto nearly three-quarters do.

In suggesting that metropolitan factors should take precedence over eastern conservatism, I am proposing that the social group of Anglicans in Montreal is more similar in attitudes and values to Toronto than to the Maritime provinces. The patterns of migration, mobility, and interaction between the two cities provide a basis for attitudinal convergence.[46] The fact that Montreal Diocese shows a substantially lower rate of acceptance of the BAS than Toronto Diocese can be attributed not to an eastern regional conservatism but to a need for the kind of stability and rootedness that can be found in the tradition of the prayer book. If the socio-political situation in Quebec had not been so threatening, and had there been higher rates of in-migration of young families over the past thirty years, there might have been greater acceptance of the new prayer book in Montreal.

In my survey, for which there were seventy returns (representing seventy congregations and a 73 per cent rate of return), 43 per cent use the BAS at all or most services, while 70 per cent use it at some or most and 31 per cent do not use it at all. In order to assess the extent to which churches were accepting other changes proposed by the national church, the questionnaire included questions about the new lectionary and the admission of pre-confirmation children to communion. Only fourteen congregations use the BAS exclusively, use the Ecumenical lectionary as well, and admit pre-confirmation children to communion. Sixteen use the BAS most of the time but do not admit pre-confirmation children to communion. These thirty congregations, representing 43 per cent of the respondents, would approximately correspond to the national survey figures for the use of the BAS at Eucharists. The national data show 53 per cent of Montreal congregations using the BAS frequently, somewhat higher than my measure, which was based on a higher rate of return. I suspect that an explanation for the difference lies in the characteristics of the parishes that returned their national surveys, characteristics generally common to those who do use the BAS.

Resistance to the BAS seems to be related to a population change that is perceived as a threat to the local church; to the characteristics of the congregation, especially in terms of age, mobility, and family histories; and thirdly, to the effectiveness of the leadership, especially the rector's success in communicating the desirability of adopting the BAS.

The degree to which the church is integrated into the wider community and functions as a focus of social interaction seems to have an important effect on the level of acceptance of change within the church. The results of the survey show that most of the churches that have refused the BAS are located in areas of significant population change. In churches dominated by "old families" and by a sense of tradition and historical precedent, there is frequently a perception of community based upon memory rather than upon active shared participation in church activities in the present. When the social group that defines these churches feels threatened by declining church membership, there tends to be a powerful motivation for retaining old and familar forms. As a generalization, it is the churches in central Montreal, in the Townships, and in the Laurentians that have resisted adopting the new prayer book. Most accepting have been churches located in areas of growing anglophone populations (especially the West Island) and areas of high mobility where youthful populations have not been strongly inhibited by older, more conservative congregations. Where the BAS has been accepted for frequent use in older and declining churches (such as St Columba in Notre-Dame-de-Grace, and St Ignatius in Mascouche), the rector seems to have played an important role in encouraging the adoption of the new prayer book.

Consideration of the twenty-one churches that do not use the BAS at all gives some weight to the suggestion that uncertainty about the future and the perception of a threat to the continued existence of the home church can inhibit acceptance of change. St Matthew's and St Thomas, for example, have experienced among the highest rates of decrease in their membership (over 80 per cent compared to the diocesan average of 66 per cent), and at these churches the red book is used almost exclusively. Traditional forms and rituals may acquire added importance as symbols of stability. Characteristics of the congregation itself, exclusive of social class, may contribute to entrenched traditional forms. Grace Church in Point St Charles and St Matthias in Westmount, at opposite ends of the socio-economic spectrum, have similar negative attitudes to the BAS. Each of these congregations has a strong nucleus of people whose histories in their churches span thirty to fifty years. Their sense of identity extends beyond Anglicanism to incorporate a socio-cultural context in which shared family histories are important.

Similarly, at several of the downtown churches, a legacy of generational rootedness gives added meaning to the membership. At St George's, St John the Evangelist, and St James the Apostle, use of the Book of Common Prayer seems to be linked to a tradition of a cultural elite with shared memories and family histories. The parishioners share a symbolic community of meaning in using the older book with its familiar order and words. Two other spatial groupings of churches that have not accepted the BAS are on the South Shore (including two in Longueil and Greenfield Park and several in the Eastern Townships) and in the Laurentians, north of Montreal. These churches, too, have experienced severe losses in membership because of out-migration of English-speaking residents, but also because of the increased spatial concentration of anglophones on the island.

Three West Island churches (in Pointe Claire and in Lachine) and several in Eastern Montreal belie these generalizations. The three on the West Island have refused to adopt the new book, while those in Eastern Montreal are using it. In both instances it appears that the incumbent rectors have had important roles in determining the liturgical form. In the West Island, despite a community of young families, the conservative clergy leadership at one church and a strong older women's group that dominates the decision-making structures at the others have acted as brakes on any initiation of change. In the Eastern Montreal area, on the other hand, a rapidly declining anglophone population characterized by a homogeneous, middle-class social group has accepted the strong leadership of young, enthusiastic clergy who have supported the new prayer book. The role of leadership in the Eastern Deanery churches has been a critical factor in acceptance of change.

Other changes have been introduced in recent years in the Anglican Church, most of which have met with opposition in Montreal. One of these is the proposal to permit pre-confirmation children to have communion. In Montreal Diocese the acceptance of this has been slow compared to dioceses in western Canada. At the Synod meeting in 1980, for the third successive year there was a lengthy debate about this issue. In the end the motion was referred back to the parishes for further study. At one church this issue was discussed for almost three years, and after about six public meetings, to which very few parishioners came (despite the church's concern that there would be an outcry if the proposal was accepted), the issue was settled at the annual vestry meeting in January 1991. It was decided that children who had received communion in other dioceses could receive communion, and if specifically requested, children whose families were active in the church would also be permitted to receive communion. Even today the guidelines are ambiguous enough to allow a rector to make on his own the decision to accept children for communion prior to confirmation, without consulting his parishioners. The only firm request on the part of the bishop has been that children who have received communion in other dioceses be allowed to continue. Possibly linked to the east-west conservative trend noted earlier, resistance to this change also appears to be related to a need for stability and tradition.

Another change for the church came in 1982 when the new lectionary, the scheduled pattern of biblical readings, was introduced. Not everyone was happy about it, and even today many churches in the diocese do not adhere to it, keeping instead with the lectionary given in the traditional prayer book. In his letter in the *Churchman* in May 1982, Bishop Hollis outlined his reasons for asking that the new lectionary be used, pointing out that it would contribute to unity in the church across the country and provide an "ampler selection of Scripture readings." Replying to an individual who asked if "change is really necessary?", the bishop said he was not "lightly abandoning the Prayer Book," but that "convenience" was not a reasonable basis for retaining the older form.[47] Nine years later many churches still do not use the new lectionary.

CONCLUSION

This exploration of the changes in the church's socio-political consciousness since 1961 and of the responses to proposed changes within the church structures themselves illustrates many ambiguities and contradictions at both the individual and collective levels of church life. There have been both positive efforts to integrate into the socio-political milieu of Quebec and defensive responses to internal change. As we shall see in the next chapter, even more profound responses have been identified in relation to the patterns of financial contributions that have helped to alleviate the reality of a serious decline in membership. Compared to the country as a whole, attendance at Montreal festival services has not fallen off as sharply and there has been a greater propensity to maintain nominal membership through the parish rolls. As William Westfall has suggested, "in times of crisis people turn to religious institutions in order to understand the problems they face."[48] Indicative of the Anglican Church's desire to be more integrated within the Quebec community are some of the new initiatives: encouragement of the clergy to learn French; presentations to the government of particular points of view; and the appointment of special committees on French-English relations. While there has been outreach towards the Quebec community, however, there has also been defensive behaviour. In apparent efforts to ensure stability within the church, some parishes have resisted proposed changes, particularly the new prayer book.

All of these attitudes and actions, both positive and defensive, reflect concerns of people whose personal histories, meanings, and identities have been threatened. An examination of the patterns of financial contributions reveals a dramatic picture of people protecting their heritage, the physical legacy defining their histories and family roots. At the same time, increased generosity is tempered by a more narrow focus of concern, as the local church assumes greater priority than the global church and Karl Mannheim's ideological religion can be seen to preside over a spirit of utopian initiative.

4 Commitment to the Church, Tradition, and Finances

Ethnicity, religion, education, and age: these are four fundamental characteristics that shape and influence man's humanistic behaviour. More subtle, but perhaps equally important, are actions and patterns rooted in how man chooses (or is ordained) to organize his life and occupy his days – lifestyle.

Samuel Martin[1]

One way in which commitment to religious faith is measured is through financial contributions. For Montreal Anglicans confronted by shrinking congregations, budgets became an increasingly important part of discussions at annual meetings and a focus of efforts to ensure the ongoing viability of individual churches. Churches throughout the diocese were worried about the impact of the high levels of out-migration upon their financial viability. Growing insecurity was apparent in the responses of the parishes to the request from the National Synod for an increase in financial commitment. In 1979, rather than accede to the request for $196,000 as its fair apportionment, Montreal Diocese agreed to only $180,000. For the second year in a row the Montreal church was responding defensively, cautiously protecting its financial security and holding back on contributions to the wider church. Resistance in the parishes to the diocesan treasurer's expressed concern that Montreal was not "accepting [its] fair share" was countered by a precedent-setting meeting of parish corporations convened by Bishop Hollis. "Underlining the seriousness of the meeting, the clergy have been told by their bishop to rearrange schedules to ensure attendance ...

The meeting, which will set the level of parish commitment for 1980, replaces the former system of target apportionments."[2]

At a time of significant pressure on financial resources and with every indication that membership would continue to decline, the church was attempting to introduce a new method of communication to ensure that budgetary commitments could be met. As the editorial on the front page of the *Churchman* pronounced: "At last a meeting has been called with real financial teeth ... A procedure of real commitment should ensue ... At last we will see a really democratic meeting of the diocese, freed from the filter of second-hand reports, freed from the delay of isolated decision-making."[3] Even the news reporting seemed to reflect the pent-up concern for financial stability in the face of social and political insecurities. The financial data are particularly interesting because the patterns they exhibit run counter to those we would expect on the basis of national surveys of philanthropic and altruistic involvement of Canadians in general and Quebecers in particular. They clearly indicate that the patterns of contributions by church members are at odds with the patterns of all charitable giving in Quebec. Interpreting the financial data of the diocese necessitated consideration of the wider question of philanthropy in Canada because the national patterns of philanthropic giving provide a base against which we can assess the significance of the Montreal data relating to donations to the church.

The decision to donate time, talents, and money to humanistic causes is grounded in cultural, social, historical, economic, political, psychological, and philosophical forces. For years Samuel Martin has attempted to discover and describe the patterns underlying the decisions and behaviour associated with humanistic activities. In his book *An Essential Grace*, Martin identifies three clusters of factors: the ability to give (wealth, income, taxation); "Level One" influences, or high-order motives, emanating from inner values, such as tradition, religion, philosophy, and altruism; and "Level Two" factors, or those that originate outside the individual, such as ethnicity, education, recognition, and social acceptance. He comes to the conclusion that, although income and ability to give are factors affecting charitable donations, the fact remains that "no force in society is more pervasive and powerful than religion in shaping man's philosophy, his feelings and behaviour to mankind, his moral conscience, his benevolence."[4] His studies and those of other researchers all confirm a strong correlation between the degree of religious commitment and the level of financial generosity to all humanistic organizations. Contribution to religious groups is the single most important factor in explaining or predicting the inclination to donate time or money to all groups. He found that more money is donated by individuals to religious organizations than is raised through donations from all sources by all other charitable organizations combined. His data support the contention that a high degree of religious commitment is the strongest single motive for giving money to the church. One of the most interesting findings, however, was that the degree of religious commitment also showed a consistent and powerful association with donations to non-religious organizations. [5]

Supported by statistically significant data, Martin demonstrates that generosity declines systematically with a decrease in a family's stated religious commitment. He goes on to point out the implications for philanthropy in Canada of fewer people maintaining strong religious ties, thereby foregoing the religious-moral philosophy that emphasizes responsibility, compassion, and sacrifice. Table 6 in Appendix A summarizes his findings.

Not only are those who have a strong religious commitment more likely to donate their time and money to humanistic causes than is the average Canadian, but the amount of their contribution as a proportion of their income is almost nine times higher than the average. In his regression model, Martin identifies a hierarchy of factors affecting the *amount* of family donations. In descending order of importance they include degree of religious commitment, level of family income, number of dependent children, and, for Protestants, affiliation with other Protestant denominations. In addition, there are factors related to the donations as a *proportion* of family income, which includes those already listed, plus the number of community organizations served, Anglo-Saxon racial origin, level of residential and occupational mobility, and education. Significantly, the level of family wealth (as distinct from income) was not strongly associated with either the absolute or the relative size of donations.

Studies by J.F. Deeg and Harry Kitchen show relationships of philanthropy to income, family life cycle, and regionalism that have important implications for the data in my study. The contributions of Montreal Anglicans to their churches run counter to the regional patterns of philanthropic activity in Canada defined by Deeg, Kitchen, and Decima Research for the Centre for Philanthropy. A study by Deeg based on income tax returns shows that the percentage of people who contribute to charitable causes has been declining since 1970. "The proportion of Canadian taxpayers claiming charitable donations (i.e. over $100) in 1980 was significantly lower in all income categories." [6] The same study shows that the most significant decrease occurred among high-income earners. Fewer than

50 per cent of families earning over $50,000 claimed deductions in 1980, compared to 78 per cent in 1970. Pensioners, on the other hand, showed the highest proportion of income given to humanistic causes.

The regional pattern of philanthropy described in the Deeg and Kitchen studies is of particular significance in relation to the patterns for Quebec and for the francophone population. Table 10 in Appendix A shows clear regional and urban differences in the amount of charitable donations per taxpayer (which provides a measure of the participation rate) and per donor (which indicates the size of actual donations). Quebec has the lowest average per taxpayer donation, less than half the national average, and the second lowest average per donor in Canada, almost 30 per cent lower than the Canadian average. In Quebec almost 40 per cent of families make no charitable donations, while in other regions non-contributers range from a high of 27 per cent in British Columbia to a low of 16 per cent in Atlantic Canada.[7] The low values for Quebec apply regardless of whether or not the receiving institution is religious (Table 13, Appendix A).

While there is a difference between the anglophone and francophone patterns within Quebec (Table 14, Appendix A), donations by Quebec anglophones still remain significantly below those in other parts of Canada. This distinctive regional pattern of contributions highlights the fact that even when linguistic characteristics are taken into account, Quebec anglophones give substantially less than people in all other regions of the country.

These statistics underline a dichotomy that makes the Montreal Anglican figures especially interesting. Contrary to the data on humanistic involvement in Canada (in decline) and to the data on relative donations made by all Quebecers, the financial data for Montreal Diocese indicates substantial levels of support and significant increases in per capita contributions, in constant dollars, especially since 1976.

Despite the fact that Quebec anglophones have a lower record of charitable donations than people in all other parts of the country, Montreal's Anglican community gives substantially higher per capita amounts than the Canadian or Toronto averages. Moreover, despite studies showing a Canada-wide decrease since 1970 in the percentage of people contributing to charitable organizations, the opposite trend is true for Montreal Anglicans.

Figure 2 in Appendix B shows the financial contributions for Montreal. These include the categories "open," "regular envelope," "special," and "regular capital account." Endowment and rental in-

come, two significant income sources, have been excluded so that the
graph will reflect a more valid index of financial commitment on an
ongoing basis. All financial data have been converted to "constant
1981 dollars," on the basis of the Consumer Price Index.

As the graph shows, there was an almost continuous decline in
total offerings for Montreal Diocese from 1961 to 1975, from a high
of $5 million (in constant dollars) to a low of just over $3 million
in 1975. The reversal after 1976 of this steady decrease is striking, particularly in view of the continued decline in membership. The increase in total contributions continued until 1980,
when contributions declined slightly for two years then rose again,
stablizing at $3,500,000.

A more meaningful measure in terms of the commitment of individual Anglicans (and one that suggests a powerful determination to
protect the physical legacy of the church) is the level of offerings per
member. As shown in Figure 3 (Appendix B), on a per member basis,
the contributions in Montreal Diocese began the 1960s with sharp
fluctuations but then showed a gradual increase to just over $98 (per
member, per year) in 1975. From 1975 there was a dramatic increase
in contributions, to $158 in 1980, $180 in 1984, and a peak of $192
in 1987. When these figures are compared to the Canadian per
capita values, the increase in Montreal's financial contributions is
even more startling.

On the assumption that Montreal and Toronto would share some
of the same urban lifestyle, education, income, and high-mobility
patterns of metropolitan centres, per member contributions for
Montreal are also compared to those for Toronto. Per capita donations in that city were higher than those for Montreal from 1966
until 1977, when the gap narrowed significantly. In 1980, for the
first time, Montreal parishioners donated more to their churches
per member than did Torontonians. Over the period 1961–75
Montreal's average contributions per capita were 8.4 per cent less
than Toronto's, whereas in the period 1976–86 they were 20 per
cent higher.

Compared to Canadian average parish contributions per member,
Montreal experienced higher average contributions in both time periods, 13.6 per cent higher than Canada in the early period but over
35 per cent higher after 1975. With regard to the average contributions, in real dollars, for the two time periods, Montreal's increased
by over 66 per cent between the two time periods, whereas
Toronto's increased by only 30 per cent.

The number of "identifiable givers" provides another measure of
the generosity of Montreal Anglicans, affording a further glimpse at

the level of commitment. Identifiable givers are those people who receive income tax receipts for their donations to the church. This measurement offers a slightly more refined indication of church commitment than membership and is slightly different from per capita offerings because it incorporates the fringe group who, as described earlier, may retain only nominal membership but nevertheless have a strong sense of the need to preserve the legacy of family roots and tradition.

Identifiable givers can be an important element in parish revenue, especially in areas where there are old families whose identity, sense of community belonging, and rootedness in historical tradition are expressed in terms of their church affiliation. Montreal Diocese has had a higher percentage of givers than either Toronto or Canada, and this higher percentage was consistent throughout the period from 1974 to 1986, with the exception of the years 1982 and 1985, when Toronto was higher. These data suggest not only that the numbers who continue to support the church financially in Montreal have remained high, but that compared to the Canadian average the percentage gap has widened, especially since 1975. It would seem that, despite high rates of out-migration, those who are still in the diocese are supporting the church in increasing proportions and at higher levels.

Part of the commitment to the church involves a global responsibility, which entails a portion of the financial contributions being directed to supporting missions and social justice endeavours outside the boundaries of the parish or diocese. The data relating to "mission commitment" provides another interesting perspective on the responses of Montreal Anglicans to the perceived threat to their survival. In offering another view on the degree to which Montrealers correspond to a national norm of mission giving, such data help us determine whether there is evidence that Montreal parishioners are reluctant to support outreach because of their concern for the apparent threat to their own churches and communities. Several sources of data were examined, including the Anglican Appeal, the Primate's World Relief and Development Fund (PWRDF), and the specially inaugurated campaign called Anglicans in Mission (AIM), which, though it ran only from 1983 to 1986, was finally closed in 1992.

The figures for contributions to the Appeal from 1974 to 1982, while not definitive in themselves, do seem to suggest that Anglicans in Quebec may be focused more on supporting their own parishes and dioceses than on outreach or mission. Lower amounts were contributed from Montreal Diocese, whether expressed as a percentage of parish income or on a per capita basis. Contributions per member were lower in Montreal than the Canadian average for every year except 1976 and 1978. The average contributions show that Montreal Diocese, when compared to other dioceses in eastern Canada and to the Canadian average, had a record of low mission contributions. On the other hand, the pattern of giving per member to the PWRDF for Montreal is approximately the same as that for Canada and for Toronto for the period 1973 to 1986. Finally, there are the data for the AIM campaign. AIM was a special effort by the national church to meet long-term mission commitments by collecting a large amount in a three-year drive for funds. Pledges were at the root of the method, heralded by commentators as a new model for institutional campaigns. The Anglicans in Mission campaign "was orchestrated at the national level by fund raising mercenaries, at the diocesan level by mercenaries and clergy, and in the parishes by volunteer lay people. The consultants produced a step-by-step plan."[8]

Despite the high parish income per member through regular offerings in Montreal, the pledged amounts for this diocese were significantly lower than in other areas in the country; they were almost 25 per cent lower than Toronto's per member pledges in 1983, a time when the per capita income in Montreal was over 4 per cent higher (see Table 12, Appendix A). Table 17 describes the amounts pledged and the per capita receipts as of the end of 1991. It can be seen that Montreal had honoured only 89 per cent of its pledge, compared to 96 per cent for Canada and over 97 per cent for Toronto.

Whether one considers the pledged amounts or the dollars actually received by AIM, the figures show a clear pattern of low financial commitment to mission in Montreal Diocese. These data, considered together with the Appeal data, suggest that indeed the diocese has been less generous than other areas of the country. The relatively poor response in Montreal to the national appeal for mission, in other words, points to an attitude of protectiveness and a certain amount of defensiveness on the part of Anglican Church members.

CONCLUSION

In our exploration of the various indicators of Anglican involvement, the documentary and statistical evidence all describe a church increasingly aware of its fragility in the face of secularization, out-migration, and a loss of control over social and economic institutions in Quebec. Chapters 2–4 have provided evidence of responses to a threatened institution through which individuals experience their life-worlds of identity and historical meaning. In the next chapters we shall look more closely at the people whose lives are intimately bound up in the church, exploring their definitions of community and the meanings the parish church has for them.

PART TWO

The Five Parishes

5 Introduction: Meanings of Community and Place

English Quebec past, present or future has been dropped from the Quebec story. Anglophones will have to tell their own story. Getting back into the community equation and onto outdoor signs will depend on who and what they decide they are and want to remain.

Gretta Chambers[1]

The historical importance of the parish church as a focus of community shared experience is well documented in academic research and in the cultural media of art and literary creativity. Its relevance today is more ambivalent. In the following journey into the private lives and public responses of individuals for whom the church continues to be important, I have endeavoured to be both objective and sensitive, to be non-judgmental and yet to offer a critique that will serve as a mirror through which we can see ourselves more clearly. It is important to recognize that in the discussions I report in the following pages, there are both "insider" and "outsider" perspectives and that these occasionally seem to be at odds. While the outsider may find it reasonable to interpret certain patterns of behaviour in accordance with diocesan trends and statistics, the insider may not recognize the explained rationale as relevant to his or her experience. For those living the everyday movements they become so fundamental that they are not even reflected upon.

Montreal's Anglican Church is not only primarily anglophone, it is also quintessentially an English church, having strong ethnic overtones. In the following pages, the stories of individual parishes strongly suggest that the English roots of the church are important to its identity and ultimately to its survival. Creole-speaking Haitians feel isolated; upper-class Anglicans cling to their prayers for the queen; and a minister offers his spare time to the Black Watch Armoury while his local food bank looks for volunteers. Even as Anglicans search for ways to affirm their identity, they appear to reject openness to the multicultural society around them. Their churches are significant places of meaning, but the meanings are rooted in times past and in active, but local, shared communities of the present. The perception of the future is inevitably one of doubt and uncertainty. In telling their stories, Anglican Montrealers show that they have not come to terms with their hopes for the future. "The relationship of the individual to God is ultimately personal, but it is mediated by the whole pattern of community life. There is a givenness about the community and the tradition. They are not normally a matter of individual choice."[2]

The following chapters examine the lived worlds of Anglican members in terms of their commitment to and participation in their community churches. For individuals, the meanings that their Christian faith, and more particularly their local churches, have for them derive from a complex interaction of community and social values, family experiences, and the broader cultural context. Religion is one important way in which Canadians participate in community life. On a pragmatic level, as we saw earlier, they give more money and donate more time to religious organizations than to all other voluntary associations put together. Commitment to the church, of course, represents far more than time and money. The local church is a community of worship incorporating the local and the universal, the sacred and the secular, and myths and stories. It is bricks and mortar as well as symbols and rituals. While reflecting the debates and tensions of the institutional church, the parish also exhibits specific characteristics related to variations of social class, mobility, age, and education, all of which are tied into particular histories. These variations on a theme define and describe communities of shared experience having histories, memories, and traditions that give meaning to church life.

The parish church contains within it three interactive elements, tangible and intangible components that define the place. First, there are the people who share activities, relationships, experiences, and stories. Second, there is the church building and its furnishings, which provide in a concrete material way, a means through which people can affirm and maintain a sense of rootedness and belonging. The third element is the compendium of formal and informal organizational and social links, the relationships that define, describe, and limit the dynamic of the church community. All of these elements interact to become churches that have distinctive characteristics of meaning and behaviour. An emphasis on the importance of these three elements working together is consistent with social theory that focuses on the importance of intragroup interaction in contributing to the development and maintenance of "self."[3] Individuals acquire shared meanings with others and in relation to place as a result of the need to affirm an identity and to develop a coherent self. The search for individual meaning, in other words, occurs in relation to reference groups (such as the church) that generate communities of shared experience, tradition, and security. This chapter will explore the ways in which individual meanings and attachments to place are intricately related to the community church.

The socio-political context of Quebec adds another level of complexity to the final outcome in these interactive structures. It has combined with the specific social milieu of each of the churches to create ever-evolving communities. In the particular context of Quebec, the local church has become for many people a place of increased significance, having meanings associated with cultural identity and security. The church is a place that can "incarnate the experience and aspirations of people"[4] and provide a sense of belonging to the social group. It has been suggested that there is a relationship between the emergence of the notion of place as a significant motif in literature, politics, and song and abrupt changes in the social and intellectual environments. People's sense of both personal and cultural identity is intimately bound up with place identity, especially under conditions of a perceived threat to loss of home. "Losing one's place" may trigger an identity crisis. Research suggests that when security of cultural identity and the fundamental values associated with any of these levels of experience are threatened, response in terms of protest about the meaning of place may erupt.[5]

The interviews and discussions reproduced in part in the following chapters illustrate differences in the ways community is perceived and differences in the corresponding responses. People spoke eloquently of the parish churches in which their life's passages had been celebrated, to which they attached symbolic importance as protectors of their culture, and from which they expected continual nourishment and affirmation. Their words reflected the many layers of individual meanings: symbolic, emotional, cultural, spiritual, ideological, and political. The parish churches are both personal and institutional in their impact and meaning. Place and community are dynamic concepts; they need to be viewed as "horizons for basic life processes rather than as artifacts or nouns."[6]

THE FIVE CHURCHES

Selected in consultation with the bishop, the five parish churches under discussion here reflect a cross-section of demographic and locational characteristics. They are not simple representations of social class or of a single social group. The churches can loosely be called "communities of meaning," and the "meaning" varies between them. Their special characteristics are exhibited in behaviour and priorities that affect their activities. Demographic characteristics of age, class, and education, as well as the residential spatial pattern of members, are concrete attributes that are reflected in the debates, choices, and attitudes presented in the following chapters. Ultimately, however, the complexity of contributing factors becomes apparent in the divisions within individual churches. Ambiguity and contradiction are inevitable for a church embedded in the social and political realities of Quebec.

Despite many attempts to establish correlations between specific demographic characteristics and various behavioural patterns in the church, almost no unequivocal statements can be made about such factors as education, family income, or occupation. Not only is it impossible to quantify spiritual commitment, it is difficult to establish statistical relationships between most of the variables and church attendance. On the other hand, as this study confirms, there are some demographic factors that have profound significance for the ways people relate to their churches. Age, for example, or more specifically the stage in the life cycle, is directly related to people's inclination to attend church. Many of the individual stories related in the following chapters provide evidence that life cycle plays a significant role in defining important structural and organizational relationships within the individual churches.

Mobility and rates of out-migration are two important characteristics of population change that have implications for the "communities of meaning." Mobility, the years lived within the parish, reflects the extent to which church members feel a sense of attachment to place and have long family histories with associated memories and traditions. In parishes where mobility rates are high, where the demographic movement of people generates new members for the parish, the old ways of doing things may be challenged. Another response may simply be that the established members are more open to change, since the church is growing.

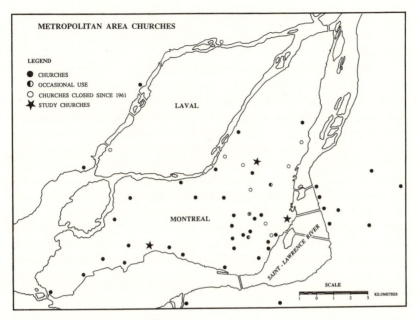

Map 3   Metropolitan Area Churches

In situations where there is net out-migration, however, where the out-going anglophones are not being replaced by potential new church members, a different combination of forces comes into play. The significance of declining membership as a factor inhibiting change and affecting "meanings" cannot be overstated. In the first place, it is statistically known that the "movers" are in the productive age groups, especially those 25 to 45 years of age. When this group leaves and is not replaced, those who remain are dominantly in the older age group. Their impact on church decision making assumes proportionately greater importance both because of their numbers and because of their existing hold on committee positions. To the extent that they perceive a need to retain familiar roles and responsibilities, and to ensure the continuance of traditional forms and rituals as ways of affirming their identities, the full integration of new members will be resisted. Age categories are one factor in mobility and net migration data; related to these are stages in the life cycle. Together these factors have implications for the "communities of meaning" insofar as they affect the extent to which new ideas and change will be welcomed. A final related demographic variable is the male-female balance, which is affected when young families move out, leaving an older population that is characterized by proportionately higher numbers of women. As we shall see, it is the women's groups, dominated by an older-age cohort, that control most decision making in parishes of declining membership caused by high out-migration.

The difficulty in exploring these relationships lies precisely in the number of contributing factors combined with the particular nature of religion as a personal framework of meaning. Belief in God cannot be quantified. The importance of spiritual renewal for parishioners cannot be measured. Ultimately, the meaning the church has for people must be accepted as subjective, and it must be described subjectively. It is important to acknowledge that the five churches selected according to objective criteria exhibit variations in the subjectively defined behaviours, and that these behaviour patterns will not necessarily be repeated in other churches having the same objective conditions. On the other hand, to the extent that the broader institutional and socio-political contexts intrude, some broad generalizations describing common relationships can be made.

6 St Matthias

St Matthias Church is located in the geographic centre of Westmount, one of the wealthiest communities in Canada, with an average (male) income of over $58,000. Whereas in Quebec only 10 per cent of the population is anglophone, in Westmount 70 per cent of the population is English speaking. A lovely old stone church perched almost precariously on the edge of the steep incline of the mountain, St Matthias welcomes visitors through two massive old oak doors. A pair of Union Jacks hanging in the chancel eloquently points to the links with Britain. Prayers of intercession in January 1991 during the Gulf War were for "our Queen's Forces." A large organ at the back of the church, in front of which is an impressive series of choir pews, testifies to the reputation the men and boys choir has earned among Montreal Anglicans. Music is important to the congregation both in terms of its perception of itself and in terms of how other Montreal Anglicans view St Matthias. The choir is a vital part of life at the church. There are 391 family names on the parish list, which means approximately 860 people are members of the church. Approximately 68 per cent of the members live within Westmount's boundaries, and 88 per cent within five kilometres of the church. The annual budget is almost $300,000 ($291,268 in 1993). Total revenues were almost $239,000 in 1993, with regular contributors providing about three-quarters of this amount. An operating deficit of over $52,000 was partly covered by income of $32,000 from a memorial fund.

There are two regular weekly services, both on Sunday mornings, in addition to a monthly evensong service late Sunday afternoon that

features the choir. The average attendance at services is twenty at the
8:00 AM Eucharist, one hundred at the 10:30 AM Eucharist, and
forty at the monthly evensongs. There is a clear majority of older
people at all services, with an average age around sixty years. The
Sunday school is small, always struggling to maintain sufficient
numbers to continue, while assurance of teachers is also a problem.
In 1988, according to a former warden, there had "been talk of pay-
ing someone to organize it." Confirmation classes seem to attract
eight to ten young people each year, but as one teacher from a private school who knows these youth said to me: "I had never seen
them at church; suddenly here they are at confirmation, 'being done.'
And we haven't seen them since." As with all of the churches in
which I involved myself, the participation of young people aged
13–30 was almost nil.

Several of St Matthias's characteristics make it distinctive in the
diocese. The wealth of its members is important, but not in an absolute sense so much as in terms of the implications for past experi-

ences of power and shared social status within the community and church. An appreciation of the values and commitment the "old families" bring to the existential meaning of their church is crucial to an understanding of the difficulties encountered by those who wish to initiate effective change at St Matthias. Most of the members have belonged to the church for many decades, and their family histories are punctuated by marriages, baptisms, and funerals at St Matthias. At the same time, in the wider community they have known the power and influence of the elite who control the economic and political institutions in Montreal and Quebec. In this period of enormous change in Quebec, during which these old families have seen many of the younger business leaders leaving the province while their own influence has been undermined by the emergent business elite of the francophone population, most of the members of St Matthias have sought to retain the familiar forms in their church, preserving a sense of continuity essential to their own identities.

Even though their wealth might protect them from the economic insecurities of unemployment and there might not seem to be a need to protect the status quo in other areas of their lives, they nevertheless bring to their worship a conservatism that eschews the desirability of a modern language liturgy, the possibility of female clergy, and the potential for a nearby drop-in centre. It is not that they are ignorant of changes in the wider church; nor that some members of their congregation do not actively support some of the new initiatives in the church. It is simply that, as a congregation, they do not accept them. Despite a short trial period at a 9:00 AM service, there has been a steadfast refusal to consider adoption of the new prayer book at any of the regular services; in appointing a new rector, the search committee understood that a female would not be considered for the position; and in discussing the possibility of a drop-in centre in cooperation with a nearby church, two members of the advisory board abstained from voting on a motion that merely asked for further investigation, while the others were reluctant to commit even moral support to the idea.

The sense of community one feels in this church is somewhat ambiguous. On the one hand, many parishioners spoke to me of the lack of any experience of community – there is a general consensus that "everyone is very separate" and that none of the parishioners see one another socially outside the Sunday morning service. On the other hand, time and time again people mentioned the choir and its importance as a nucleus of strength and commitment in the church. I shall return to this issue because it is crucial to an understanding

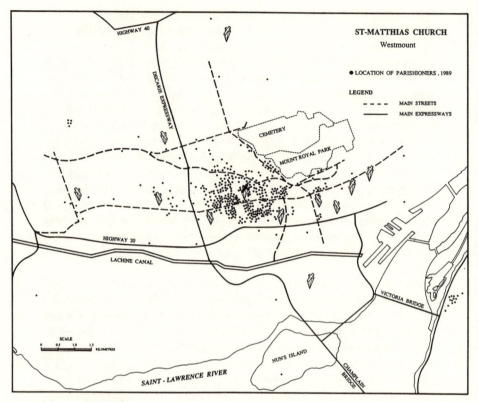

Map 4 St Matthias

of the meaning St Matthias has for its members. One active member said that he saw "two parishes," one which turns out for the funerals of the elite and another, a committed group of one hundred or so regular attenders, who support the church through active participation in worship services and social events.

In most churches, one group that usually functions as a focus of community sharing is the women's association. Understanding the role of the women in the church and the ways women perceive their relationship to the church involves the examination of a complex variety of elements. I shall present them here as they apply to St Matthias. Out-migration and secularization, as well as increasing numbers of women entering the work force, have had an enormous impact upon the women's activities. The past four years have been a period of great insecurity for the women's association, which has not been able to fill its executive positions on a consistent basis. A recent newsletter included the following comment from the current president:

When I was elected to the position of co-president of the A.O.W. [Association of Women] after only being in the church for a few months (in itself an indication of desperate times!), I accepted the post with great enthusiasm and with the hope of being able to bring in some new blood and vigour to the group. After only nine months in this position, I must admit to being very discouraged and pessimistic as to the future of our organization. Aside from a few handfuls of very dedicated and hardworking individuals, it is becoming increasingly difficult to get people to take on jobs and to see them through, without constant supervision ... This creates an enormous burden on an already aging and dwindling group of people and puts us all in an untenable position ... As it now stands, only six out of a slate of twelve members of our executive, are prepared to return to their jobs next year, leaving the top three posts, in particular, unfilled.

This articulate description of the situation for the women's association at St Matthias is not unique. All of the churches exhibit similar concerns for the aging population and for the lack of commitment to the volunteer duties, with much being done by few. St Matthias is different not only in the degree to which no one seems to be forthcoming and in the recognition that the organization may cease to exist, but more particularly in the reality that the numbers are in fact there. The potential for an active women's group exists. This is not a church surviving on an attendance of thirty or forty, as is the case at Grace Church (described in the next chapter). The membership of St Matthias includes a large pool of well-educated women who are not all working during the day at paid employment. While at some of the churches, such as Grace Church and Resurrection, the women's groups serve the important role of bringing people together to share in the social and altruistic experiences of community, at St Matthias the women's group seems to be a "duty." There is little sense of enjoying the shared commitment or of wanting to enhance the experiential meaning of their Christian faith. Many of these women are involved in competing activities (volunteering as museum guides, for example, or working for hospital guilds), which provide outlets for their social, altruistic, and intellectual needs.

At the annual meeting of the Association of Women in January 1989 there were thirty-two ladies present. I sat at the back next to a delightful 78-year-old lady who was busy knitting and alert to everything going on around her. She wondered why I was there – I was "so young!" Another woman I talked to said that she was not a very regular attender at church because she and her family are away on weekends at their house in St Agathe. "Weekenders" are a frequently mentioned problem for St Matthias. This woman was surprised at the good attendance at this meeting; last year there had been only about six people, she said. At the end of the meeting, when the president asked how many would be at the next one in a month's time, only eight hands were raised. The struggle of the women's group is related not to potential numbers but to the attitudes and values of church members who do not seem to need a church community for their social sharing.

The determination of the president to ensure the continuance of a fund-raising and fellowship group compelled her to propose at the annual vestry meeting in January 1991 to form an "all members" group, not restricted to women. Arguing that "we must all be accountable if we hope to build momentum and growth within our congregation and community at large," she initiated a committee to define the guidelines for the new group. In the spring of 1991 the Association of Women was disbanded, and a new fellowship group, including both men and women, was formed in its place.

The decision to include men as part of the women's group at St Matthias is not unique; other churches have also discussed such a move. As the women's groups have increasingly come to be dominated by retired-age people, many of whom have retired spouses who would benefit by the shared socializing, there is a recognition of the need to redefine the rationale for these groups. At the same time there are paradoxical struggles to retain old forms that served particular power interests. For some women, especially those whose histories span many decades in the church, the church has provided a means for self-affirmation and public recognition. Strongly established relationships, sometimes known as cliques, become the basis for a powerful informal structure of control. The women's group wields enormous power in terms of its role in providing a community ambience and organizing social functions and receptions for special occasions; through their very presence in the church, the women know more about the details of administration and organization than any new warden who takes office for a three-year term. Their power is real even if it is not acknowledged by church officers and the clergy, as frequently it is not.

The irony in their struggle to form a new type of organization is that new young women in the church have great difficulty being integrated into these groups. Even assuming that a new female member is introduced into an association meeting, it would take her years to understand the many informal rules, traditions, and stories that guide the "way things are done." In this St Matthias is not alone. It is a situation, however, that seems to be exacerbated in Quebec by the lack of large numbers of new young members who can act as initiators of change. In churches dominated by the older age groups, the women retain their power as a way of perpetuating their identity and sense of belonging.

Despite these problems, the women at St Matthias have continued to provide important sources of funds. Their fund-raising bazaars enabled them to contribute $24,000 to various causes in 1988, almost 50 per cent of which were outside the parish. One interesting aspect of women's groups in all the churches is that they tend to retain complete control of their finances; their funds often do not appear in the audited financial reports and are contributed to the total church revenue at the discretion of individual executives. This issue is one of the most delicate ones for any rector to address.

As mentioned earlier, the evidence for a sense of community at St Matthias is ambiguous. Two groups, organized mainly by women, that exhibit a degree of commitment and significant elements of community through shared responsibility are the Meals-on-Wheels organization and the team of Pastoral Care visitors. What is interesting about these groups (one of which is not strictly a St Matthias organization, though it is based in the church) is that they have had consistent leadership, directed at specific goals within known time frames. They have achieved an outreach into the Westmount community and in serving the elderly population have fostered a sharing of common experiences of the past and have carried these experiences into the present.

Despite a powerful presence in the church, the women's groups are often overlooked in general discussions about the future direction of the church, and at vestry meetings their reports are short, their particular concerns given little attention compared to that given the choir, budget, and building renovations. In the autumn of 1988 a special meeting at St Matthias was called to discuss stewardship and develop a questionnaire that could be the focus of a parish-wide campaign. It was almost two hours into the meeting before the women's groups were acknowledged. This happened when one lady – we'll call her "M." – pointed out that the proposed questionnaire hardly mentioned them. Since her family history was deeply rooted in the church and she was respected for her strong faith, the meeting gave her its attention when she said that "some activities are glossed over. Meals-on-Wheels is not even mentioned." She went on to say that "there's too much emphasis on music. This [the questionnaire] is asking for facts. But we need 'feel.'" [1]

After the meeting acknowledged her concern, however, the next question refocused attention on stewardship visiting, asking whether its ultimate objective was to solicit money. The reply that money should "not necessarily" be the primary objective in the initial contact illicited no further discussion of women's roles. Someone said he hoped that at least a year could go by before a financial campaign was begun, since he did not believe they were about "to close this place down. Our job is to look ahead two or three years, and to be self-sustaining." While the definition of stewardship provoked discussion, there was always a return to a focus on money. No one returned to the comments of M. or acknowledged an awareness of the potential importance of women in stewardship.

At a second meeting on stewardship, M. clearly expressed her concern for the lack of community commitment at St Matthias, particularly in the women's association, which she described as "a very nebulous group" with "nothing to bind them together except the rummage sale and bazaars." [2] One man suggested that in view of the problems keeping the women together, "why not cancel the women's group and put them under 'parish support'?" The problem was perceived to be an organizational one that could be solved by rearranging the pieces. The meeting did finally acknowledge the significant contribution of the women through their fund-raising activities and agreed that they should be encouraged to continue.

Another important group in most churches is the Sunday, or Church, school for children aged 4–12. Its very existence is perpetually threatened by small numbers, and in one year recently (1987–88) there was no school at all. Each Sunday six to twelve youngsters file out early in the service, accompanied by several parent-teachers. At an advisory board meeting in 1988, Mrs J. reported on their activities: "The good news is that we have an increase in the number of teachers who are helping; but unfortunately they don't come every week. We have 7 teachers, so there is always someone there. But it would be better if they weren't different every week. Combined with intermittent attendance of the children, it is very difficult to generate any sense of community." [3]

Typically, the reports on the Sunday school and youth group activities did not generate any questions or comments. The apparent lack of interest was in contrast to the many questions directed to the financial report. More recently, in 1990–91, an increase in the number of Sunday school teachers and young people has generated some optimism. As one man said to me, "The increased interest of young fathers who have volunteered as teachers is a good sign."

Any discussion of a sense of community at St Matthias inevitably focuses on the choir. One relatively new church member described the basis for his family's decision to join St Matthias: "I think back to when we were looking around for a church, and we had gone to St Stephen's for awhile. There were a lot of very attractive things about that church. But, really, when we looked at the congregations, we realized that we wanted one which was rooted, where there was a sense of community and long-term commitment. St Stephen's is a very transient population."[4]

There is no question that the population of St Matthias is rooted, that there are intricate links in family histories and a strong feeling for the legends of times past and for significant family celebrations and rites of passage. To conclude, however, that there is a strong sense of community is to understate the meaning of that word. The young assistant priest commented that "my wife wouldn't feel comfortable with our three-week-old baby in church. We would need a less formal, freer kind of environment."[5] An ex-warden pointed to "a solid core of commitment amongst the one hundred people who come to church every Sunday." He described the "enormous potential" among the parishioners but said he felt that the church was putting its "head in the sand." In describing his own strong sense of loyalty, he admitted that he did not feel truly part of a "community" church. He summed up by saying, "I enjoy it, I love it, but I may leave tomorrow!"

At one meeting someone said that the church needed to make people feel more welcome but that they did not know each other well enough to share their emotional selves. When it was pointed out that St Matthias members become enthusiastically committed when there is a specific goal, such as an organ fund, it was suggested that everything be broken down into projects. Again, the choir was held up as an example of a group with clear goals, with a mandate. Someone said that "everyone at this meeting is connected in some way to the choir. In the choir there is a very strong sense of community. The men share a lot."

The question of the choir and its role at St Matthias is particularly interesting, with profound implications for the functioning of the whole church. Most of the church leaders are associated with the choir. It is the choir that epitomizes community. It is the choir that accounts for the single largest expenditure from the budget. It is special services featuring the choir that attract the largest congregations. The reality of the choir's participation in the life of the church, however, is at odds with this common perception of it as a community builder. The only meetings or events that choir members attend are those directly affecting them. At a major parish retreat held over an entire weekend in November 1989, the purpose of which was to discuss and formulate a mission statement, there was only one representative from the choir. Nor do choir members participate in social events such as the Patronal pot luck luncheon or the Shrove Tuesday pancake supper. As important as the choir is perceived to be in generating a sense of community, there is little evidence of its participation in the church outside the regular services.

A series of meetings held to consider a replacement for the choir director of eighteen years provided an illuminating perspective on the role of the St Matthias choir and on the ways it is perceived. The meetings highlighted the extent to which the choir is both the greatest strength and the greatest liability for St Matthias. At two parish meetings called for the express purpose of discussing what the congregation would like in a new director, the overwhelming majority of those attending were choir members. Using the search for a new choir director as an opportunity to examine the needs, priorities, and the possible choices, the corporation asked members to consider four issues. Presented to the meeting on a flip chart were the following:

1 Assess the nature of the music programme
2 What is the long-term vision?
3 Viability – a. recruitment of men and boys;
            b. costing
4 Possible future composition of choir

Implicit in this outline for discussion was the possibility of changing the type of music, altering the form of services, and even introducing girls or women into the choir.

Some choir members responded with hostility, but all were unanimous in arguing for the status quo. Their presence dominated both meetings. Presenting an alternate view was a member of the congregation whose two boys had been active in the choir for many years:

We've been very fortunate having two boys in the choir, stretching over twenty years, and we feel they've both benefited enormously. Moreover, they have involved us in our attachment to St Matthias; and that experience has multiplied through many households. And I suppose one reason I've felt very positive about the music program is not only the beauty of the music, but also because it fills the church, it builds the parish. So when I find that the very person who has been the sparkplug behind so much has found recruiting a problem, then we should take a hard look at it. In fact the tradition of the men and boys choir may no longer be supportable.[6]

While several people acknowledged there was a recruiting problem, no one was willing to discuss the possibility of introducing girls or women into the choir. One parishioner who sings in the choir described a church in Boston where the explicit emphasis on the arts as a means of communicating the gospel seemed to offer a model for St Matthias. He said that the importance of the men and boys choir was that it offered "a music program that does this sort of thing that goes with the liturgy and is a strong part of our service."

The question of cost was raised by a parishioner who pointed out that

the music program last year cost us 16 per cent. In the cathedral, with costs only 15 per cent more than us, it cost only 10 per cent of their expenditures. Sixteen per cent for St Matthias, that shows you where we have our priorities. Ten percent for the cathedral, which considers itself the heart of the diocese and runs a music program because it feels it has to demonstrate it is the heart where the Anglican liturgy is highly important. Eleven per cent at St George's; 11 per cent in St James; and 4 per cent in St Barnabas. The point is these churches feel there should be a limit on their music. The question is, do we in St Matthias with the deficits we have, really want to spend our money in this way on the choir?[7]

Continuing at some length in his analysis of the budget and of the issues he felt needed to be addressed in deciding on the future music program, he asked, "Is it practical, desirable, necessary, that we should restrict the spiritual instruction that our boys are getting just to the boys? If it is so desirable, should not the girls be included? They're 50 per cent of the youth of the parish. Why shouldn't they be entitled to some of these benefits of this education?"

Although there was an articulate presentation of the choices and issues, in the end the views of the choir, which favoured maintaining the traditions, were accepted. One choir member said that they should be looking at "value provided," while a choir mother suggested that they should be taking into account as extra benefits the Christian education and fellowship offered through choir participation. Taking another perspective, the man quoted above who was challenging many of the church's traditions expressed the opinion that the choir often dominated the worship services, precluding participation by the congregation. He questioned the overall goals of the church: "I wonder if we have our priorities right ... we need to consider how music is integrated with the mission of St Matthias as a parish church. Do we also think of the refugees? What about the mission to singles? We need to widen our horizon, to become less static, to be a growing parish. I do feel that a challenge is necessary."

His views were not supported by others at the meeting. No one was interested. Choir members diverted attention away from the issue of finances and priorities towards consideration of who the next director would be. When a warden suggested there would have to be expenditure cuts because of an impending deficit, a choir member offered this response: "There is not a balance sheet on the choir; the income might go down if the choir were not here." Focusing on the qualifications of a new director, one choir member said that since "we're staying with a men and boys choir for the time being ...," thereby assuming a decision that had not been taken on the criteria for selection. The choir was injecting a subtle but effective form of coercion into the discussion to ensure that its composition, leadership, and traditional music would all remain intact.

The influence of the choir at St Matthias does not end with decisions concerning the music. Choir members actively seek to influence other important norms within the church. I was told of an episode that illustrates this sort of intervention: a member of the choir was so upset when the rector included the recently consecrated – and female – Bishop Harries in the prayers of intercession that he "stomped out of the church" before the beginning of the final hymn.

Two weeks after this incident, St Matthias celebrated its Patronal festival followed by a potluck luncheon. Not a single member of the choir came to the luncheon, as they were all being entertained at a choir member's home. Their lack of interest in a social church event puts their claims for the choir's contribution to a feeling of community (uttered just two weeks earlier at the choir hearing) at odds with the reality. The power of the choir is real and is exercised in terms of enriching the services, but the reality is that the choir does not involve itself in community sharing among the wider congregation. The lack of participation by choir members in social events or in discussions concerning the direction of the church detracts from efforts by others to strengthen a sense of community and shared experience at St Matthias. When this was suggested to one of the former church wardens, he expressed surprise, saying, "I admire the choir. It used to be the drawing card for the church, and the centre of its creativity." He added that he felt the choir was trying to adapt to the wishes of the congregation, that it "no longer" acted in relative isolation.

In addition to the choir and the women's groups, there are less tangible experiences of community that define the relationships at St Matthias. An important majority of parishioners have family roots extending through several generations within the parish. The experiences these families bring to their relationship with St Matthias strongly influence the ways they respond to many of the proposed changes within the Anglican communion. The possibility of changing the music program met with resistance not only from the choir but also from several of the long-time families, who equate the traditional music with their definition of the meaning of spirituality. For them the traditional music is the central focus of worship. A conservative chord is apparent in other responses to innovation, such as the reaction to female clergy, the new prayer book, and the possibility of admitting pre-confirmation children to communion. While about eight or ten individuals who are active in the church are willing to look at some of these options for change, their voices are rarely heard.

The role of women is significant from several points of view. While they are more involved than the men in organizations and fellowship, their participation in leadership roles is less, even taking into account that two recent wardens have been women. At advisory board meetings men outnumber the women and dominate the discussions, and the core of sidesmen are exactly that, men. At the

Easter service in 1989 eight people took up the collection – all men. One of the servers at communion is a woman who is also a leader in the altar guild and active in mission projects outside the parish. There are men who still refuse to accept communion from her. Her particular involvement in the church is unique at St Matthias, and it is visibly rejected by the males in the church.

This public dominance of the men is one important aspect of the internal structure of St Matthias. There is a second element, however, that is more subtle, less public, but nevertheless very significant. It is the female network based in the women's organizations and consolidated through family histories and traditions. This informal network uses its power to control decisions, influence activities, and ensure that traditions are maintained. Two forces seem to be operating here. One is the need of individuals for control. The second is a natural tendency, seen in all the churches, for seniority and especially family roots to be given status. While neither of these forces is inherently harmful, in combination they are potentially enormously damaging. One situation at St Matthias involving a very powerful woman epitomizes situations in countless other churches in Canada. This woman was able to dominate all activities and decision making in the church through a powerful combination of circumstances. As secretary to the rector for over twenty-five years, and therefore at the hub of all communications, and as leader of one of the organizations and plus having the status of long family connections, she expected and was given extensive control over all aspects of church community life. Her support became a necessary requisite for all action.

Such exercise of power reflects a not uncommon element of church life. It has roots in the intimate nature of church community, but also in the dearth of alternative outlets for women who have a need for power. The existence of such entrenched interests is particularly apparent in churches having a long history and pride in family roots. The circumstances that allow such women to acquire and exercise control are exacerbated in Quebec owing to the high rates of out-migration that preclude an inflow of new, younger members. In the churches described in the following chapters, which have a more mobile and younger population, status acquired through family connections and generational contributions to the church is much less significant. Another factor in Quebec that contributes to the creation of these powerful individuals is the diminished number of opportunities for community service for older anglophones who have not learned French or integrated into the francophone milieu.

Another aspect of church life is Bible study. Commenting on the interest in Bible study at St Matthias, one person said quite simply: "We've tried discussion groups, Bible study, and small group meetings [Cursillo]. But there isn't much interest in this kind of thing here." One family has hosted a Bible study group in their home for several years, without any success in attracting more than three or four regular attenders. Viewed by others in the congregation as a separate and distinct group, they themselves do not feel they have the same spiritual values and needs as others in the congregation. Indeed, there are few ties between the group's members and the larger congregation. They admitted to knowing very few of the parishioners. When one woman in the group had a major exhibit of her artwork, the parish was scarcely aware of it. Despite the hosting family's strong spiritual commitment and participation in diocesan activities, they represent the isolation of St Matthias members from each other.

Social relationships outside regular church services and activities may reinforce a sense of community within the church. The social mixing of members, in their overlapping circles of friendships and contacts, is limited at St Matthias. Parishioners agreed that the church does not function in an integrative role, that friendships are neither formed nor developed among other church members.

In Toronto everyone goes to church; it is the done thing; it's for show. Church is part of the networking system. That's not the case in Montreal. Anglophones have other institutions for their social networks. In Quebec Anglicanism does not have the clout the way it has in Toronto where being an Anglican implies status. Here the Anglican Church is in such a minority position, it in no way reflects the prevailing culture, and no one cares if you're an Anglican or not. We don't have our friends amongst the church members.[8]

The sense of community at St Matthias is ambiguous. There is pride among members in their choir and a common perception that the choir is essential to the identity of St Matthias and to the continuity of tradition. Women are active in fund raising, in attempts to maintain a sense of fellowship, and in the altar guild. Their acceptance as leaders and decision makers by the men and their visibility in support roles such as greeters and sidespersons are very limited. Spirituality is rarely mentioned at meetings and is not evident in the activities of the membership. It is rare for parishioners of St Matthias to participate in conferences on prayer and renewal, a particular focus of Hollis's tenure as bishop. Shared family histories have contributed to maintaining a sense of belonging and continuity, but have contributed as well to an exclusiveness that intimidates new members. The strong resistance to change seems to be related to the dominant role of the male choir, as well as to the pride in tradition.

Despite the significant lack of true community at St Matthias, two indicators suggest an ongoing determination to ensure its continuation. First, there is no lack of financial commitment. Secondly, even as people move out of the immediate vicinity of the church and are presented with alternative places of worship, they are inclined to retain membership. These two concrete demonstrations of further meanings attached to the church will be explored later, in chapter 11. First I shall describe the community experiences in four other parishes.

7 Grace Church

Grace Church is located in Point St Charles, a working-class area that used to be home to hundreds of British immigrants who in the late nineteenth century worked in the emerging industrial complex along the Lachine Canal. The church building is an imposing red-brick structure built in 1871, but it is now in need of major repairs following years of deterioration through benign neglect. Land was given for the building of the church through the "kind assistance of the general manager of the Grand Trunk Railway," and therefore "the committee decided that the church should be named after his daughter, Grace."[1] Its location in the middle of a run-down, poverty-stricken area (the unemployment rate of 25 per cent is the highest in Montreal) sets it at the opposite end of the economic spectrum from St Matthias.

Average family income in this area is $20,000, and almost 40 per cent of the population over the age of fifteen have less than a grade 9 education. There continues to be a high percentage of English-speaking people, almost 50 per cent in the area immediately around the church. The district is also characterized by a high number of elderly people; about 15 per cent of the population around the church are over 65 years of age, while the Montreal average for this age group is 10 per cent.[2] The large church has a capacity for about 650 people, although average attendance at Sunday services is only 50. The parish list includes 158 names, of whom 46 per cent live in "the Point" and 53 per cent have pledged regular donations by having envelopes. There is no rectory, and the rector has chosen to live in a

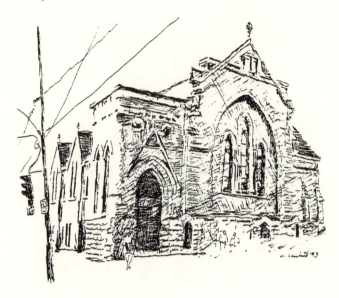

middle-class area about seven kilometres from the church. For twenty years, until 1990, there had been a retirement home associated with Grace Church, located just a block away.

The following description of the 1988 Palm Sunday service suggests a sense of shared community very different from that experienced at St Matthias. Even a half-hour before the service was to begin, twenty-five people had already arrived. Everyone greeted each other in an atmosphere of relaxed informality. Two men at the door greeted people as they entered, but all others in the church were women, widely scattered in pairs throughout the church. The people chatted with each other across the backs of pews. Everyone was in dress attire, the women wearing felt-brimmed hats and the two men in three-piece suits. As people were heard coming in, those already seated would turn to see who it was, and would often nod, smile, and even wave a hello. Then a big robust lady appeared, talking to people, distributing envelopes, and generally acting as though she was the hostess. Even as she came over to talk to me, she continued to keep an eye out for others coming in, and she would occasionally call out to someone. She told me about a problem with the roof caving in, and remarked that they could not afford to have it fixed. With still fifteen minutes until the service was scheduled to start, the woman's husband appeared on the chancel steps to announce the three hymns selected for the pre-service hymn sing. Some sang; others continued to talk. Then in the middle of all this, a couple came in with their pet poodle, who was all dressed up in a neat little jacket. No one paid any attention. At exactly eleven o'clock the songs ended and the rector appeared and began the service. There were now almost seventy people in the church, eighteen men and fifty women, as well as four children who later went out to the nursery.[3]

In the attire of most of the women, in their hats and dresses, and in the three-piece suits of the men, there was a certain formality that was carried over into the traditional Book of Common Prayer service. Indeed, in the mode of dress there was no indication of the poverty that defined the area around the church. There was no sign of the new Book of Alternative Services, and the service itself was somewhat muted, perhaps in part because of the average age of those in attendance – well over 65. Even though the seventy-odd people were scattered all through the large interior, everyone seemed aware of who was present – and thus perhaps also of who was absent!

Despite the small percentage of males present, it was men who filled the formal, public roles of greeter, sidesperson, and server. The wardens whose names were listed in the bulletin, were also all men. The records compiled since the 1870s show an overwhelming dominance of men. There has never been a female warden, and the congregation's delegate to Synod has been female only in the three years 1966–68. Revealingly, in the church's unpublished history, the lists of "Our Parish Laymen" include treasurers, auditors, secretaries, wardens, and delegates, completely omitting officers of the women's associations.[4] At the service, notwithstanding the greater number and more lively presence of the women, it was two men who stood at the chancel steps to help any of the elderly who might require assistance at the time of communion.

Despite the contrasts of social class, there are interesting parallels in particular behaviour and patterns of participation between Grace Church and St Matthias that reflect similar concerns for tradition and commitment to the survival of the church. Like at St Matthias, a high proportion of parishioners of Grace Church live outside the immediate area of the church and a very high proportion have family ties extending back over many decades. Again like at St Matthias, there has been strong resistance to adoption of the new prayer book. As one parishioner expressed it, "The BAS has hardly been mentioned here. No one wants it!" The strong conservatism of the congregation extends to other proposed changes, such as communion for children prior to confirmation. "The rector has not even suggested it. It's a watering down of confirmation. I don't like the kids up at the altar." Also similar to St Matthias practice, there is very little participation in diocesan events such as Cursillo or the bishop's

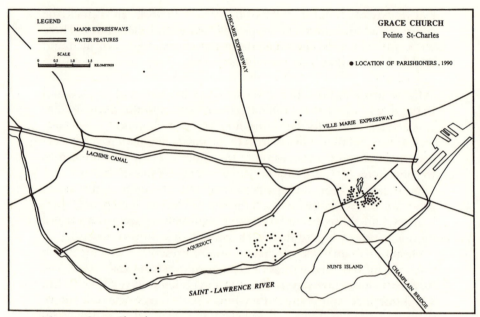

Map 5   Grace Church

conferences on prayer and renewal. Another similarity is in the dominance of formal male leadership. While the women contribute the hours and the organizational leadership for fund-raising events, the men invariably fill positions of public responsibility. On the other hand, several men at Grace Church are always available to help at the rummage sales and church suppers, putting up tables, arranging chairs, and helping pack boxes. The informal presence of women, so significant at St Matthias, is in evidence but remains much less important at Grace Church. All of the executive and public roles (such as delegate to the annual Synod and warden) are firmly held by the men.

There are several ways people are brought together at Grace outside of the regular services. Most important are the twice-monthly rummage sales, at which about twenty faithful workers pull out boxes of clothes, books, and odds and ends from a large room behind the stage and carefully lay the items out on tables around the large basement hall. For three hours local people come to find needed coats or shoes or skates or slacks at prices ranging from fifty cents to a couple of dollars. The ladies of the church chat; a small coffee room provides refreshments; and another hundred dollars or so is earned for the church. These rummage sales provide an important opportunity for social sharing in a common cause, and over many years a strong sense of loyalty and commitment has evolved. There is also an opportunity for reminiscing and sharing memories of the days when the church had many more members and parishioners lived in the immediate neighbourhood.

One of the ladies sitting behind a heavily laden table at the rummage sale was a tiny, frail 83-year-old who had been baptized in Grace Church in 1905. Another woman remembered the days she had participated in the Sunday school in 1918. According to her account, five hundred children were enrolled. Children were everywhere, she said, filling the nursery and the hall, and after church they went upstairs for Bible study. Today the aging population, mainly over 65 years old, is highly dispersed, living in communities as far away as fifteen kilometres, in Notre Dame de Grace (N.D.G.), Verdun, and Ville LaSalle. As one woman pointed out to me, many former Grace Church members became the nucleus for newer churches in the suburbs of Montreal. When N.D.G. first began to grow, "a lot moved out of the Point; St Matthew's Church was half from here in its early days." But many others who moved out of the area continued to maintain their links with Grace Church, sometimes as active members and sometimes as financial contributers or as visitors at special events.

Community at Grace Church is strongly associated with memories of the past and a long association with the church. Everyone remembered the "old days" with fondness for the vibrant community and lively social functions. One of the women described the activities of Gord, who she pointed out to me as he helped to organize the rummage sale, move tables, and count the money. Gord had been in Sunday school with them back in the 1920s and through the years had taken on a multiplicity of roles in the church. He has sung in the choir, played the organ, and served as warden, treasurer, and delegate to Synod. He continues to influence virtually every role, committee, and event. His parents had been active church members, and his own commitment is almost legendary among the congregation.

Church suppers, to which the wider community is frequently invited, are another very important source of community sharing. These are always very well attended. An annual anniversary dinner each October, which includes entertainment by a local amateur group, usually attracts over a hundred people. The importance of these events was made clear when I arrived fifteen minutes early for the 6:00 PM dinner in 1988. Most people were already seated, quietly chatting as they waited for dinner to be served. The rector was nowhere to be seen. At the precise time on the ticket he emerged from a back office, leading a small group of invited guests, who in-

cluded other local clergy and the bishop and his wife, to the head table. Gord acted as master of ceremonies, introducing the head table and inserting jokes that helped everyone feel they were included in the community of sharing. One couple had driven over a hundred kilometres from St Agathe in order to attend the dinner. The husband explained that he had grown up in Point St Charles, and even after he had left, spending years in Britain as a Rhodes scholar and later in Toronto as a dean at the university, he has always retained his connection with Grace Church. The couple support the church financially and usually attend services about once a month. While this is perhaps the most extreme example, many of the people on the parish list have never been members of any other church, and many continue to return to Grace even after moving into other neighbourhoods. Another couple who return each year for the anniversary celebration live about ten kilometres away and are active members of another church. But they maintain their links with Grace to the extent that they are on the residence board of directors and always attend the important social functions. The entertainment for the evening was a local "kitchen band," including washtub strings and kazoo, which kept the dinner guests entertained for almost an hour and a half with songs familiar to the elderly assemblage.

Another dinner held annually is the potluck dinner before the Ash Wednesday service at the beginning of Lent. Typically a group of six women work all afternoon at the church, baking "extras" and sharing the social time together. By 5:30, a half-hour before the dinner is to be served, people begin arriving, some carrying casseroles or desserts, immediately seating themselves at tables. Of the thirty-eight people who came for dinner in 1988, no one was under 60 years old. All of the men were in suits, and the women all wore neat dresses with jewellery. Three women were particularly striking because of their chic clothes, one wearing a fur coat and hat, another a navy wool coat, and the third a smart-looking snood over her head. Two of them worked closely together on the Grace Church residence over many years, and only one of the three actually lives in Point St Charles near the church. At these dinners, although everyone is known to each other, there are distinctive groups: the three chic ladies, the lively workers in the kitchen, a few elderly ladies from the residence, the men, and finally a group who always seem to come in pairs and who never talk at all.

Despite the cheerful chatter of the rector and a particular sense of persistent community, there was also a sense of resignation among most of the people. At the anniversary dinner in 1989, a francophone city councillor was one of the invited guests. He gave a short but comprehensive presentation, completely in English, on an issue of special interest, the proposed changes in the local bus routes, which would greatly facilitate transportation to the downtown. He was thanked by only polite clapping. More successful in generating an enthusiastic response were twelve women from a neighbouring church who provided old fashioned entertainment in the singing of such classics as "White Cliffs of Dover', and "Hello Dolly." Their average age was about 66, and their obvious enjoyment was transmitted to the audience.

One important part of the life at Grace Church was the residence for the elderly that was opened in 1969 but was finally closed early in 1990 because there were too few residents. It provided room and board for women who did not need nursing care and who could dress themselves. It was a house with nine bedrooms, a living room/ dining room, and a large kitchen. While it was still in operation, it was explained to me that "the people are not all Anglican, but they must all go to the monthly communion service, even if they're Catholic. Bruce [the rector] is very fussy about that." When it closed after all attempts to attract new residents had failed, there were only three women living there. It also provided a significant focus for the organizational energies of one long-term Grace Church member who has lived in the Point since 1942 and had been a nurse until her retirement in the mid-1970s. She and another woman had managed the finances of the residence, arranged for all maintenance, and supervised the person who cooked the meals. They also helped the residents with some of their shopping. Its closing was a blow to the church's sense of direction and service in the community, as well as to the individuals who had taken it on as their special mission.

The monthly "select vestry" meetings are very low key and extremely short, being mainly a presentation of the rector's activities and a financial report from the women's association. Typically there is no discussion of broad issues concerning the overall direction of the church in the community, attention being focused on the amount of money brought in by the rummage sale or on the problem of finding an organist. There is a pervasive sense of the need to survive, of having to hold on to the declining community and the church building as a way of preserving the remnants of a past, though without any real hope for the future. The interviews, while reflecting this atmosphere, also indicated a depth of strength and perseverance that seemed almost heroic in this time of alienation and cynicism. To the sense of fatalism was added acceptance without bitterness.

One of my conversations illustrates how family ties are used as a way of ensuring the survival of Grace Church. The woman I talked to attends Grace Church "most Sundays," especially for the sake of her 80-year-old parents who still live in the Point. She had moved out of the area after high school, but while she had lived there, she had not realized that the Point was "blue collar." When she was first married, she lived in an adjacent community, but for the past twenty years she has resided in a middle-class suburb about twenty kilometres from the Point. Her own daughter is now a teacher at a school located even farther away from Point St Charles. When her daughter gets married in June, it will be at a church close to the suburban home she and her husband will settle in. As her mother told me, despite the distance factor, the daughter had considered having her wedding at Grace Church, "cause you'll never find a nicer church anywhere ... not with the lovely decoration." Only with the granddaughter is there a reluctant break with membership at Grace Church.

In addition to generational ties, links through participation in church events help in the church's survival, even after parishioners move out of the parish and into other churches. This was made apparent at a service in September 1989 as I witnessed the active roles of two couples who had returned for the anniversary service. One man, who had arrived a half-hour early, went up one aisle and down the next, greeting everyone in the church before the service started.

The second man, Ron, stood helping people down the chancel steps all during communion. Said one parishioner to me, "The single most important thing about the church is the people, regardless of whether they are educated or not. They are good people, and that gives me hope, a good feeling. They provide a sense of support. I'm sorry I didn't go to functions earlier. I never used to go. I might have been better off with them, in the forties. Their heads are on right. Relationships were cemented in the 1920s and 30s."

One long-term member who has lived in the Point for almost fifty years was resigned to the probability that Quebec would separate from Canada, and his response was to "let them have it." He would probably move to the Maritimes. Typically many of the older people have children and grandchildren living outside Quebec, such as Faith, whose children live in Winnipeg and Kitchener; the Watts, whose children are in Nova Scotia; and the Mitchells, whose daughter had moved to Vancouver. Said one lady: "If I were younger I would leave the province." But she went on to add, "If it separated I would stay: I don't give a damn, as long as my friends stayed." Among those who have stayed there is a sense of resignation and an apparent feeling of powerlessness to effect any change. When the city councillor came to the dinner to describe the plans to improve transportation, no one asked any questions. When I enquired about who had been elected in their riding two days after the provincial election in 1988, no one seemed to be sure. And when the rector announced that there was a petition on the notice board to be signed by those wishing to protest Bill 178, very few added their signatures.

I asked the rector about the parish involvement in the Point community projects. He said that when he had arrived in the parish in 1983, he decided to stay away from any involvement because they were all "Marxist-Leninist" groups. The anniversary and Lenten meals, the residence, and the twice monthly rummage sales are the focus of interest at Grace. The survival of the community of Grace Church is the overriding goal. Loyalty to this community is of paramount importance. With its many parishioners who have been members for over fifty years and who have family ties going back even further, Grace Church may have the highest proportion of long-time members of any church in the diocese. The other side of this is the absence of any growth through new and younger family members.

While one sees in the heroic struggles for survival at Grace Church the extremes in the diocese, elements of these can be seen at many other churches in varying degrees. In the determination of the women to retain control of their finances and to carve out a niche of self-affirmation, in the rejection of a modern prayer book, and in the return of members for the anniversary services, there is a tangible demonstration of a need to belong and, in the context of a community, to ensure that identity is nurtured and affirmed.

8 St Paul's Church, Knowlton

In many ways St Paul's Church is the most complex of the five churches. Within it are several distinctive groups defined by interests, historical experience, theological concerns, and socio-economic backgrounds, with the result that interpretation of the meanings St Paul's has for people is more difficult than for the others. Unlike the fairly homogeneous populations of St Matthias and Grace Church, which have maintained a consensus concerning liturgical choices, the parishioners of St Paul's are from diverse backgrounds, experiences, and traditions. This fact, combined with a period of significant change in both church and community, has meant that St Paul's has had a recent history of tension and acrimonious debate, but also one of growth and renewal.

St Paul's is located 125 kilometres from Montreal in a formerly rural environment, in the town of Lac Brome (formerly and more commonly known as Knowlton), which has a population of five thousand. "Formerly rural" is an important description because it underpins some of the variable responses within the church, reflecting a rapidly changing social context. Located on a beautiful lake and surrounded by the rolling hills and mountains of the Eastern Townships, Knowlton has been a second home to many wealthy anglophone families for generations. Many of these families own estates and wooded properties, and over the years they have made substantial contributions (including endowments) to St Paul's. Some of them have moved permanently to Knowlton following retirement from active employment. For some parishioners Knowlton is their

only home, where they work and go to school. Among these people are some whose family roots go back several generations, while others have moved to Knowlton in the past decade to set up new businesses, taking advantage of the growing local economy. Finally, a significant impact upon the landscape of Knowlton and its environs has been made by a new and growing group of two-home "yuppies," many of whom choose condominium living. The changing landscape and social fabric of Knowlton are factors in the tensions and changing congregations of St Paul's.

The conflicts and tensions we see in the church are reflections of those permeating all aspects of Knowlton's economic and social life. Evidence that the social milieu of Knowlton is changing, with concurrent impacts upon the landscape, can be found in newspaper articles and letters to the editor. In response to a newspaper article critical of the new "obligatory antique-looking wooden signs," which were seen as a new "yuppie image," one resident and businessman defended the changes, pointing out that "dozens of business people have worked together restoring dilapidated turn-of-the-century buildings."[1]

His defence of the changes in Knowlton articulated the conflict of values and interest groups that have characterized Knowlton's social milieu especially during the late 1980s. As described in a travel article in the summer of 1990, "This once sleepy village by the shores of Lac Brome has become a hive of entrepreneurial activity, mainly thanks to the efforts of out-of-towners who have come here to start new businesses ... a complex of historic clapboard homes converted into boutiques, art galleries and restaurants."[2]

The author describes many of the new entrepreneurs who have recently arrived from Toronto, New York, and Montreal, to "get off the fast track." "It seemed as if every second person was from somewhere other than Knowlton. The newcomers have brought new blood to the village, but despite their entrepreneurial successes, many are resented by the old guard." The definition of "newcomer" varies. When I asked one long-time resident if she had family roots in Knowlton, her reply was, "Oh no. We've been here for only thirty years." But she remembered seeing the mother of one church member "driving in a horse and buggy with a small black hat on her head." Since she seemed to feel she was really "from the city," I asked if that meant she was part of the "Westmount group" I had been hearing about. No, she did not feel there was an association there either. Describing a different group of newcomers, she said to me, "The people who have bought the condominiums are the ones who come out only on weekends. They haven't integrated into the community at all. And there's a lot of French. It's quite alarming."[3]

The perception that there are different groups is accurate and significant. The subject frequently comes up in discussions about the community and church. Another woman described the farm she had lived on for many years, near the "old cattle trail" that goes up over the Glen towards the railway tracks. "Now there are trails all over the place. The area of West Bolton is known as 'Little Westmount' – or they would like it known as that! They bring their city out here with them." Said one member to me: "We have a very strange mixture of locals and Montrealers here." Then she went on to define herself as a local, while her husband was certainly a Montrealer, transplanted a year earlier following his retirement.

Newcomers and old guard; young families, couples, the elderly; the wealthy and the middle class; farmers and retailers – all are part of the new mosaic of Knowlton and of the stone Anglican church situated just behind the city hall. The church itself was established over 150 years ago in 1840, but it was rebuilt following a fire in 1941. It holds about 250 people. About one hundred parishioners attend on an average Sunday, most of whom live within three kilometres of the church. The parish list includes 155 names, of whom about

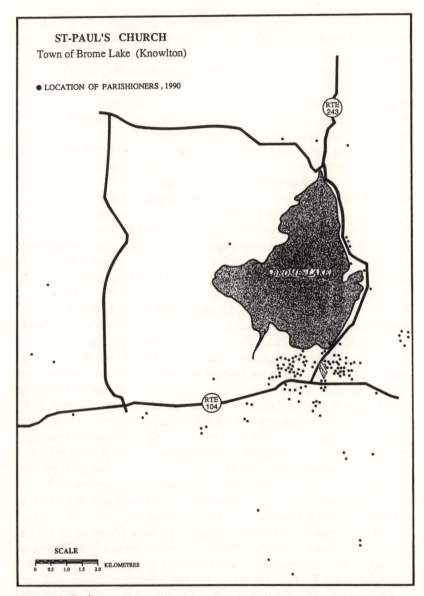

Map 6   St Paul's

75 per cent are in church at least once a month; 140 are identifiable givers; and about 100 have envelopes.

A description of the characteristics of St Paul's is a study in contrasts compared to the diocese and the two churches already described. Echoing these contrasts are highlights of the church interior itself, beautifully framed by vaulted dark wood beams and lit by softly sculpted lamps. At the chancel steps a proud eagle mounted on a lectern sits under a handmade banner inviting the congregation to "Come and See." The traditional windows bearing family names such as Graffety, Foster, and Buchanan light a book display at the back of the church, which includes titles dominated by themes of evangelism, prayer, and family life. Evidence of the important presence of young families can be found at another lectern at the back, where a visitor can leaf through an album of photographs recording significant events in parish life such as a tree planting and parish barbecue. The divisions within the congregation, however, are illustrated most tellingly by the two sets of bulletins, one for a traditional 8:00 AM service, the other for the 10:00 AM service, which includes an extra sheet with "Songs of Praise and Worship."

Divisions aside, the church is alive. Attendance, membership, and offerings all show significant increases since 1980. Membership in the period from 1981 to 1986 rose by 75 per cent, compared to a decline of 15 per cent in the diocese. In contrast to the few children in Sunday school classes at both Grace and St Matthias churches, the St Paul's school has an enrolment of more than fifty, with an average weekly attendance of thirty-five. The Sunday congregation at St Paul's is strikingly younger than most, dominated by couples in their thirties and forties. While all of the other churches I studied have a youth group that is barely surviving, at St Paul's there is an active ecumenical group involving about twenty-five young people. Small group Bible studies and "house churches" involve about seventy parishioners in weekly meetings. The parish profile sent to a prospective clergy applicant in 1987 for the position of rector described the church this way: "A Christian community ... A biblical church ... A worshipping community ... A service church." It is a church that seems to have defied all the trends in Montreal Diocese. Nevertheless, there has been a cost.

A persistent decline, from 1971 to 1981, in membership and offerings was reversed at St Paul's with the arrival in 1982 of a young, energetic, and charismatic priest who initiated significant changes, that ultimately lead to a growth in membership. The growth was accompanied by severe stress within the congregation as older, conservative members reacted to the evangelical nature of the new ministry. Changes in the music, challenging preaching from the pulpit, unwavering acceptance of new liturgical forms with the introduction of the Book of Alternative Services, Bible study in homes, and an active healing ministry all combined to threaten the tradition of Anglican conservatism. Seventeen people are known to have left the

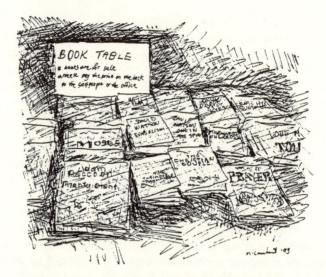

church, although several continue to contribute financially. When members were asked to characterize those who left, the response was "the cocktail circuit." Clearly they were people who could not accept the introduction of non-traditional forms and styles. The decrease in revenues was more than compensated for by an increase in the number of smaller weekly contributions, and most people I talked to, while unhappy about those who had left, felt that on balance the new situation was much more hopeful for the future. They initially told me that those who had left St Paul's had been very active in the church, but on reconsideration the consensus seemed to be that "they weren't really very regular attenders." It seemed that their real commitment was "in their wallet." On the other hand, any time there had been a real need for something in the church, such as a new carpet, "they were informed and it just appeared." Their main participation had been in their attendance at the annual vestry meeting each January.

When the young priest left for a church in Winnipeg in 1987, a search committee was formed to choose the replacement. The selection process itself provides an interesting commentary on the changing nature of both the congregation at St Paul's and the community of Knowlton. At the meeting where six members of the search committee were to be named through an election process (two wardens would fill out the complement to eight members), twelve people were nominated for the six positions. One woman who ran for a spot and failed had not attended church for four years; she was highly disgruntled and has not appeared at St Paul's since. However, she had wanted to serve on the committee, recognizing its importance in establishing the criteria for selection on the basis of parish priorities and, ultimately, in finding a new rector. The clergy, in part determined by the leadership in the lay community, can have a profound impact upon the growth or decline of a church, particularly during periods of change. The statistics clearly show that clerical leadership can have a significant impact on attendance, financial contributions, and membership. These statistical data reflect the ways in which people respond to the ministries, personalities, and capabilities of the clergy. The data show how styles of leadership relate to the degree of acceptance of spiritual and theological questions.

One of the most significant areas of change initiated by the new priest in 1982 had been the introduction of "home churches" (see Appendix E). As a significant basis for community and fellowship, these provided a concrete vehicle for strengthening commitment to the church beyond the Sunday services. Their downside was described to me by one participating member: "People get comfortable in their groups, and they don't want to split them up in order to form new groups. After a while they are seen as being cliquish, and they don't grow." Many of the older, more conservative people in the church do not participate in these small group meetings, finding them divisive and exclusive.

The language of the parishioners clearly reflects the deeply spiritual meanings they attach to their church. The 1987 parish profile referred to earlier was prepared for prospective new priests. It described the community around St Paul's, its congregation, and the various ministries that are offered (the church school, youth ministry, house churches, visitation, overseas mission, family life, music ministry, prayer chain, tape ministry, and so on). Each activity in the church is viewed as a special ministry guided by people whom "God has gifted" in those areas. At the annual vestry meeting in 1989, there was a discussion about how decisions should be made in the parish. One man said that they must "take these issues and talk about them ... pray about them, and see where we stand in the Lord, to ensure that we are more Christ-centred." This is not the language of Grace Church or St Matthias.

In many ways, however, St Paul's reflects the discussions, debates, and problems common to other churches in the diocese. The members of the Anglican Church Women (ACW), verbalized the frustrations and dilemmas that seem to plague all of Montreal's Anglican churches – young women are not joining; many young women work and cannot attend midday meetings; older women prefer daytime meetings because they do not like driving at night; young women are not interested in bazaars and knitting; and so forth. As with other churches, the women's association at St Paul's has difficulty filling its executive positions and there are fewer members each year. In 1991 about fifteen women attended the monthly meetings, which tended to be mainly social gatherings following a short Eucharist. Because of the social nature of these gatherings, there was friction with the new rector, who would have liked to insist upon theological content in all church activities. Resistance by the women to any redefinition of their activities was immediate and unequivocal.

A characteristic of the St Paul's ACW, one that is typical of the women's associations I encountered everywhere, is the way the women retain control over all fund-raising decisions and the eventual disbursement of funds. The thousands of dollars raised by the women through bazaars, rummage sales, and coffee parties does not enter the records or budget of the corporate church; the accounts are not audited; and the women decide how the money will be spent. These arrangements seem to reflect not only a need to exert control in a particular area of church affairs, but also the situation of women in society. There was real antagonism towards the rector when, soon after his arrival in 1987, he "suggested" that rummage sales and bazaars did not meet his criteria for "Christian action." The women's antagonism was directly related to the way they defined their roles in the ongoing work of the church and its mission to those in need in the community. At their annual meeting in November 1988 the group of twenty women decided how they would allocate over $2,000. For the sister church nearby, in desperate need of repairs, there would be $1,000; $100 would be given to the Sunday school; $100 would be given to each of two residences in other areas. They continued in this way until most of the balance had been allocated. There was a strong sense that the rector's intervention in the process would not be welcome. Within a few months of his arrival, the new rector did intervene, with the result that two executive members resigned. His fundamentalist theological position put him at odds with raffles, the serving of alcohol at meetings, and the celebration of Hallowe'en by the Scouts and Cubs in the church basement. The women were accustomed to serving sherry when acting as hostesses for the deanery meeting. To be advised by a new rector, after years of this practice, that this would no longer be acceptable was seen both as unreasonable and as a rejection of their self-defined roles. Many of the women were unwilling to accept any restriction on their activities. The ACW clearly feels it should be allowed to define its areas of contribution without interference.

Opposition to the new prayer book, which precluded its introduction at both Grace Church and St Matthias, is manifested at St Paul's by the existence of two congregations: one older, traditional group at 8:00 AM, when the 1959 Book of Common Prayer is used, and another younger, family-centred one at 10:00 AM, when the new Book of Alternative Services is used, together with modern songs and guitar accompaniment. Part of the concern over the BAS focuses on the modern language and on the informality of the service. But there is also antipathy towards the exchange of the Peace. Said one of the older women: "People would come flying over to me, give me a hug and a kiss! I never knew what to expect. It was awful." On the other hand, even though she usually attends the early service, she admitted that the new rector has "toned [the BAS service] down a little" by suggesting that people shake hands and not move around the church as much. Her objection seems to have been to the bodily contact (hugging) rather than to the actual exchange. There are others who will not acknowledge, even by a handshake, the exchanged prayer of Peace, saying that it is "such an invasion of my private space."

On one occasion the rector implicitly acknowledged the reality of two congregations when he announced at the eight o'clock service that there was to be a baptism by immersion in the afternoon at one of the nearby farms and that everyone was invited. "This isn't only for the ten o'clocks," he said, "it's for the eight o'clocks too!" During the announcements he also noted the upcoming picnic the following weekend, stressing that he hoped they (the people at the eight o'clock service) would feel welcome.

Even the style of dress at the two services points to the contrasting meaning systems of the two congregations. At the early service, suits on the men, dresses on the women, and generally smart attire describe the dress style. The young families and couples who arrive for the ten o'clock service, on the other hand, wear slacks, casual sweaters, and plaid shirts. The informality of the later service is apparent even when the traditional BCP service is followed, as for example in June 1991 when most of the hymns were "Songs of Praise," part of the liturgy (the Venite) was taken from the modern songbook, and guitar accompaniment was used. The response from the older members of the congregation is their absence. At this service very few in the congregation were from the older age groups or represented long-time residents. In the autumn of 1991 I asked the organist about the modernization of the BCP service. Without openly criticizing the form of service, she admitted that there was no clear direction and that many people felt a sense of unease and confusion.

In addition to the controversy around the use of the new prayer book, there has been some apprehension about the introduction of pre-confirmation communion for children, mainly among the older, more conservative members of the parish, those who attend the early BCP service. Baptism has also been an important issue in the Anglican Church in the past decade, with clergy having different opinions on the criteria for accepting or rejecting a "candidate." At St Paul's the two most recent incumbents have taken a fundamentalist stance towards the ritual, feeling that non-church attenders should not expect to have their children baptised at St Paul's. This has generated concern among some of the older members who would like to have grandchildren baptised in the church but whose own children may not be practising Anglicans.

Despite the evidence of divisiveness, there is a significant sense of shared community and common commitment among all groups in the church. Although there is an inevitable separateness in activities such as the women's bazaars and the younger families' ski day, there are also opportunities for shared participation. At a spaghetti supper in the winter of 1988, more than 130 tickets were sold, and although the majority of those who attended were young families (including about thirty children ranging in age from 2 to 17 years), there were also a significant number of older people. Organized by the young people with exuberance and informality, the evening included entertainment by old and young alike – skits, songs, and jokes – which all contributed to a lively shared experience of community. One contribution to the program was a poem read by a mentally handicapped girl who is always included in church activities. Abandoned as a child and brought up in a series of foster homes, she is obviously very comfortable with the community at St Paul's, and her poetry reading was well received by everyone. One noteworthy aspect of these informal social occasions is that they are scheduled for Saturday nights. At most churches social events carefully avoid Saturday nights when "people might be busy."

Other avenues for social interaction are provided in the monthly hymn-sings at the nearby sister church, which is being maintained but is not used for services. The hymn-sings are organized by one of St Paul's long-time members in order to help fund the church's maintenance and for the pure enjoyment of community sharing. They run from June through October and attract about seventy people, which is all the tiny church can hold. There has been a sporadic move on the part of the men to organize a "men's breakfast" on Saturday mornings. In general, however, the most active men in the church recently have been the younger men who participate in the Sunday school and help to organize family social events such as the ski day and the spaghetti dinner.

The budget is a problem common to all churches, and especially the challenge of ensuring it has a positive balance at the end of each year. At St Paul's, in contrast to the other churches, even the discussion of money is in words and language strongly tied to religious faith. Discussion of the budget usually takes up a major part of annual vestry meetings. In 1989 at St Paul's, however, the budget was not introduced until three hours into the evening meeting, by which time some people had left. Among those who stayed there was concern that they could not afford a deficit, as it would absorb endowment interest, but they expressed this concern over a purely financial dilemma as follows: "We need teaching on what God wants, and how to apply the biblical teaching," and "When the spiritual life improves, the giving will increase ... that's the Lord's work." There was some discussion about tithing and about the possibility of a parish letter asking members to consider that as an option in their pledges. In the end no action was taken in terms of a parish letter, but it was agreed that more planning should be done in future to avoid overspending.

Mission is another area of church involvement that helps to illuminate the meaning behind church participation. I suggested earlier that the extent to which parishioners feel threatened will influence their willingness to contribute to causes outside their own community. Parishioners at St Matthias have given a substantial degree of financial support for mission outside their parish, particularly for several women's centres in Montreal, both directly and through the apportionment system of the diocese. At Grace Church, on the other hand, there has been almost no mission support outside the parish. St Paul's provides another variation on the way parish churches consider their responsibility for Christian mission beyond their individual parishes. In financial terms St Paul's has allocated approximately 20 per cent of its budget to mission, a figure that is suggested by the diocese, but it has contributed to a specific project in Africa, aimed at providing a rice mill for a village. But in fact, and not in any sense atypically, there has been very little discussion of or expressed concern for outreach at St Paul's. The following exchange at one parish council meeting, at which the group was trying to establish a budget to be presented at the annual vestry meeting, illustrates the attitudes of many parishioners in many churches. The ambivalence on the part of most discussants towards a commitment to mission is a strong thread throughout the discussion.

J. – Under ministry beyond the parish, we didn't quite know what to do here. The local youth is what C. was asking about a minute ago. For mission outreach there isn't a place in the budget. If there was a category, then people could occasionally put money into an envelope especially for outreach – for SAMS, or the rice mill, or whatever.

K. – But maybe it would be better to simply allow it to be an "in and out" amount, and not be included as a budgetary item.

C. – But what does that say about our church, in the sense that our budget doesn't include anything other than the church's assessment for mission. When I give a dollar to the church and none of it is spent on mission outreach except for what the diocese has asked for, we have no control over how that money is spent. But I'm suggesting we put aside money in the budget for mission outreach. Why can't we look after mission the way we look after building maintenance? Why can't we set up a mission fund just as we're proposing to set up a capital fund for the building and a computer?

F. – Do you want to take money away from something that is already in there? Or do you want to add it on? We're already looking at an 18 per cent increase ...

J. – Should we make it a budget item and increase the budget?

C. – My point is that, even though twenty cents of my dollar goes to mission, I wonder how much of that money actually gets to the people it is supposed to help. I wonder if it is eaten up in administration.

F. – I would rather have no figure than a minimal figure.

The discussion continued. In the end no decision was reached, and there was neither a mission category nor a special fund created. For over half an hour C. persistently presented his view that outreach should be a budgeted item, but in the end his argument was ignored, since that option would mean having to increase the financial commitment of the parish.

St Paul's is a parish with distinctive characteristics in terms of its youthful congregation and strong emphasis on commitment to spiritual values and small Bible study groups. The impact of the new priest in 1982 was profound, and his arrival coincided with significant changes in the demographic characteristics of Knowlton itself. Together, a challenging priest and a changing local community have had significant implications for the nature of the parish. On the other hand, the women's determination to retain control of their activities and finances is indicative of needs unrelated to liturgical or demographic change. Their response to the possibility of change has been to protect their traditional roles and relationships within the church, thereby ensuring continuation of an area in their lives where they have a degree of control, which gives meaning and structure to their lived experience. One member said that the purpose of the women's association was mainly camaraderie and that she liked the mix of people from all sorts of backgrounds, though she acknowledged that the age range was narrow. Despite explicit recognition of an aging membership in their association, which is not being renewed through younger members joining, the women are unwilling to change the nature of their meetings, even to the extent of holding evening rather than daytime meetings. The experience of one young president a few years ago ended with her "leaving in tears." The older woman who described the incident to me was puzzled: "I still haven't figured out why she thought we were so awful." Their dilemma is typical of many churches.

Interviews suggested an uneasiness among church members about the changing nature of the Knowlton community, especially regarding the "condo people," who are not perceived to have compatible community values. There seems to be less concern about the increased numbers of non-anglophones, and certainly few people at St Paul's believe there is any real threat to their own church. Indeed, the dominant attitude was one of confidence for the long term. When I asked one parishioner how she felt about the French ministry in the church, her response was "I've never heard any of it." She thought it was a "good idea" but wondered if there were "any French people interested in the Anglican Church." She expressed the view that perhaps it was "just numbers chasing." When asked whether or not she thought of the Anglican Church as being part of the Church of England, she acknowledged that as a child she had, but that she no longer incorporated this idea into her perception of what the church is. Bilingual signs in the church were okay, she felt – "After all, we're in a French province." Her roots in the Townships extend back to her great-grandparents, who were buried in an Anglican cemetery a few kilometres away. She feels a strong sense of continuity both with the area and with the church, but expressed the view that the rector is "unhappy" with those like her who want to maintain the traditional forms. She had this to say about the young people who attend the ten o'clock service: "They're nice, ordinary kids. I like them." But she prefers the eight o'clock service and its traditional words and form, and like many of the older people in the congregation, she has separated herself from the main service in order to maintain the traditional links.

St Paul's is a complex church, with several distinctive groups of parishioners who have difficulty coming together in worship but who seem to enjoy their differences in other activities. It is a church that seems comfortable in its Quebec milieu, mainly because there has been neither a direct threat to its existence nor a challenge to change its way of doing things in relation to francophones or ethnic minorities. On the other hand, the diverse life experiences and histories in the church have created a particular dynamic which, together with the leadership and ministry styles of two rectors, have contributed to tensions around the issues of change within the church itself. In common with other churches, St Paul's is reluctant to commit itself to mission and justice issues; also like others, its women's group exhibits the need to retain its independence of church officers and budgetary rules. David Martin's description of "local quirks and quiddities" in association with common "dykes and contours" never seemed more appropriate than in relation to St Paul's.

9 Church of the Resurrection

Church of the Resurrection is our fourth church, located in Pointe Claire, a suburb thirty kilometres west of downtown Montreal. The village of Pointe Claire began as a summer community of anglophones on the shores of Lac St Louis, becoming incorporated in 1911. While it retains some of the ambience of a quiet old village since the building of highways in the 1950s and improved public transportation by both bus and train, the suburb has become an important city of thirty thousand population with a balance of residential, commercial, and industrial land uses. It offers an impressive range of services, including a large hospital, nursing homes, indoor skating rinks and swimming pools staffed by Olympic-calibre coaches, facilities for summer programs in baseball, soccer, and tennis, one of the best public libraries in the province, and both English and French schools. The population is predominantly anglophone (75 per cent); average family income is $50,000; and the unemployment rate in 1986 was about 9 per cent, lower than the Montreal average of over 10.3 per cent in that year. Pointe Claire has a slightly higher proportion of older people, with over 11 per cent being over 65 years old. While there is a high rate of mobility (over 40 per cent of the population moved between 1986 and 1991) many residents have lived in the community for several decades. There is a mix of all types of housing, with 57 per cent of the population living in single detached homes, 13 per cent living in highrise apartments, and 27 per cent living in other rental accommodation such as townhouses and low-level apartment buildings. The rapid growth of

Pointe Claire which accompanied the highway construction in the 1950s meant that a high proportion, about 40 per cent, of its housing was built at that time.

In the census tract immediately around the church, the population has a higher proportion of young families and a higher rate of mobility (44 per cent) than Pointe Claire itself. Approximately 75 per cent of the membership of Church of the Resurrection live in the census tract immediately around the church. Built in 1964, the church is of a modern architectural style. Many of today's members were active in the fund-raising campaign at the time of its construction. Despite the diversity of age and mobility characteristics in the congregation, in socio-economic terms the population is homogeneous, middle class, with expectations and attitudes reflecting a conservative, family-oriented tradition. In 1993 there were 209 names on the parish list, which includes 145 families and 64 individuals. Altogether total membership is 533 persons, of whom approximately 130 attend church regularly on Sundays. As with the other churches there are two services: an early service at 8:00 AM using the Book of Common Prayer, and the later 10:00 AM service using the BCP and the Book of Alternative Services alternate weeks. The two sides of the prayer book debate seem to have made a more equable accommodation at Resurrection than at the other churches examined here. While there are certainly some people who attend only the early service because they are assured of the BCP, the kind of antagonism towards the new BAS still apparent at St Paul's or an outright rejection of it, as experienced at St Matthias and Grace churches, cannot be detected here.

General acceptance of a variety of liturgical and musical forms seems to be related to a variety of demographic, community, and leadership factors. The meanings of the church are different from those in the other churches because of different life experiences and differing levels of apprehension for the future. Important consequences of the high mobility at Resurrection, for example, seem to be the ease with which new members are integrated into the congregation and the concomitant lower profile for "entrenched positions." The negative side of mobility is that those who accept positions of leadership (such as wardens) are often unable to complete their terms because of job transfers. The rector noted that the turnover of executive positions, particularly among the younger members, is a serious problem for Resurrection. The diversity of age, on the other hand, has meant that there is a wide variety of activities. At this church the socio-economic homogeneity and the secure anglophone environment of the congregation have had an impact upon many relationships. While there is some diversity of perspective on the meaning of faith, for the most part the members of Resurrection cannot be labelled by one of the main streams of today's Anglicanism. The rector said to me:

I look at a map of the other churches in the area. What are they doing well? One is a fundamentalist church, and getting more so all the time; the two northern neighbours are wildly charismatic, and we have the refugees from there, who don't like the touchy-feely business; and Dorval is from the point of view of social awareness. So now, what sort of ministry can I do here? Basically we've opted for a good liturgical ministry. Doing what others are not doing. This church has always been slightly old-fashioned, leaning towards the liturgical tradition, because of the people it serves.

A few people who are involved in the evangelical Cursillo movement lead Bible study in their homes, but most of the membership look to the church as a community, sharing in social activities and friendships. This is a church in which everyone is known and people are welcomed. It is a democratic church, with monthly meetings where all groups contribute. Above all it is a relaxed church in which everyone is encouraged to participate. The spatial distribution of its members is the most compact of all the churches, with 75 per cent of the congregation living within two kilometres of the church. This nucleated pattern is reflected in the functioning of the church as a centre for community participation, drawing upon both parishioners

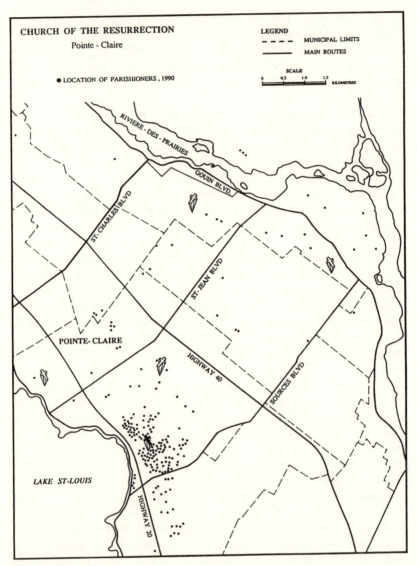

CHURCH OF THE RESURRECTION
Pointe - Claire

● LOCATION OF PARISHIONERS , 1990

LEGEND
– – – – MUNICIPAL LIMITS
———— MAIN ROUTES

SCALE
0   0.5   1.0   1.5
KILOMETRES

RIVIERE - DES - PRAIRIES

GOUIN BLVD.

ST - CHARLES BLVD

ST - JEAN BLVD

POINTE- CLAIRE

HIGHWAY 40

SOURCES BLVD

LAKE ST-LOUIS

HIGHWAY 20

Map 7   Resurrection

and local residents who are not church members. Despite the concentrated distribution, some of the parishioners come from a secondary area about six kilometres away, passing several Anglican
churches on the way. One woman who lives in this more distant area
and who has served as a warden and delegate to Synod described the
experiences she had when attending the other churches when she
first arrived in Montreal five years earlier:

I came from a church which was very similar to Resurrection. The other two parishes, which are closer to my house, are what you might consider ministering churches, and those people are the kind who stand up and affirm, "I am a Christian." When I walked in there it scared me to death. I've been in lots of churches, but you'd never stand up and say that. You'd never go out and knock on someone's door and ask them to come to church. When I walked into those churches I felt like I was in a foreign land. I had to find my way back to Resurrection, in a comfortable setting. It wasn't long after that that the BAS came in, and I grew with that. I love it now. It's something that grows; when the changes come slowly you can accept them and adjust to them. But if you turned to the parishioners tomorrow at Resurrection and asked them, "Okay, what's your special ministry?", well, you'd see the church just clear right out! I'm not going to start preaching the gospel and knocking on my neighbours' doors![1]

The main groups and activities include the Sunday school, in which there are about fifty children registered and approximately twenty-five who attend regularly; the ACW; a monthly "Tea and Topics" (a meeting to which speakers are invited and tea is served following the presentation); a struggling youth group; a group that does pastoral visitation; and an informally organized young families group. There are, of course, also the altar guild and choir. The Bible study group involves about four of the members at Resurrection.

Resurrection's congregation has several distinctive characteristics. First of all, there are overlapping memberships insofar as the groups traditionally run by women are not as segregated as in many other churches. Women and men work together in various activities such as stewardship, social events, and fund-raising bazaars. Moreover, with respect to specific roles and positions, such as wardens, Synod delegates, and greeters, there is no strong gender bias. Secondly, there are many opportunities throughout the year for the various age groups to mix together. These characteristics, examples of which will follow, are related to the homogeneity of the congregation and their common understandings of meanings, to the high mobility combined with a nucleus of long-term residents, and also, at least in part, to the interaction between the rector and the congregation. In encouraging the adoption of the BAS and new songs without rejecting the traditional hymns and use of the familiar "red prayer book," the rector has accepted a middle-of-the-road approach to liturgy and music. He has also supported the need for community social gatherings without any apparent theological content, another policy that has endeared him to his parishioners.

The church members convey a sense of community that is founded upon the security of the larger anglophone community of which they

are a part, but they are also conscious of the need to protect and enhance the shared fellowship. A woman described her concern for her 78-year-old aunt living in the Eastern Townships who is "afraid of dying in French." The aunt's background actually was French, her original forebears being Deschamps, but the family name had been changed four generations earlier to Fields. When I asked what she herself thought about having bilingual signs in Anglican churches, she replied that she was "all for them," but added "There's so much fear among the older people."

The amiability of the Resurrection community has not always been thus. In the late 1970s, for five years until 1982, the incumbent priest was a man who had uncompromising ideas about liturgy, elements of communion, and the theological commitment of every church member. His approach caused a major rift in the congregation. During his time there was a devastating drop in membership and financial contributions, both of which were a direct result of the difficult priest-congregation relationship. At a time when other

Montreal churches were experiencing significant increases in their revenues, the parish income at Resurrection fell precipitously. This was also the time period of the greatest out-migration from Quebec of young anglophones, with the result that this priest had an inordinate impact upon those who stayed in the church. Even today many speak with deep resentment about his inflexible approach to his faith and the difficulties he caused. Said one member to me: "Everything stopped when he was here. Once he called us 'hard-boiled eggs'!" When we look at the ways in which members participate in the church, it is important to take into account not only the relative roles of society, culture, and community relationships, but also the special role of the incumbent minister.

Business meetings offer interesting views of the church-in-action, as they reflect attitudes and values of the parishioners. At the monthly advisory board meetings, a sense of participatory democracy is apparent in the arrangement of chairs in a circle, with no head table. Occasionally, this informality carries over into the presentation of important reports, such as the financial report. At the 1988 annual vestry meeting, this report was presented unaudited and the treasurer was unable to answer fully some of the questions asked. The attitude seemed to be that the financial report was a mere formality. The nominating committee report at this meeting proposed increasing the number of deputy wardens from two to three because of the problems experienced when church officers moved unexpectedly. In thanking the out-going warden at this annual meeting, the rector commented that when she was appointed in 1986 she became the first-ever female warden at Resurrection.

One area in which Resurrection is typical of other churches is in the congregation's general lack of interest in the wider church and, particularly, in outreach or mission. There is almost no discussion about or allocation of money for outreach. The student assistant who served with the rector in 1987 made note of this when she presented her final report to her college. She pointed out that Resurrection is served very well in the areas of fellowship and worship, but that there has been very little concern for outreach into the community and beyond.

Serious concern over the youth of the congregation has been expressed at many meetings. Despite efforts by several parishioners to form and lead a youth group, and despite discussion about the possibility of a paid youth worker, the church has not been able to generate enough interest among the young people to sustain a group. At the 1988 annual vestry meeting the discussion on the needs of youth illustrated the frustrations experienced by many churches. One woman wondered if they could "pool the resources of the three Anglican churches in the area" and hire someone to lead a youth group. When someone wondered how "that would affect our budget," the response was that "even if it [the cost of a youth leader] seems to be major, we need the children for the future!" But some people felt that if "parents can't get kids to church, how can we expect a stranger to?" Others argued that the needs of the young people should be a priority. "The money is important, but we also need faith. God will find the means." When someone suggested asking the teenagers what kind of program they wanted, a man said, "They don't seem to know what they want. They may be interested, but there always seem to be other conflicting activities. Church is at the bottom of their list."

Although the parishioners agreed overall on the importance of a youth leader and that the cost should not matter if the youth get involved, in the end there was no vote on allocating money to a youth project. Despite being located in a community of young families, Resurrection has been unsuccessful in building a youth program.

The women's groups, however, are active and growing. While the ACW is experiencing some of the same problems as in the other churches, there is an enthusiastic group of about twenty women who form a core group. The ACW raises about $15,000 each year through bazaars, a giant garage sale, a military whist, and a fashion show. It is also responsible for catering special events such as the Harvest Supper, and in one case the ACW women hosted a shower for someone who was about to be married and would be moving to Toronto. The ACW membership overlaps with the Tea and Topics group, who arrange for speakers to come once a month to give talks on subjects of general interest to seniors, such as financial planning, antiques, and travel. The number of men and women involved in this monthly activity has grown in two years from about thirty to over seventy-five, many of whom do not belong to the church. It has evolved into a broadly based community activity, providing fellowship for seniors who live in the vicinity of the church.

After one of the ACW meetings one member expressed concern about the group's inability to attract younger women and to fill one of the executive positions. The conversation that ensued was described to me as follows:

S. – And I remember asking one of the ACW ladies, how do you see your role? She said that they are the ones who earn the extra money for the church. But that wasn't all. They're also friends. So in other words, and this was the complaint of one of the young mothers, "I can't afford to hire a babysitter just to come out to socialize." The ACW sees itself as fund raisers and as a group for fellowship. Their concern is, what if it falls apart? And yet, we have the young couples group springing up. Maybe this problem will take care of itself. It might look as if things are being done "because they've always been done that way," but they do change.

The Sunday school is strongly supported, with a core of about six teachers who meet regularly to discuss the curriculum. It has a regular attendance of about thirty children. One of the teachers initiated an Advent event a few years ago that has had success in bringing together the many ages within the church. From grandparents to young children, all are invited to participate. It is essentially a craft fair after church at the beginning of Advent, and everyone has an opportunity to make a variety of decorations, wreaths, and ornaments for Christmas. After a hectic hour and a half, during which time about seventy people, including thirty children, make their decorations, everyone is invited into the church for a short service of dance and blessing. This event typifies the distinctive warm and welcoming community at Resurrection, in which people from all age groups share their faith in mainly social settings with a strong family orientation. Another way in which the young families have begun to emphasize their need for community sharing is in their informal bowling nights. This activity attracts about twenty-five adults and some teenagers.

The lively and relaxed atmosphere of a Thanksgiving dinner in 1988 was very different from the quiet, seated group I had encountered at Grace Church. The participatory democracy already mentioned was evident at this social event in the method of determining which table would be invited to line up first at the buffet table: numbers were chosen from a hat. An auction later that evening provided for more shared fun and laughter. Bidding was fast and furious for the services of fellow parishioners (such as a dinner for four or help with home repairs). An informal sing-song led by a new church member brought the evening's fun to a close.

Other community-oriented programs at Resurrection include the summer day camp for children 4–12 years old and a pastoral visiting program. The latter is supported by about fifteen parishioners – both women and retired men – who visit about twenty hospitalized and shut-in people. The day camp attracts about seventy-five youngsters from the neighbourhood, including many who are not affiliated with the church. These shared community-of-interest activities seem to be related to the high degree of homogeneity in the community at large. Most people are of middle-class and anglophone backgrounds. On the other hand, there is evidence of lack of interest in and support for outreach beyond the local community.

During one of the advisory board meetings at which the motions to be presented at the upcoming Synod meeting were on the agenda, someone asked, "Should the church be involved in politics at all?" The rector firmly pointed out that the church is part of society, is affected by it, and should be active in it. Someone else expressed concern about the motions opposing free trade and the nuclear submarine program. All the views expressed reflected conservative, middle-class perspectives.

At another meeting, called to discuss a critique of the parish prepared by the student assistant, there was barely disguised hostility to his assessment that "Resurrection is not working at reaching out beyond its immediate community." In part, the congregation resented the student's assumption that church members should feel "called to a ministry." There was a consensus that the concept of ministry carried threatening evangelical connotations and that "only a minority of people see their Christian commitment as a ministry." One woman at the meeting said, "Most of the people at Resurrection regard what they do as a bloody duty. The ACW is putting on this; I'm a member, so I'd better turn up and take my station, whether it's at the kitchen sink, or whatever. They certainly wouldn't talk in terms of a ministry."

The idea of developing a mission statement for the parish was unequivocally rejected as being unnecessarily wasteful of time and energy. In defending their "many quiet ministries behind the scenes," the members expressed a sense of frustration that an outsider had seen only the reported events, apparently remaining unaware of the informal network of support providing drives, visits, and meals. Concerns for youth and continuity of lay leadership were viewed as internal problems that came out of the societal context but that should ultimately be solved within the framework of the existing structure of Resurrection.

In arguing for ongoing growth in the church, one woman used the example of Tea and Topics, pointing out that this event "has been enormously successful" in reaching out into the community. The hostile tone of the meeting gradually moderated as everyone began to focus on the perceived strengths of the parish.

S. – There's a continuity here, isn't there?

B. – Well, I'll tell you this. There's quite a few here who I went to school with; that's when there was a huge youth group and nothing else.

S. – And now we have all these young children all over the place. It's getting better. I think you can start to look out of the parish when you're sure the roof over your head is going to hold. I think that's the stage we're reaching. We're starting to feel secure and confident, not only financially but also our numbers are growing.

J. – It's much easier to absorb gradual growth. Because each church has an ethos, and in a way you want the people to make that ethos theirs ... the joining of stories.

L. – And yet we've come a long way in ten years. It used to be that you knew when you walked in what book you would be using, which hymns would be sung, and you could fit in comfortably. We've moved a long way from that, but at our own pace, not feeling we're radically changing. We're maybe not running, but we're moving, steady, like the tortoise. Dependable. You know where you're going to be when you go to church. There's not going to be any big surprises pulled on you, which is important in our changing society.

J. – Some sort of continuity with the past, and recognizably Anglican.

B. – Therein lies my security.

S. – I had a little concern when I first read it [the student's report], and I was concerned about this word "status quo." Many of the people I've spoken to were so worried at one time about losing the whole shooting match, the whole church as they knew it, that they were clinging in many ways to the status quo, because they were afraid of losing it. But we're starting to feel comfortable now, secure enough with the parish and fellow parishioners, with the minister, with the community, that we can start to grow now.

The parishioners recognition of the church's vulnerability and hence of their need to protect it is woven into the larger community context in which they feel confident in their commitment and mutual responsibility. As one loyal parishioner expressed it, "If a request goes out that somebody is needed to help, I think you'll find that they'll be there. Something I'd like to say is that if old people were encouraged to form a prayer ring it could be an incredible dynamic. And I would be prepared to go out and visit people, and talk about this. We haven't tried that, have we?" As the meeting came to a close, the student asked for an overall reaction to his report. Replied one woman, "A little bit over-critical, I think."

The Church of the Resurrection, with its mobile, economically and linguistically homogeneous membership, reflects the community within which it is located. The parishioners span all age groups and live, for the most part, in the immediate vicinity of the church. Insofar as its location alleviates the immediate threat to survival that haunts Grace Church, for example, Resurrection can enjoy a security that frees its members to approach liturgical changes within the church more equably. The variety of activities and the membership overlaps indicate a connectedness between community and church that is less definable in the other churches I investigated. While interviews and discussions revealed a conscious awareness of the problems inherent in the minority status of anglophones in Quebec and the importance of the church as an anglophone institution, there is no real sense that imminent demise was possible. The importance of the church to the identities of some parishioners is apparent in their stories of past events, from the original fund-raising campaign in the early 1960s to the problem of the rector in the late 1970s. There are attachments to rituals such as baptism, and discussions were intense as to where they should take place in the church. But always there is a sense of openness. There are few signs of entrenched interests and few examples of a concern with the status of old families. Compared to other churches, there is flexibility and democracy, but still no utopian initiatives. The security of community location does not encompass a global confidence.

10 La Nativité

La Nativité is unique in the diocese. It is an Anglican Haitian congregation without its own church, relying instead on the rented premises of an anglophone church in Rosemount. The large, red-brick church, St Luke's, was built in 1908 and continues to be the spiritual home for a small congregation of English-speaking parishioners on Sunday mornings. Like that around Grace Church, the community around St Luke's is no longer dominantly English speaking; rather there is a multicultural, multi-racial mix of languages and religions. The church is situated in a landscape of semi-detached brick houses and rows of duplexes and triplexes, most fronted by old trees and cracked sidewalks.

The congregation of La Nativité, totally Haitian, rents use of the church on Sunday afternoons and other occasional times when they have special events. Attending one of their services is an experience in cultural transformation. Apart from the architecture of a large old Anglican church, there is little that is familiar. The prayer book is a French translation of the American Episcopal book, and the hymn book is a Creole photocopy, recently brought from Haiti. The language of the service moves back and forth, from Creole to French, in the singing, the sermon, announcements, and liturgy. But language is not the only distinction that gives La Nativité an ambience unlike that of the other Anglican churches in the diocese. More important is the informal behavior of the congregation, as well as the way they interact with one another, as they enter the service, often up to an hour late, and make their way to the front of the church,

chatting quietly. Until the recent introduction of the new hymn book, the music had been a lilting, unaccompanied singing of Creole songs. The Peace is exchanged as a rhythmic song-dance, during which everyone is greeted. The sermon frequently lasts more than half an hour, and throughout it people continue to enter the church, all the while greeting their friends. The service usually begins on time at about 2:15, when there might be ten people in the church; by the time the sermon begins, typically about fifty people are there; and by the end of the service perhaps seventy people have gathered.

There are about a hundred families on the parish list, of whom about half are represented on any given Sunday. Unlike at other parishes where the majority of parishioners live within two kilometres of the church, at La Nativité the majority live between ten and fifteen kilometres away. Widely dispersed in outlying, low-rental areas, most must depend upon public transportation.

The parish was originally established in 1975 when a few Haitians began meeting in the home of a Haitian priest. A few months later they began to hold services in a hotel room, a situation that continued for about a year. St Luke's was then chosen as a location because of its availability for afternoon services. In 1978 a new priest, White and anglophone, was appointed. According to the present incumbent, he "n'a pas reçu bon accueil lors de sa première messe à la paroisse." [1] However, during his eight-year tenure he became a loyal friend to many recently arrived Haitians and the trusted spiritual leader of the Haitian church. Interestingly, his replacement, Père Joseph from Haiti, provoked some concern among the congregation.

According to a knowledgable priest, they feared that a Haitian priest would represent the authoritarian style of Haiti. The congregation wanted someone who would help integrate them into North American life. However, following an interview by members of the congregation, Father Joseph was accepted in 1985, and La Nativité has continued to serve a small but loyal group of Haitian Anglicans. In 1990 two other small Haitian congregations were established in the Montreal area, one in Montreal North and another in Lachine.

Members of La Nativité were all active in their churches in Haiti before immigrating to Canada, and their social relationships within the church reflect their Haitian culture. In a report he prepared about his parish, Father Joseph described his congregation, noting the important role of women:

Il est important de mentionner dès maintenant que les femmes actives constituent environ 90 à 95 pour cent de l'assistance régulière. Elles forment l'épine dorsale de la paroisse. Leur âge varie entre 25 et 50 ans. Si certaines sont infirmières et d'autres secrétaires de bureaux, la grande majorité travaille dans les manufactures. Les hommes ont entre 25 et 60 ans et sont tous mariés. Ils travaillent dans les manufactures. Les jeunes ... sont impreignés de la culture québécoise. Les enfants sont ceux dont l'âge se situe entre 0 et 14. Ils sont nés au Canada. Ils parlent tous le français mais comprennent le créole. [2]

The distance travelled to get to church and the desire to socialize result in most people staying after the service for a reception in the basement hall, at which home-made meat-filled pastries are served with coffee and juice. The elderly people sit quietly, while the children dash about with exuberant energy. The ladies prepare the food in the kitchen while the men, remaining separate from the women, stand about talking.

The gender separation is apparent in all aspects of life in La Nativité. The younger women, who are very conscious of this, provoked a confrontation over the issue at a vestry meeting in 1989. It had been decided that a committee should be formed to formulate a plan to ensure that the parish was self-supporting within five years. After a great deal of lively, noisy debate, volunteers were requested. Instantaneously seven men materialized on the committee, and someone announced that no more volunteers were needed. One young woman jumped up to say that women formed the basis of the church, that they had not been given adequate opportunity to be part of the committee, and that they demanded representation. One man, described to me as the resident "comic," said, "If she wants to be on

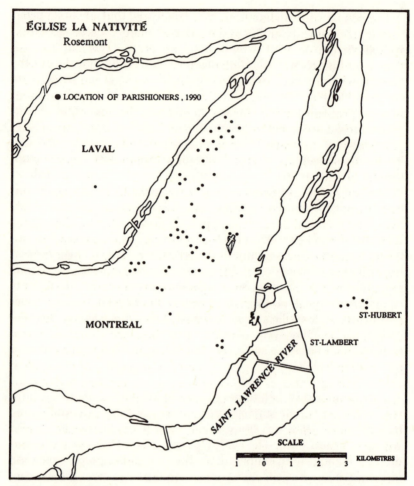

ÉGLISE LA NATIVITÉ
Rosemont

● LOCATION OF PARISHIONERS , 1990

LAVAL

MONTREAL

ST-HUBERT

ST-LAMBERT

SAINT - LAWRENCE RIVER

SCALE

KILOMETRES
1   0   1   2   3

Map 8   La Nativité

the committee that badly, she probably wants to be a man." He was shouted down, and three women were subsequently elected, in addition to the men already on the committee.

Meetings usually begin quietly and with apparent respect for the chairmanship of the rector, but inevitably discussion and debate become lively as more and more people offer their strongly held points of view. There is a very loyal core of commitment. Despite this, Father Joseph complains that it is difficult to widen the group of active parishioners. He attributes this in part to the widely dispersed congregation and in part to the need for reliance upon public transportation. There are other factors as well. Many people are on shift work, for instance, and others are single parents with full-time jobs.

The people of this church are not concerned with the issues that have divided other churches in the diocese. There has been no discussion about the Book of Alternative Services, for example, because they continue to use the American prayer book, translated into French, which is very similar to the BAS and with which they are comfortable. Another source of conflict for Montreal Anglicans that is not a problem for the Haitian members is the admission of children to communion before confirmation. This has been part of their practice for many years. Their acceptance of exuberant children during business meetings is typical of their acceptance of children in all aspects of church life.

The congregation's primary concerns are the fact that they do not have their own church building, one located closer to where they live; their financial dependence upon the diocese for subsidies (they would prefer to be financially self-supporting); and their sense of isolation from the diocesan (anglophone) church. Together these missing elements in their church life appear to affect their sense of participation in the fullness of Canadian society. Because most of the congregation speak no English and some do not read, they are reluctant to attend diocesan events, especially formal meetings such as the annual Synod. There is also a belief that the diocese does not know or care about their existence, let alone their problems. The question of a church building, giving the congregation a sense of place, identity, and recognition, as well as more control over their activities, is crucial. The problem of finding a central location is almost as difficult to resolve. Because of the widely dispersed Haitian population, the current solution, as already mentioned, has been to open up new Anglican Haitian congregations close to where Haitians are living. Because the new groups are drawing in members who were formerly attending French Catholic churches in their areas, La Nativité's membership has not suffered. Nevertheless, in a decision regarding the location of a permanent structure for La Nativité, at least three widely separated areas might be considered as possibilities. While St Luke's represents an improvement on the hotel room, the congregation's isolation from diocesan life is magnified by their sense of alienation within St Luke's itself. The two congregations, the resident one and La Nativité, are totally separate, meeting in combined services only once a year.

Father Joseph commented in his report that the original goals of the Haitians in coming together for mutual support through their faith are continuously affected by the "institutional politics" of Montreal diocese: "C'est une communauté qui se rassemble pour continuer les gestes de foi commencés en Haiti. Le début de cette paroisse a été marqué par le besoin de se réunir pour partager les

nouvelles expériences, identifier ensemble les défis et surmonter, dans la solidarité, les obstacles rencontrés dans le nouveau pays."[3] Prior to Father Joseph's arrival in 1985, the parishioners formulated a job description for him. The elements of this document indicate some of the key areas of concern for the members of La Nativité. The members wanted, for example, counselling support for families, help with immigration problems and unemployment, and assistance in the formation of self-help groups, such as for the elderly. They also thought the diocese should be sensitized to the particular needs of the community and that there should be consultation with the bishop on ways to achieve other "stations" (congregations) for Haitians. All of these indicate a strong desire on the part of the congregation for a strengthening of their community through more opportunities for meeting together and improving their security in Canada. Two meetings I attended were devoted almost entirely to plans for upcoming social events that would involve not only the congregation but also the friends and relatives of members.

Father Joseph, on the other hand, sees a need for the Haitian community to reach out to and become engaged in the society around it. He has tried, unsuccessfully, to involve the congregation in such current issues as free trade, refugee policy, and the goods and services tax (GST). "J'aimerais aussi que les acteurs soient vraiment des acteurs et non des spectateurs."[4] His objective is to encourage both the strengthening of the church community and the congregation's more active engagement in social action. He has expressed disappointment in the congregation's lack of interest in issues not directly related to

their situation. At the annual vestry meeting in 1989 he introduced
a motion to oppose the expulsion of illegal Haitian immigrants from
Canada. To his dismay it was unanimously rejected.

An important area of difficulty for La Nativité is the cultural bar-
rier its members experience in their relations with the diocese. "On
y trouve toute la culture anglo-saxonne et toute la vision ecclésiale
britannique."[5] Father Joseph is concerned that rival churches such
as the Baptist and Pentecostal churches, which frequently offer services in French, might offer stronger cultural ties. They have, in fact,
attracted some of the Haitians who might otherwise become members of La Nativité. The common experiences of adjusting to a new
country and culture can be more important than the ties to the
Anglican faith, and in many cases parishioners of La Nativité attend
other churches as well. Some members return to La Nativité only for
the main festivals like Easter and Christmas. The Baptist church services attract the Haitians because they seem more familiar culturally
– liturgy, for instance, is less "rigide et fermée." The relationships
between one's culture, socio-political milieu, and church are strong
indeed.

In strengthening the commitment to La Nativité, the youth group
and the women's association are especially important because they
are active and growing groups, with strong elements of community
sharing. These groups, too, face the problems of a membership living
far from the church and, as Father Joseph explains, of the Haitians'
different cultural perspective, which seems to be a factor inhibiting
active social and political engagement. The paternalistic socio-
political system of Haiti has influenced the "mentalité et l'attitude
qu'on rencontre dans le milieu ecclésial."[6] The Haitian acceptance
of hierarchy and "blind obedience" has implications for the attitudes
of the members of La Nativité. In the acculturation process, "ils ont
dû épouser de nouvelles valeurs."[7] The return of many Haitians to
Anglican services at Christmas illustrates the importance of tradition
and ancestral ties. "Ils pensent pouvoir continuer l'oeuvre de leurs
pères et surtout être en lien avec les parents et les grands-parents
épiscopaliens décédés."[8] Despite the links to tradition, however,
there is evidence of alienation that the Anglican Church in Montreal
has not addressed:

Face au diocèse, les fidèles pratiquants de La Nativité n'ont pas plus de sens
d'appartenance que "les distants" face à la paroisse. Ils se montrent très ré-
ticents quand il s'agit de participer à des activités diocésaines en raison des
barrières culturelles et linguistiques mentionnées plus haut. Ils se sentent
comme des étrangers ... Il n'y a donc pas de communication entre eux et le

reste du diocèse. Tout se fait selon anglaise pour répondre aux attentes des canadiens anglais et des Britanniques.[9]

La Nativité is a church founded on the need of newly arrived immigrants to share with one another their faith and their problems of adjusting to a new culture. It continues to struggle, not with the concerns of Quebec nationalism or changes in the liturgy, but with an Anglo-Saxon-dominated church that does not seem responsive to its needs. As a community, La Nativité offers weekly fellowship and the opportunity to share the experience of adjusting to the North American way of life. But it is also concerned with the need for a more centrally located church and for greater financial independence from the diocese. One warden told me that her elderly mother does not attend regularly simply because it is too physically demanding to make the journey, and so she attends a nearby French Catholic church instead. The isolation and alienation these Haitians feel have as much to do with their cultural distance from the Anglican Church as with their cultural distance from the greater society around it.

The Five Parishes:
An Overview and
Some Statistical Indicators
of Commitment

AN OVERVIEW

These five parishes reflect differing perspectives on church life. Concerns for family roots, the language of the liturgy, the needs of youth, and how to balance the budget are common in all congregations, but with different emphases and different implications for people's relationships in the church. In the four anglophone parishes concern was expressed about the out-migration of anglophones, particularly as members left and wardens had to be replaced. But despite evidence at Synod of strong feelings against the francization of Quebec, responses in the parishes varied according to the community and social group defining the parish membership. Another area that was shown to be especially significant was the role of women. In every parish women were in an ambiguous relationship with the church. On the one hand, their commitment to fund-raising and community-building activities were crucial to the life of the church. Their daily activities in the church have given them knowledge and, with it, power to control many of the decisions made by others in the church. On the other hand, women were frequently excluded from positions on the corporation, and during public presentations men almost always officiated. Particular coping strategies have been developed by women, such as maintaining the independence of their budgets, in order to protect their "domains." Complicating these relationships further were the attributes of life-cycle and an aging population, especially in relation to family histories and traditions in the church.

For women in all parishes the church has been an important vehicle for self-realization and a sense of self-worth. At a deeply personal level for each parishioner, the potent combination of a need to feel needed and a desire for the security of rootedness in tradition has meant that women have had a central role, and therefore that they have been at the centre of all controversies in the parish churches.

The tensions generated by the debates over the Book of Common Prayer and the Book of Alternative Services varied among the churches, depending on the sense of history and importance of tradition within each parish. The variations are difficult to characterize because they do not relate directly to social class, age of parishioners, or the social organization within churches. I have suggested that the variations appear to be related to two key factors, the mobility patterns of the church membership and the extent to which parishioners felt threatened by an incursion of francophones into the community. Mobility incorporates several dimensions, including the history of the individual parish, the average age of parishioners, and the degree to which young families have been welcomed into the congregation. In other words, "change" and a willingness to hear the voice of new members were crucial factors in the debate over the BAS and the BCP. The extent to which a sense of threat pervaded individual parishes seemed to affect the acceptance of the BAS insofar as the survival of a church might have been seen in terms of the need to ensure stability.

The spatial distribution of individual parish members was an interesting variation as well. In most churches the nucleated pattern, which relates to a minimal distance to travel, was an adequate descriptor. Some parishes, however, exhibited somewhat different spatial patterns, related, as in the case of La Nativité, to a specific cultural choice, as well as to historical ties to a community church (Grace Church) and to a desire to avoid a more radical (charismatic) form of service (Resurrection). This is to say that parishioners are not necessarily concentrated in well-defined population distributions around the local church. Their spatial pattern varies according to differing degrees of importance associated with historical roots, traditions, culture, and liturgical form.

All of these factors affect both the meanings that people attach to their church affiliation and the dynamic relationships that reflect these meanings. I will next examine some of the statistical expressions of church affiliation, which also show both commonalities and divergences among the five parishes.

SOME STATISTICAL INDICATORS
OF COMMITMENT

As we have seen, the five parishes show differences in organizational structures, age and mobility characteristics, relationships between men and women, and perceptions of the importance of community and tradition. These distinctive characteristics are reflected in various measurable attributes of church participation. The distinctive patterns of participation shown in Montreal Diocese after 1976 seem to be related to specific provincial socio-political changes. We will now examine the same figures at the level of the parish, comparing them to each other and to diocesan averages. While some anomolies arise because of the arrival of a new priest or the establishment of a special capital fund for a new building, certain fundamental similarities can be attributed to the socio-political context. Timing and magnitude of variation reflect the special characteristics of each congregation. In certain cases, reporting discrepancies in parish records affect comparability, notably with regard to the attendance figures for St Matthias. For most of the period from 1962 to 1983, the rector recorded only the attendance at Eucharist services, with the result that about half of the actual attendance was not recorded. It has been necessary, therefore, to estimate attendance at 190 per cent of the actual figure recorded in the vestry books. The estimates also affect offerings per person, a measure calculated from attendance figures. Despite this caveat, what is most important (and is not affected by the estimates) is the general patterns rather than the specific values.

La Nativité has been excluded from most of the tables because of its special character associated with its ministry to the Haitian community. Its temporary location in rented facilities and the short duration of its existence are other factors making statistical comparisons with the other parishes somewhat irrelevant. Data for La Nativité are discussed separately.

While the socio-political environment of Quebec is reflected in the broad patterns of both the diocese and individual parishes, it is the distinguishing "quirks and quiddities" that are of concern here. The factors that seem to define most strongly the differences between the parishes are those that reflect different social groups and lived experiences. They can be summarized as "characteristics of community," and they include demographic change, especially out-migration, and the histories of the church and community, especially as they relate to family histories, shared memories, and traditions. The statistical reality of out-migration does not in itself account for the apparent impact of out-migration upon a church congregation. A decrease in numbers is accompanied by a non-quantifiable sense of perceived threat that is particularly significant when mobility options are constrained by lack of alternative employment opportunities. Differences in community characteristics are also defined by the history of the church itself. Where there is a long history and where memorial windows, plaques, and needlepoint kneelers are important symbols of family belonging, there is a profound sense of continuity and of the need to preserve the myths and shared stories that underpin personal and collective identities. It is the potent combination of this sense of place, defined by tradition and historical memory, and the intense perception of threat to its maintenance that seems to affect acceptance of change and the propensity to contribute time and money. The data for individual parishes help to illuminate some of these factors and their interactions.

The relationship between priest and congregation has a marked effect on membership and attendance, as the annual statistics demonstrate. Over the period from 1961 to 1986, apparently erratic patterns may reflect the arrival or departure of a priest. During an interregnum, for example, when visiting clergy serve the parish between clergy appointments, attendance usually drops significantly. When this period extends over several months, decrease in the size of congregations may persist over an even longer period. More or less popular appointments are reflected in attendance data. At St Paul's, for example, the impact of a new priest in 1982 can be seen in the sharply rising attendance figures, and at St Matthias a new priest attracted new members in the period 1983–85, but his subsequent involvement in a scandal caused a marked period of decline. In the 1977–82 period at Resurrection, on the other hand, there was a continuous decrease in membership and offerings; the priest at that time had antagonised many parishioners.

Tables 21–27 (Appendix A) summarize the changes in membership, attendance, Easter communicants, and offerings (in constant 1981 dollars) for the period 1961 to 1986 in four parishes. The numbers of "census Anglicans" decreased in Montreal Diocese by 32 per cent from 1961 to 1981, and in three of the four parishes decreases ranged from 35 to 62 per cent, the highest decrease being around Grace Church in Point St Charles. The only parish in which membership increased was St Paul's in Knowlton, where growth can be attributed to increased population, related in turn to a new highway that improved access to the area in the mid-1960s. Comparable decreases occurred in attendance and the numbers of Easter communicants. Even at St Paul's, despite its increased membership, attend-

ance decreased by 17 per cent and Easter communicants by over
50 per cent.

The broad patterns of giving in all parishes reflect those of the diocese described earlier, with an increase in financial contributions
after 1976. Figures 7–11 (Appendix B) show a significant change in
1976 in all parishes except Resurrection, where change seems to
have been moderated by the clerical problems noted above.

Tables 21, 22, and 23 show some interesting similarities between
Grace Church and St Matthias, parishes that have experienced the
most severe losses of membership (73 and 70 per cent respectively,
1961–88), attendance declines (58 and 34 per cent, 1961–88), and
decreased offerings from the peak year (45 and 41 per cent, respectively). Part of the explanation for these figures, of course, is directly
attributable to out-migration (Grace Church lost 53 per cent and
St Matthias 45 per cent of their census Anglicans between 1961 and
1981). What is particularly interesting is the extent to which these
similar statistical patterns in St Matthias and Grace Church can be
seen to reflect other similarities. Both parishes have long histories, a
high proportion of older families, and a pervasive belief in the importance of tradition and rootedness. Their histories combined with
their high losses in members seem to reinforce expressed needs to ensure continuity.

Despite the outward threat to the viability of the parish church especially during the 1970s, attendance did not drop as precipitously
as membership. At St Matthias, for example, whereas membership
decreased by 50 per cent in the period 1971 to 1981, average weekly
attendance increased from 210 to 223. Similarly, at Grace Church
total offerings (in constant dollars) actually increased throughout
the period 1971 to 1981 despite membership losses of 50 per cent
and a location in a very low income area. In other words, severe
losses of membership seem to have been countered by greater efforts
to maintain the church. In the period 1971 to 1988 both St Matthias
and Grace Church show similar patterns of response. While membership decreased by 64 and 72 per cent respectively, offerings decreased by only about 15 per cent. In the "crisis years" in the
mid-1970s both churches show a cluster of peak value total contributions (in constant dollars), indicating a sharper and more immediate reaction to events around them. (See Tables 23 and 24.) Their
sense of threat seems to have been more profound than at
Resurrection or St Paul's. It appears that the financial contributions
have acted as a barometer fluctuating with the pressures of socio-
political change.

Another element affecting the actual level of financial support is the relative wealth of an area. The neighbourhood of Grace Church, with high unemployment and low educational levels, has only limited ability to increase its giving. This makes figures for Grace Church even more remarkable, indicating in the persistence of high donations a strong commitment to its survival. St Paul's and St Matthias, on the other hand, are located in high-income areas and have members with histories in the area who have given endowments or large donations, although they may not participate actively in church life.

The data for St Paul's (see Tables 21–27, Appendix A) are generally positive: an increase in membership between 1961 and 1988; compared to other churches, a smaller decrease in average attendance at services; and the greatest rate of increase in total offerings. Despite this growth, there has been a significant decrease in the size of individual contributions. Between 1961 and 1981 contributions per member more than doubled, but since then there has been a decline of almost 40 per cent. (See Table 24.) This decrease is especially remarkable in view of the overall increase in donations in the diocese and for the other parishes in this study. Several factors appear to have caused this. The characteristics of the community of St Paul's may account for part of it. As the interviews confirmed, there is little evidence that people in Lac Brome (Knowlton) perceive an imminent threat to their church or to their cultural identity in this community. In fact, the community has experienced growth, albeit in the numbers of predominantly English-speaking young professionals and entrepreneurs. However, the clerical leadership has also been an important factor. The nature of the ministry and beliefs of the two rectors who have been at St Paul's since 1982 have affected all aspects of church life. The uncompromising introduction of the new prayer book and a charismatic ministry drove away approximately seventeen people who were also major financial contributors. While this number may seem small, accounting for about 15 per cent of an average Sunday congregation, these individuals represented a significant component of the membership and their contributions a significant proportion of total contributions. For the active congregation there has been greater emphasis on a sense of community through prayer, as well as a certain pride in the vibrancy of services and the active youth participation, which incorporates a feeling that "people with money" are not important if they do not bring a "commitment to Jesus" with them. The active membership seems unwilling to accept any meaning of belonging to the church other than that which "proclaims Jesus as Lord." I heard concerns expressed by a few of the older members, and by the clergy, about the loss of the affluent members, but many others did not acknowledge their departure as important. Fewer people of wealth and a youthful congregation that puts less emphasis on financial commitment have resulted in a growth in attendance and a decrease in the size of individual donations. Despite the overall decrease in per member contributions, however, this parish exhibits the same temporal pattern as other parishes: in 1978 and 1979 absolute contributions rose by almost 75 per cent, and per member contributions almost doubled.

St Matthias, like St Paul's, had a sharp increase in offerings after 1975: absolute offerings rose 75 per cent in one year alone (from 1975 to 1976), and per member contributions rose by about 50 per cent. As we saw earlier, St Matthias had experienced high membership losses (70 per cent from 1961 to 1986) partly owing to outmigration of anglophones from the province. During the same period the level of donations was increasing significantly, on a per member basis increasing almost two and a half times from 1961 to 1988. Losses in membership were compensated by the increased financial commitment of those still there. The perceived threat to the cultural community and a need to affirm the continuity of St Matthias seem to have provided added impetus to already-increased contributions after 1975. Today the determination to compensate for member loss may not be enough to sustain the church, since the absolute contributions have been declining since 1985. In 1988, in constant dollars, the total offerings were about 30 per cent lower than they had been in 1961, and 41 per cent lower than the peak in 1976. As described in the previous chapter, there is a real concern about the future ability of the congregation to continue to maintain this large church. Covering operating deficits through withdrawal of capital from endowment funds is feasible for only a limited period, and wardens at St Matthias recognize the problem.

At Church of the Resurrection all data show a persistent downward direction. The 1960s membership of 1,500 and a peak in total offerings (constant dollars) in 1963 have never been matched. Per member contributions at Resurrection approximated the diocesan values until the difficult years of 1977–82. Although the congregation at Resurrection did increase its contributions during the late 1970s to $9.00 in 1978 and $8.40 in 1980 per attending member, this represented an increase of only 35 per cent over the 1961 value, whereas at St Paul's the donations had more than quadrupled and at St Matthias they had doubled. The arrival in 1982 of a new priest had an immediate impact: in 1983, for the first time in the church's history, per member figures reached over $100 and once again were approximately the same as the averages for Montreal.

At Grace Church we see temporal patterns similar to the other churches, with a steady increase in per capita contributions, especially after 1976. Total offerings peaked in 1981, and on a per member basis, the offerings at Grace have increased over two and a half times, comparable to St Matthias and Resurrection. Measured with respect to the numbers of people who attend services, the offerings are substantially higher than those of either Resurrection or St Paul's and have tripled since 1965. All of this suggests that even among parishioners whose employment or pension income is severely limited, the determination to ensure the survival of Grace Church has produced high levels of contributions.

Variations among parishes also exist for patterns of attendance. Two measures of attendance provide another way of assessing the meanings the church has for people. The ratios of average attendance to membership and of Easter communicants to average attendance suggest differences in participation rates and the distinctive behaviour of a "fringe" group who retain membership despite minimal participation in worship service. In the early 1960s, at a time when Knowlton was still a rural and relatively isolated community, St Paul's had a higher participation rate than any of the other parishes, with one-third of the membership attending church compared to 15 per cent at St Matthias and 20 per cent at Resurrection. The higher level of participation might have been related to the importance of the community and social interaction in this rural environment. The trends in participation rate show interesting differences between parishes through time. While at St Paul's there has been a steady decrease since 1961, at Grace Church and St Matthias the opposite is true, indicating that a higher proportion of members are actively attending worship services today than in 1961. In other words, these churches have a smaller fringe group, a situation that also exists with respect to Easter communicants. By 1986 all churches had a participation rate (average attendance as a proportion of membership) of about 20 per cent (see Table 26).

As discussed in chapter 2, there has been an ongoing debate about the meaning of secularization. Many people point out that declining church attendance does not necessarily reflect loss of faith. One element in this debate is the continuing affiliation of people with a church even though they do not attend regular services. The large congregations at Christmas and Easter give some support to the argument that many people regard attendance once a year as sufficient commitment to their faith. As I discussed earlier, after a period of declining figures for Easter communicants in Canada, there has been a trend of increasing numbers at Easter services since 1975, even as membership has continued to fall. In Montreal the ratios of membership to Easter communicants have dropped at half the rate of Canada, indicating that Montreal has retained a higher proportion of occasional attenders (Table 20). In the parishes under study here there are discernible differences in the size of the fringe group, which I measured by comparing average attendance and Easter figures (Table 27).

The high figures in the 1960s show that there was a larger number of people attending the Easter service in relation to those who attend regularly than has been the case in more recent years. These ratios decreased as the numbers of Easter communicants decreased in relation to average attendance. Expressed another way, among those who continue to be members of the church today, there is an increased likelihood that they will attend regularly. There are fewer fringe people attending only at Easter. St Matthias and Grace both have a fringe group that continues to be a significant part of the membership and probably accounts for the continuing financial viability of the church, particularly for St Matthias. This fringe group, I suggest, is smaller in the two churches in which a strong community ethos prevails, St Paul's and Church of the Resurrection. The higher ratios at St Matthias and Grace, indicating a larger fringe group, appear to reflect the tendency for historical ties to draw nominal members back into the church fold at times of special celebration. For this reason, there is also a relationship between the size of a fringe group and the spatial patterns of membership. Because nominal members may retain links despite a move out of the vicinity of the church, the larger the fringe group constituted by these people the more dispersed is their spatial distribution. Those who remain active participants, as described in the previous chapter, have felt frustrated in their attempts to encourage a more participatory community of shared experience partly due to the nature of this fringe group.

Spatial distribution of the congregations in relation to their churches is a most interesting dimension of church membership. Maps 4–8 (on pages 84, 100, 110, 124, and 136) depict a much greater dispersion of the members of La Nativité than of the members of other parishes. For the La Nativité parishioners (Map 8), who travel up to twenty-five kilometres to attend a Sunday service, the need for a more accessible place to worship is of paramount concern. Fewer than 40 per cent of the members live within five kilometres of the church. Especially in view of the low average incomes and the fact that few members own cars, the distances they travel make their commitment all the more impressive.

The residential pattern of Grace Church members is also remarkable (Map 5). Only 46 per cent of the members live within two kilometres of the church, and over 15 per cent live beyond ten kilometres. High out-migration of anglophones from Point St Charles throughout the period after the Second World War could have resulted in the closing of the church. Instead, because many of the people who moved into adjacent municipalities have continued their affiliation with the church, Grace Church has survived. Fully half of those who attend regularly live several kilometres away. Others who remain on the membership list are people who grew up in the Point but moved into middle-class neighbourhoods after marriage. A young man from this group recently became the new treasurer of the church; he lives about ten kilometres away and passes three other Anglican churches on his way to Grace each Sunday. A unique commitment to Grace Church seems to spring from a loyalty to working-class roots and the shared belief in affirming the importance of those beginnings.

Resurrection shows the most concentrated pattern, reflecting the sense of celebration and extension of the local community described in chapter 9. Some members live about seven kilometres away and have intentionally chosen this church for its conservative, middle-of-the-road liturgy, eschewing the charismatic services of two closer churches, but over 90 per cent of the members of Resurrection live within five kilometres of the church. This pattern is reflected in the community-based activities described in chapter 9. St Matthias also shows a fairly nucleated pattern and has been described by one parishioner as the "first church out of the downtown which can be considered as a family church." However, the fact that more than 12 per cent of its members live over five kilometres away suggests that many members have maintained links with the church for historical reasons. During one interview a woman told me that she came from four kilometres away, passing two other churches, because her "family had always gone here" and she "loves the music."

Finally, the distribution of the congregation at St Paul's is clearly related to its location in the middle of Knowlton. That there are more than 20 per cent who live farther away than five kilometres is owing to the rural nature of the setting, there being no reasonable nearby choice, and the generally dispersed residential pattern of the population.

The spatial patterns add one more dimension to an understanding of community relationships and the factors people weigh in deciding where to worship. Contiguity or extension of community is certainly one important factor. However, family ties, an identification with known liturgical forms, shared social experience and memory, and the music all contribute to people's sense of belonging. The relative importance of these factors varies in accordance with the dynamics of the social group in the particular community environments.

12 Anglicans in Quebec: Community, Identity, the Future

In common with churches across North America, the Anglican Church in Montreal has struggled in the face of declining attendance. Even among those who declare themselves to be Anglican, fewer attend regularly. Regardless of one's definition of secularization, there is an undeniable trend away from regular attendance at Sunday services everywhere in Canada. In Montreal, however, the Anglican Church has experienced a more complex series of changes than simply secularization. Its situation as a church dominated by the English-speaking minority within an increasingly nationalistic francophone province has been a critical factor in many of the struggles and activities of parishioners. The central contention of this book has been that the socio-political context of Quebec, especially since 1971, has had a profound impact upon many aspects of the church in Montreal Diocese. As the out-migration of anglophones accelerated in the mid-1970s, church members whose family histories were rooted in Quebec experienced a double threat, from declining church attendance and from the out-migration from the province. Their social groups and communities of meaning were shrinking, and with this came a diminished sense of control. Daily life-worlds were being restricted, and former understandings and practices were being challenged.

As Charles Taylor has argued, a person's identity usually relates to "not only his stand on moral and spiritual matters but also ... the defining community."[1] In addition to a quantitative loss in their numbers, Montreal Anglicans have experienced a threat to their qualitative life as former understandings and practices have been radically altered. At the level of the individual church member, the formerly taken-for-granted world of such daily contacts as English forms, signs, and telephone enquiries has been challenged. When Taylor defined practices as "more or less any stable configuration of shared activity, whose shape is defined by a certain pattern of do's and don'ts,"[2] he was referring to the ways in which our inner beings, our concepts of self, are developed through "being embedded in practices." In attempting to illuminate the ways in which the "self" and individual identities are related to social practice, I have focused on differing interpretations of community and expressions of faith in five churches. While society and the institution provide important structural determinants of action, the social group in the context of community relationships is crucial to the development of meanings and a commitment to place. The social group, precisely through contiguity and daily shared experience, is important to the evolution of a prevailing ethos.[3] The question of the development of an identity, personal and collective, is inextricably tied to social relations and the development of social practice within the local community.

MEANINGS OF COMMUNITY: CONTINUITY OR CHANGE

As was discussed in the first chapter, Durkheim and Weber adopted different perspectives in their analyses of the role of religion in society. Durkheim emphasized the importance of the collective society, in which religion was the glue holding society together. His more functionalist perspective has provided a useful basis for analysis, and supports the present argument that the church in Quebec has served as a source of personal identity and a means of cultural affirmation, especially in the face of political and social change. An additional level of analysis seemed to be crucial to understanding the roots of Quebec's Anglican experience, and therefore an important aspect of this study has been the illumination of different responses to socio-political change in accordance with differing communities of meaning. Weber's analysis focused on the individual meanings of religion, arguing that religion could be radical and innovative, an initiator of change rooted in the individual. Recognizing that social groups are intimately related to their locales, he went on to show that their religious commitment may have different political meanings. Through the window of five parishes we have seen that individual meanings of church membership have distinctive patterns of relationships rooted in different historical experiences and shared memories.

The past is crucial to how people in Montreal Diocese perceive and respond to the present, particularly because of the historic role anglophones had in Quebec until 1961. Accustomed to their status as a majority (despite being a numerical minority), dominating the social and economic levers of power, anglophones have had to readjust their perspective as their roles have been redefined for them and they have been forced to acknowledge their minority position. In the transformation of Quebec society, anglophones have experienced a discontinuity that has had a fundamental impact upon their concept of self and upon the ways they have expressed their church commitment. We know that tradition and the past can have opposite effects; they can allow the possibility of "meaning, freedom, identity or beauty" or they can amount to nothing more than "an excuse for inaction."[4] These two effects are reflected in two religious responses described by Mannheim as ideological and utopian.[5] In the responses of Quebec Anglicans there has been a strong thread of defensiveness, a tendency to protect rather than renew the church. The resistance to changes in the liturgy and the reluctance to contribute to mission and social justice causes are the two most obvious illustrations of these responses. The lack of innovative or utopian initiative has acted at the diocesan level as a significant inhibitor of institutional changes introduced by the church leadership. The dominance of an ideological religious expression has been relied upon to legitimate the existing social order, defend the once-dominant values, and create a sense of security and stability. There are areas in which innovation and energy seem to be providing hopeful signs of renewal, particularly at the diocesan level through youth activities organized by Crosstalks Ministries. However, the long-term impact of such initiatives is unknown.

It is at the parish level that we look for positive signs of change and growth. Ultimately, religious faith rooted in the individual and in the reality of community is a key element in commitment to faith and the believing community. The degree of importance people attach to the concept of community and the ways in which this concept is manifested in their behaviour reflect both experienced meanings and the perceived threat from the society around them. In some churches the importance of community seems to have evolved through a *longue durée* in the context of which families share memories of past histories. Community is rooted in traditions, symbols, and artifacts that contribute to the meaning and significance of shared relationships,

and protecting these has become an integral part of identity maintenance. In suburban areas, where there is both a high proportion of
young families and high mobility rates, church community is defined
by a participatory shared experience that is of today. Traditions and
shared stories of the past play relatively minor roles. The emphasis
is on activities that bring people together, not to celebrate tradition
but to build community.

Both definitions of community incorporate the ideas of identity
and belonging, but according to the first, the church is a symbol of
continuity and stability, while according to the second, the church is
a place more focused on the present. That there should be two fundamental meanings of community in Montreal Diocese is related to
the different histories in space and time of the parishioners. The context of socio-political change in Quebec has magnified the differences in these meanings of community. Similarly, the issue of
changing majority-minority relationships for Quebec anglophones
has been reflected in the question of power and status in the church.
For those accustomed to dominant roles in their parish churches, the
double threat of secularization and out-migration has introduced the
possibility of losing a significant base for individual status. There are
fewer and fewer ways for anglophones to become involved in setting
and accomplishing community goals. The loss of control in daily activities has had implications for the church, which continues to be
predominantly anglophone.

POWER AND IDENTITY

Power contributes to collective and personal identity formation in
different ways. For anglophones, in addition to the changes in social
and economic power relationships directly related to their new minority status, there are power relationships at a more intermediate
level that directly affect individuals and become more important as
loss at the higher level is perceived to be significant. The relationships between young and old, male and female, were seen to constitute important interactions that both described and defined roles
within the churches. The relative importance of these interactions is
dependent to a large degree upon the meanings attached to community. In other words, the structural tensions in Quebec society have
been communicated to the individual level, exacerbating the personal conflicts issuing from a need for self-definition and identity
through particular roles within the church.

Those parishes that have incorporated a broad range of ages and
stages of family formation seem to have fewer difficulties adapting

to more egalitarian gender relations than parishes that are characterized by high average age and few young families. It seems possible
that a higher proportion of young members, with values associated
with greater acceptance of female leadership, constitutes a significant element supporting change. Where young members represent a
small fraction of the active parishioners, there seems to be less inclination to accept change. However, the causal factor may not be age
as much as it is the community relationships and sense of cultural security dominant in the congregation. For those social groups, such
as at St Matthias and Grace Church, that have experienced significant loss of social power and the possibility of less control over
choices in their lives, there may be a greater propensity for defending
the status quo at the level of individual activity in the church.
Therefore, in these churches the continuation of disparate degrees of
power and status between the young and the senior members, and
between male and female, may be in the interests of the long-term
decision makers in the church. When a senior parishioner argued
that surplus funds should be kept in the parish because she knew of
a parish that had been "overly generous and now has to close," she
was expressing the concerns of older members who felt that the past
must be preserved and that younger members do not have the same
understandings and should not have the same power to decide.
Seniority confers symbolic and real power in all churches, not only
because of proportional representation, but also because of the accepted norms and practices that define the rules. In Quebec the role
of seniority has taken on added significance.

THE QUEBEC CONTEXT

The analysis of Synod *Proceedings,* including the bishop's charge
and the motions presented at Synod, and a review of the *Montreal
Churchman* through the period of the study show a church that,
through the 1960s, gradually awoke to the changes of the Quiet
Revolution. There is, however, no evidence until 1970 that the
Anglican Church in Montreal expected to be a participant in this evolving society or that it understood the import of the changing balance of power. All of the documentation prior to the election of the
Parti Québécois in 1976 shows a church that is essentially unrespon-
sive to the society within which it is located. It took the challenge of
a separatist government, the passage of restrictive educational bills,
and the reality of out-migration of anglophones to force the church
into a pro-active position. Even so, despite calls for a French ministry
and bilingual priests, the concrete actions of the church have been

cautious. The reasons are open to debate. Some people have pointed to the leadership, noting that the bishop continued, throughout his sixteen-year tenure, to import clergy from Britain, and that despite his announced intent that the church become more bilingual and in closer touch with the realities of Quebec, his actions spoke of continuing links with the Church of England. Others have said that the bishop was intentionally, and wisely perhaps, cautious about bilingualism because so many parishes were extremely apprehensive about French in their churches. As late as 1988 the annual Synod meeting refused to request bilingual signs outside churches. There has been an ongoing dialogue between the leadership and individual members, many of whom regard the church as the only institution in Quebec in which they still retain full control.

In all the churches, parishioners expressed support for many of the changes in Quebec, while at the same time refusing to accept French initiatives in their own churches. "There isn't any need for a French ministry," some said, or, "Francophones are not interested in Anglicanism." Until 1990 there had been little concrete action, with the exception of initiatives at Christ Church Cathedral, to support the argument that the Anglican Church is actively involved in integrating into Quebec society. The election of a new bilingual bishop in 1990 may have important implications for the role of the Anglican Church in Quebec. Indeed, the differences in theological outlook and priorities between the two bishops indicate that many of those voting delegates who selected Bishop Hutchison in 1990 were aware of a need for strong new directions. It is significant that during the election process itself an ability to communicate effectively in French was seen as important. Within two years of his incumbency the new bishop had made it clear that all clergy should make an effort to become bilingual and that new appointments would consider bilingualism mandatory.

While La Nativité is the only truly French-speaking (with Creole) parish, there are regular services in French in other churches in the diocese. The most successful ministry involving both languages seems to be in Montreal North and in Rosemere, where the priests conduct separate French and English services. An attempt on the West Island to open up a French ministry, aimed especially at immigrants from Zaire and Haiti, did not attract new parishioners, and special funds from the diocese supporting the initiative were not renewed in 1993. Even at Christ Church Cathedral the introduction of French has not been without difficulty. In response to protests from members of the congregation, services in French were moved to Saturdays, and they are now conducted by a layperson, Gavin

Elbourne. The attempt to use the fifth Sunday of the month for French services had resulted in the non-attendance of regular attenders.

The experience of La Nativité, as a French-speaking and culturally unique parish, is especially instructive insofar as significant cultural dimensions have clearly affected behaviour and issues within the parish in ways that are different from the other four parishes. The male-female relationships within La Nativité reflected the tensions of cultural adaptation among members, tensions inherent in change from a male-dominated Haitian society to a somewhat less authoritarian, more egalitarian North American context. The gathering of parishioners after church, with the separation of males and females, young and old, bubbled with community spirit even as it suggested different social traditions. The issues of concern to parishioners at La Nativité also differed from those of the other parishes discussed in this study. The order of service, prayer books, and hymn selection were never considered problematic. For La Nativité the overwhelming concern was the lack of their own place of worship, a place they could call "home." A second major problem for them was their relationship with the Anglican Diocese in Montreal. Unlike anglophones, who could relate to their churches as symbols of their English roots, the French and Creole-speaking Haitians felt like outsiders, both within their church and in terms of Quebec's francophone society. Theirs is a struggle for self-affirmation made more difficult by the insistence of Quebec's anglophones to retain strong English traditions and to resist the francization of the diocesan structures.

THE BOOK OF ALERNATIVE SERVICES: RESISTANCE TO CHANGE

Resistance to change in Montreal Diocese was most apparent in the reaction of Montreal Anglicans to the proposed new prayer book. Results of the surveys on the use of the new prayer book indicated reluctance and even hostility to the changes proposed by the national church. With the exception of the Atlantic provinces, the two dioceses in Quebec (Quebec and Montreal) have shown the greatest degree of resistance to the new book, with significant implications for parish relationships as we saw in three of the parishes described earlier. While acknowledging that there is an attitude of eastern conservatism apparent in all social statistics, the metropolitan character of Montreal should moderate the eastern conservatism to an important degree. This study suggests that the cautious leadership of the church and the need for stability in the face of changes in society encouraged a more traditionalist stance. However, the church leadership has had an influence both for and against change. The bishop adopted a deliberately cautious position in asking the parishes to try the Book of Alternative Services, and some felt this approach implied rather lukewarm support among the church leadership for the BAS. In some parishes where members were resistant to change, however, priests who were enthusiastic about the new book have been crucial to its introduction.

The most characteristic response to the BAS, however, was the profound antagonism expressed by individuals. The resistance in Montreal was essentially rooted in the individual parish member, reflected at the diocesan level, but coming out of a personal need for continuity of a traditional form of worship represented by the Book of Common Prayer. Hostility to the BAS was real and it was profound. That people changed churches, altered their habitual time of attending services, and even withdrew their financial support testifies to the intensity of feeling around this issue.

In Montreal the social characteristics of the community and congregation were important indicators of the parishioners' willingness to accept changes in the liturgy. Of key importance in the resistance to change were the degree of threat perceived by parishioners and the extent to which historical memory and shared family traditions dominated relationships in the church. As David Martin points out, "the sacred rite links the local congregation with the wider scope of the church," but there are also local "quirks and quiddities." "People cling to the signs of their identity and their history."[6] For the parishioners of La Nativité, on the other hand, time and place have not afforded an opportunity for the adoption of traditional symbols of historical meaning.

Kneelers, lovingly designed and created by members of the congregation, family plaques and memorial windows, regimental and Union Jack flags hanging in the chancel, a donated computer system for the office: all of these represent symbols of commitment and belonging, sources of pride in family roots and cultural heritage. The combination of perceived threat because of out-migration and long family tradition is a potent force inhibiting change. Where this combination is strongest in Montreal, especially in the centre of the city and in the Eastern Townships, the possibility of change depends upon strong leadership. Whereas the local community of meaning is an important predictor of acceptance of change, the relationship the priest is able to develop with a congregation can be the key to new forms of worship. Churches in Eastern Montreal where out-migration has been most significant have adopted the new liturgy in large measure because of the strong, enthusiastic leadership of young clergy.

SACRED PLACES AND SYMBOLIC MEANINGS

With the notable exception of La Nativité, all the churches represent more than a place to worship on Sunday. The churches are a focus of the sense of community, a community that not only is religious and cultural, but also incorporates family traditions and personal, private meanings. In the discussion at Resurrection about when baptisms should be performed, the parishioners explored the meanings attached to community sharing and responsibility and came to a new understanding of the baptism ritual. Baptisms are now conducted as part of the Sunday services rather than as separate, private services. This kind of new understanding is not apparent at St Matthias, for example, where the congregation is not perceived to have a role in the event and where the status quo is more likely to be taken for granted. At Resurrection there is a strong link between the community and the church, and involvement in the church represents a celebration of the wider community rather than historical traditions. The church as place is viewed as a dynamic extension of the community, in contrast to St Matthias, where the church represents a place of historical roots, and to St Paul's, where the sense of place focuses on spiritual meaning. The ways in which people relate to their churches reflect their life experiences, the social group to which they belong, and the particular contexts of locale. Memory is crucial to our sense of identity, and in those churches having strong family traditions there has been a tendency to conservatism more pronounced than in churches characterized by a mobile population. Stories and myths associated with the old families have become part of the baggage and the heritage of the church. In one instance the relocation of wall plaques from the front to the back of a church was tantamount to a "fall from grace" of the family who had donated the plaques, and some church members expressed their dismay in a letter to the rector.

The spatial patterns of residence in relation to the church provide another interesting perspective on differing meaning systems. While proximity and shared experience have been dominant factors in the community building at Resurrection, there is evidence that some parishioners chose Resurrection because of liturgy and style. They made a conscious choice in their style of worship (in the same sense

R.W. Bibby used with reference to fragmentary options, discussed earlier). The community was not only spatially concentrated, but also socially cohesive as a result of shared meanings associated with a homogeneous middle-class background. In sharp contrast, the spatial pattern of Grace Church members is one of high dispersion because of the high rate of out-migration from Point St Charles. Despite the lack of spatial concentration, the attachments and long family histories of parishioners have caused members to retain their affiliation with Grace Church. The affinity for the social group, held together by shared memories, has been a potent force there, enabling the church to survive. In the case of La Nativité, the scatter is related to the dispersion of a small ethnic community. As the community grows and new congregations are formed (two new congregations in 1990), this spatial pattern will change. The ambiguity of the meaning of community is exemplified in these differing spatial patterns and degrees of social cohesion observed in the five churches.

One particularly important focus of this study was the relationship of the congregation to the surrounding community. At Resurrection the homogeneous middle-class neighbourhood has provided a stable milieu as a focus of community sharing, while at Grace Church the community suffers instability as a result of out-migration. The most complex parish is St Paul's because of the social heterogeneity of the community and the profound changes that have occurred there in the past decade. One change has been an increase in the number of francophone residents. Although none of my interviews indicated any sense of threat to their church on account of the changing linguistic balance, one member did express the feeling that "there's a lot of French. It's quite alarming." Of much greater concern to long-term residents has been the influx of young professionals who spend weekends in Knowlton but who do not seem to have any long-range commitment to the town. Social group rather than social class defines the membership of St Paul's, and the definition of social group is changing. At St Paul's, the determining characteristics of social groups are less a combination of class, linguistic, and church affiliation, and more age and stage in the life cycle. Even as the community itself has changed, affecting the meaning of the place, so too have the meanings that church members attach to St Paul's. St Paul's has become less a repository for family histories, a symbol of English heritage in the area, and more a youthful centre of shared worship. It is less a private space and more a place for public sharing of spiritual commitment. As the symbolic qualities of Knowlton have changed, so too have the symbolic meanings attached to St Paul's. People within the church who have served as important links in the process of change are those who came to Knowlton twenty or thirty years ago. Many still do not consider themselves "of" the community, but they have adopted the old myths and meanings that defined Knowlton when they arrived. It is these people who, despite their rejection of many of the changes in the liturgy and their dislike of the informality of the new service and hymns (the "ditties," as one parishioner called them), continue regular attendance at church. For them the response has been to attend the traditional service at 8:00 AM, thereby creating two congregations. The profound changes in St Paul's, initiated by the new priest who arrived in 1982, were most enthusiastically adopted by new Knowlton residents and younger church members. Although there are exceptions, for the most part it has been those who have arrived in the past twenty years who have led the changes towards house churches and the modern liturgy. They have not adopted the old stories and myths of Knowlton as their own; they have defined new meanings and symbols for their church and their community.

WOMEN: INCLUSION AND EXCLUSION

Despite the common suggestion that people to an increasing degree are relating to a global rather than a local community, there is strong evidence in these churches that people value the intimate ties of local churches and are emotionally committed to their local parishes. One of the most common manifestations of this local loyalty is apparent in the activities of the women's groups, which concentrate almost exclusively on events and causes in their own parish. The community of meaning for these women is predominantly their own church, not the wider church in Canada or the world. One woman, in relating her experience at a diocesan meeting (she had driven 150 kilometres to attend), complained that the wider church had no relevance for her in terms of her parish. "They were interested only in Toronto," she said. "They don't seem to care about the local churches." The sense of place she was describing provides a psychological tie between the biography of the individual and the locales, communities, and churches that are the settings of existential experience.[7] This was most strongly evident at Grace Church among the women who organized the dinners and the twice-monthly bazaars, their small group continuing to come together despite long journeys for many of them.

While the roles and relationships of women in the churches had not been part of my original research design, the significance of their experiences soon became apparent. The dominance of patriarchal values is an acknowledged characteristic of internal relationships in the church. I was startled nevertheless to encounter strong emotional and articulate resistance to many aspects of changing female roles. The opposition to female clergy at St Matthias and a choir member's public response to prayers for Bishop Harries were two of the more obvious examples I cited. Less dramatic but no less significant examples of the ways women are excluded from full participation in the life of the church continually presented themselves throughout the study. In many churches the exclusion of women from positions on the corporation and as representatives to Synod is still an important institutional practice. Women's exclusion from public and official roles concurrent with their significant informal power most accurately describes female participation in church life. Women may not be proportionately represented in the decision-making and financial committees of the diocese, but their informal power in the context of the parish church is real. The problem, of course, is that communication between the two levels is dependent to some degree upon a correspondence between them. In terms of institutional change, there is little evidence of change towards greater equality and acknowledgment of women as decision makers. Despite a letter from the new bishop requesting that parishes consider gender-neutral language, no parish has shown any concerted effort to address the issue of "women in the church." Change is slow. On the other hand, through the presentation of awards by the church leadership, the contribution of women is being acknowledged at one level. Both nationally and at the diocesan level, in 1990 women received most of the awards for outstanding contributions to the church. The ambiguity reflects a certain discord within the church leadership. There is the desire to recognize the contributions of the work-a-day parish individual, but a reluctance to encourage accessibility for women to public and decision-making roles at all levels.

In all the churches studied, women's groups exhibited a profound sense of identity that was related to their shared commitment to self-defined goals. Their activities, events, and aims were not defined by the corporation or by the rector; they were generated by the women themselves, were usually social, and were almost always linked either to traditional roles, such as baking and crafts, or to fund raising. The women spent large amounts of time in their churches, and their accumulated knowledge and experience gave them status and power. This status and power were usually informal and invariably unacknowledged. They tended to guard their independence from the dictates of the corporation and to insist upon maintaining a separate budget that was not factored into the annual budget of the parish.

The nature of activities, the timing of events, and the disbursement of funds raised at bazaars and rummage sales were decided by the women. Interference by wardens or even by the rector could be hazardous to the health of the church (the attempt by St Paul's rector to redefine the women's activities is a case in point). It is tempting to compare this institutional praxis with that of society and the family, in which women are the decision makers and arbiters of social relationships.

Another important aspect of the way in which women function in the church, revealed in many conversations, relates to their unwillingness to welcome new members and give up positions of authority to younger women. Young members reported feeling intimidated and unwelcome in the long-established domain of the Anglican Church Women. Though often feeling the weight of a double handicap in being new to both church and community, they have the potential to offer energy, enthusiasm, and new ideas, underpinned by different values, all of which may appear to conflict with those of older members. At St Paul's one long-standing ACW member wondered "why she [a new member] thought we are so awful." The new member had come in with new ideas that did not fit the prevailing ethos and traditions of the women's group, and they were rejected. Not surprisingly, the women's groups in all the churches are experiencing problems of declining membership. It is only since 1990 that they have begun to examine how to redefine their roles, but without addressing the problem of their relationships with new and younger members. Their solutions have been tentative at best. In one church (St Matthias) the women's group has been disbanded altogether in favour of a "fellowship group" for both men and women.

Despite their powerful presence, the women's groups are often overlooked in general discussions about policy considerations or new directions for the local church. In the consultations on stewardship at St Matthias, for example, the contribution of women was virtually ignored in the formulation of a parish questionnaire. At Grace Church as well, where all of the fund-raising is under the leadership and initiative of women, rarely has a woman sat at the head table at parish suppers or been included among the names of church officers in the parish history. The situation is more egalitarian at St Paul's and Resurrection, where community has a stronger family dimension and there is greater emphasis on activities that involve a wider range of ages.

Despite the failure of the church to correct its gender imbalance, it has continued to be a place of significance for women who need to express their talents and leadership in the context of shared community relationships. That there are serious problems facing every women's group with which I had contact is indicative not only of an increase in the number of working women, but also, I believe, of the church's failure to come to terms with the urgent need to change its relationship with women. After a difficult debate at Synod in 1988, there was only grudging acceptance of the need to specifically address women's needs by the creation of a new staff position. Even today that position remains only a part-time appointment.

CONTRIBUTIONS AND MEMBERSHIP

The most solid evidence of the impact of social and political tensions can be seen in the levels of financial support of the church. Throughout the diocese a significant increase in contributions measured on a per capita basis occurred after the election of the Parti Québécois in 1976. Despite national surveys that indicate a consistent pattern of low Quebec contributions for altruistic causes, the Anglican Church in Montreal has, since 1976, shown consistently higher donations than anywhere else in Canada. While the threat was strongest in the years leading up to the referendum in 1980, the contributions continued to grow after that year. After a brief levelling off in 1981–82 (also a time of recession), contributions per capita increased until the peak in 1987.

At the same time as Montrealers were exhibiting generosity within their own churches, they became less generous in their support of missions or outreach beyond diocesan boundaries. After 1976 churches gave less than they had previously, and they gave less than churches in other parts of the country. There seems to have been a strong tendency to protect themselves by directing increased proportions of their dollar support to themselves, thereby assuring the continuity of their symbols of family heritage and community roots. In their resistance to change within the church, their strong financial support for themselves, and their withdrawal of financial support of outside missions, the parishes in Montreal have been responding to the threat to their cultural identity; they have been protecting an institution that has symbolized the historical sense of belonging and family roots. Their churches are significant places, not only of worship but also of shared experiences giving meaning to their lives. The loss of their churches would symbolize the end of their existence in Quebec, and the loss of any real community of meaning.

The evidence contained in the membership and attendance data has proved more difficult to interpret because the data must be compared to a base population of census Anglicans, a statistic that is available only every ten years. For the census year 1981, when additional data were available because of a special tabulation done for the Long Range Planning Report of the national church, data suggested that, as a percentage of the total possible, there were approximately the same numbers of people on membership rolls in Quebec as in the rest of Canada. The only difference appeared to be in the balance between those who attend regularly and those (the fringe group) who attend infrequently or only at the special festivals. Everywhere in Canada there has been a diminution of the numbers of people who allow their names to stay on church rolls but who do not attend church, and in every region outside Quebec there is a closer correspondence between average attendance and the numbers of Easter communicants than in Quebec. This probably indicates that formal affiliation with the church today is a more conscious decision, less affected by the expectations of society. As the ratio of Easter communicants to average attendance has declined, there are fewer people in the fringe group as potential regular attenders. In Montreal these ratios tend to be higher than for other parts of Canada, indicating that there may be a tendency to retain membership even though attendance is minimal, in recognition of the church as a cultural institution having significant ethnic homogeneity. The higher ratios at St Matthias and Grace Church where the perceived threat is great and family traditions are strong lend support to this idea.

In the *Montreal Churchman* and the *Proceedings* of the annual Synod meetings there was substantial evidence of a church in the throes of adaptation and challenging compromise. The gradual recognition of change in Quebec society and politics was forced upon the church leadership in the early 1970s, at the same time as it was having to adjust to forces of secularization and new directions in the church itself. These documents provide unequivocal evidence of the tensions and conflicts caused by these changes. The more ambiguous data were those generated from individual church members, through interviews and participant observation. While most of the parishioners expressed openness towards francophone culture, their stated views often contradicted their actions. For example, their apparent support of bilingualism expressed in interviews belied the result of the vote at Synod on the issue of bilingual signs within the church, the signs being rejected by a wide margin. Church members did not seem to be conscious of any ambiguity in their behaviour. Most would have been surprised that they were seen to be acting in a protective way, despite the frequency with which their committees became engaged in discussions about the future of their churches.

Members made no conscious connection between their resistance to change and their socio-political environment, and without exception everyone was surprised to learn that their per capita donations were among the highest in Canada. No one had considered that their lack of engagement in the world church was unusual or in any way reflected a predominant concern for their own interests at home. My interviews with parishioners clearly brought to light their awareness of the importance of a community church and their commitment to ensure its survival. In 1994 the reality of dwindling resources and numbers of church members raises crucial questions for the diocesan bishop. Reorganization, merging of parishes, and closure of some churches appear to be inevitable consequences of the changes we have been discussing. The choices will be difficult because the communal church continues to be central to the self-definition of its members. The spatial and behavioural dimensions of participation are directly related to the meanings that individuals, within their social groups, attach to their church.

A FINAL SERVICE: METAPHOR FOR THE CHURCH IN MONTREAL

Special invitations were mailed. Past and present parishioners, friends, and clergy by the hundreds were invited to a "Service of Thanksgiving" marking the closing and deconsecration of a downtown Montreal church in May 1991. People came from across the city, drawn by past associations and memories, by the unusual nature of the occasion, and perhaps by a degree of empathy for the church members confronting this situation. No one would be unaware of the significance of closing a church; every person could relate to the factors that had contributed to the final decision. Many, especially in the downtown areas, are faced with a similar possibility. The service itself mirrored many of the significant responses to the problems faced by the diocesan church. It was a metaphor for the fears, traditions, family roots, and heroic determination seen in other parishes in the diocese. The service also reflected the church's isolation from its milieu.

A former rector of the parish (now a bishop) gave the address, in which he reminisced about his own "happy" tenure of four years in the early 1960s. He did not, however, mention the many social and political changes in Quebec since then. Next to me was an elderly woman who had been a member for over sixty years and whose loyalty brought her each Sunday, via public transportation, past three other Anglican churches, a distance of over eight kilometres. She talked about the old days, expressing concern that their new church did not seem to be very welcoming. It will be almost as long a journey for her, but she allowed that she would "try it until September."

Of the more than four hundred people attending the service, about 75 per cent were women and the average age was over 60 years. Despite its location in the middle of an ethnic minority neighbourhood in downtown Montreal, the church did not seem to have attracted any of the visible minorities, all noticeably absent from the service. Furthermore, notwithstanding the high proportion of women in the congregation, it was men who were wardens, men who acted as sidesmen, and men who took up the collection. Finally, the traditional processional hymn was followed by the traditional communion service from the Book of Common Prayer. The beautifully carved woodwork of the interior and the glowing colours of elaborate stained-glass windows will now grace the premises of a municipal library.

Religion is not neutral. It is implicated in social practice and has profound political meanings. In Quebec the social and political changes since 1961 have affected the Anglican Church in ways that are apparent at both the diocesan and individual levels. The relationship between the church and the social milieu is reflexive, in a constant process of change. The community of the church has provided many parishioners with a way to make a significant affirmation, an affirmation rooted in the symbols of place and the landscape of tradition. In a reflexive process, the roles of society, institution, and social group mediate the ways in which people behave and the choices they make. Historical memory and shared stories provide significant underpinnings to the ways people respond to the wider socio-political and institutional environments. The complex relationships between religion and society and between the community and the individual have been explored in terms of the particular Quebec milieu in a time of profound change. The tensions generated within the socio-political milieu have had consequences for the Anglican Church and in turn for individual members in their parishes.

Appendices

APPENDIX A: TABLES

Table 1
Chronology of Key Socio-political Events, 1959–93

1959	Death of Premier Maurice Duplessis
1960–61	Quiet Revolution; "Maître chez nous."
1967	Publication of Bilingualism and Biculturalism Report.
1968	Riots in Italian district of St Leonard (Montreal) as a school board eliminates English as the main language of education.
1969	Bill 63: the government affirms right to choice of language of education.
1970	Kidnappings of James Cross and Pierre Laporte; imposition of the War Measures Act in October.
1974	Bill 22: French made the official language of the province; access to English schools limited to those who already have a working knowledge of French, and establishes programs for francization of firms doing business with the Quebec government.
1976	Election of the separatist Parti Québécois.
1977	Bill 101: restriction of access to English schools; intensified francization programs; elimination of most English signs; French the sole official language of the National Assembly.
1980	Referendum: Sovereignty-association is rejected.
1982	Constitution repatriated without Quebec's signature.
1987	Provisional acceptance of the Meech Lake accord.
1988	Bill 178: using the notwithstanding clause of the 1982 constitution, the bill overrides a decision of the Supreme Court that affirmed the rights of stores to have a second language on outdoor signs.
1990	Rejection of the Meech Lake accord, leading to renewed nationalism and support for separatism in Quebec.
1993	In the federal election, the Bloc Québécois wins 54 seats in Quebec.

Table 2
Estimations of Quebec Interprovincial Migration, 1966–67 to 1982–83

Year	Entries	Exits	Net Migration
1966–67	44,737	59,215	–14,478
1967–68	40,457	56,183	–15,726
1968–69	39,071	57,766	–18,695
1969–70	36,226	72,067	–35,841
1970–71	34,633	72,628	–37,995
1966–71	195,124	317,859	–122,735
1971–72	38,810	59,271	–20,461
1972–73	35,594	55,666	–20,072
1973–74	40,773	55,909	–15,136
1974–75	37,834	47,133	–9,299
1975–76	32,915	45,557	–12,642
1971–76	185,926	263,536	–77,610
1976–77	28,867	55,233	–26,366
1977–78	23,945	70,374	–46,429
1978–79	25,524	56,408	–30,884
1979–80	22,018	51,994	–29,976
1980–81	22,905	45,746	–22,841
1976–81	123,259	279,755	–156,496
1981–82*	20,722	44,844	–24,162
1982–83*	27,452	50,020	–22,568

Source: M. Baillargeon, "Évolution et caractéristiques," based on sources in Statistics Canada.
* Provisional figures.

Table 3
Interprovincial Migration to and from Quebec According to Mother Tongue,
1966–81

	Mother Tongue			
Migration	French	English	Other	Total
Entries				
1966–71	33,400	46,900	4,600	84,900
1971–76	37,200	41,900	4,700	83,800
1976–81	31,875	25,220	4,210	61,310
Exits				
1966–71	46,900	99,100	14,400	160,400
1971–76	41,300	94,100	10,400	145,800
1976–81	49,940	131,530	21,560	203,040
Net				
1966–71	−13,500	−52,200	−9,800	−75,500
1971–76	−4,100	−52,200	−5,700	−62,000
1976–81	−18,065	−106,310	−17,350	−141,730

Source: Baillargeon, "Évolution et caractéristiques linguistiques."

Table 4
Five Study Parishes

Name	Location	Average family income surrounding census tracts (1986 Census)	No. on Parish List
St Matthias	Westmount, mid-city	$86,000	860 indivs. 391 resids.
Resurrection	Pte Claire, suburbs	46,000	533 indivs. 209 resids.
St Paul's	Knowlton, rural	35,000	755 indivs. 159 resids.
Grace Church	Pt St Charles, mid-city	20,000	274 indivs. 158 resids.
La Nativité	Rosemont, mid-city	15,000 (est.)	377 indivs. 160 resids.

Source: Statistics Canada, Cat. 95–130; Cat. 94–110.

Table 5
Anglican Membership, 1961–91 (000's)

Year	Canada	Montreal
1961	1,358	95
1966	1,293	80
1971	1,109	62
1976	1,008	51
1981	922	38
1985	856	33
1991	802	25

Sources: Bibby, *Fragmented Gods*; Synod reports.

Table 6
Family Donations by Degree of Religious Commitment, 1981

	Strong Religious Ties	Frequent Attendance	Infrequent Attendance	No Religious Ties
Donating more than $100	88 %	69 %	45 %	37 %
Family Donations				
Religious	$1,105	$264	$ 84	$ 21
Non-religious	378	133	202	189
Total	1,483	397	286	210
Percentage of Income	4.3 %	1.3 %	0.8 %	0.5 %
Hours of personal service	118	94	63	50

Source: Samuel Martin, *An Essential Grace*, 192.

Table 7
Measures of Involvement of Anglicans by Diocese and Ecclesiastical Province, 1981
(percentage of census Anglicans)

Diocese	Members	Confirmed	Givers	Attendance
Fredericton	67.9	40.5	14.5	14.0
Quebec	73.7	53.7	21.2	14.2
Montreal	38.3	27.1	11.9	10.8
Province, Canada	67.2	41.3	17.8	12.2
Toronto	25.0	17.0	7.6	6.8
Province, Ontario	33.5	22.3	9.7	8.0
Province, Rupert's	33.5	19.2	8.1	8.4
Province, B.C.	19.1	13.1	5.3	5.9
Total, Canada	37.8	24.0	10.3	8.6

Source: "National Long Range Planning Report".

Table 8
Members on Parish Rolls, Montreal Diocese and "Province of Canada" 1961–91

Year	Members		Mtl., % "Canada"
	"Canada"	Montreal	
1961	368,654	94,891	25.7
1966	355,392	80,249	22.6
1971	333,950	62,154	18.6
1976	337,662	51,126	15.1
1981	317,774	37,735	11.9
1986	300,919	32,131	10.7
1991	290,404	24,773	8.5

Source: National Synod reports, 1962–92.

Table 9
Numbers of Members on Parish Rolls, Percentage Change, 1961–91

Years	Canada	Toronto	Montreal
1961–66	–4.8	–7.1	–15.4
1966–71	–14.2	–20.8	–22.8
1971–76	–9.0	–16.8	–17.7
1976–81	–8.6	–12.3	–26.0
1981–86	–9.5	–8.0	–14.8
1986–91	–4.7	–6.0	–21.6

Source: National Synod reports, 1962–92.

Table 10
Charitable Donations by Province and City, 1980

	Donations, $ per person	
	per Taxpayer	per Donor
Quebec	$ 31.3	$491
Yukon/N.W.T.	47.9	557
Newfoundland	56.3	499
Nova Scotia	65.4	513
P.E.I.	73.7	485
B.C.	79.3	739
Ontario	84.3	619
Manitoba	88.6	662
New Brunswick	90.0	615
Alberta	93.7	824
Saskatchewan	108.7	669
Canada	71.1	689
Quebec City	43.7	491
Montreal	55.5	635
Vancouver	83.0	718
Toronto	90.6	755
Winnipeg	90.3	648
Halifax	92.2	588

Source: Deeg, "How and What Canadians Contribute to Charity."

Table 11
Percentage Change in Financial Contributions and Membership, Montreal and
Toronto Dioceses, 1961–86 (in constant 1981 dollars)

	Percentage Change			
	Total Contributions		Membership	
Year	Montreal	Toronto	Montreal	Toronto
1961–71	–27.9	–24.0	–34.4	–26.5
1971–76	–5.0	+2.5	–17.7	–16.7
1976–81	–2.2	+9.4	–26.2	–12.3
1981–86	+1.0	+13.0	–14.8	–8.1

Source: Annual Synod reports.

Table 12
Average per Capita Offerings, Montreal, Toronto, and Canada, 1961–86
(in constant 1981 dollars)

	Montreal	Toronto	Canada
1961–75	89	97	78
1976–86	148	127	109

Source: Annual Synod reports.

Table 13
Variations in Median Amount Donated by Type of Organization, 1987

	Canada	Outside Quebec	Quebec
Non-religious	$ 42	$ 47	$26
Religious	137	155	73

Source: Decima, *Nation-wide Survey*, 12.

Table 14
Charitable Donations by Mother Tongue of Head of Household and Region
as a Percentage of Gross Family Income

Mother Tongue	REGION					
	Atlantic	Quebec	Ontario	West	B.C.	Canada
English	1.26	.55	.92	.90	.75	.91
French	.84	.32	.47	1.48	.35	.38
Other	.60	.35	.77	1.75	.93	1.01
Total	1.22	.34	.86	1.11	.77	.78

Source: Kitchen.

Table 15
Average Attendance as a Percentage of Membership, by Diocese, 1973–85

Year	Mtl.	Fred.	N.S.	Ott.	Tor.	Rup.Ld.
1973	16.7	23.8	15.6	20.0	20.0	21.6
1974	16.5	22.1	15.6	19.8	20.1	20.7
1975	17.4	19.7	14.7	20.6	20.7	20.8
1976	17.8	19.4	15.4	19.3	21.5	21.1
1977	18.1	19.8	14.9	18.2	22.2	21.8
1978	–	20.0	15.1	20.8	26.1	25.5
1979	–	20.6	15.2	22.0	25.9	23.4
1980	–	21.1	16.2	24.0	26.2	21.2
1985	–	23.8	19.6	23.3	28.1	23.7

Source: Annual Synod reports.

Table 16
Anglican Appeal: Percentage of Parish Income and Contributions per Member,
1974–82

Diocese	Average	
	1974–82 % Parish Income	1974–82 $ Per Member
Montreal	.0088	$0.83
Quebec	.0085	0.69
Ottawa	.0184	1.60
Toronto	.0098	1.05
Canada	.0115	0.91

Source: Annual Synod reports.

Table 17
Anglicans in Mission: Amounts Pledged and Realized per Member, 1983, 1986,
and 1991

| | Pledged, 1983 | | Realized, 1986 | % Realized of Total Pledge | |
| | | | | | |
Diocese	% Income	per Cap.	per Cap.	1986	1991
Montreal	30.6 %	$59.26	48.36	77.3	89
N.S.	42.6	41.30	38.93	92.1	94
Toronto	43.0	76.40	81.05	95.3	97
Canada	45.9	59.50	59.93	91.9	96

Source: National Comptroller documents; Synod reports.

Table 18
Percentage Change in Church Populations in Four Parishes, 1961–81

	Census Anglicans	Membership	Attendance	Offerings	Easter Comms.
Grace	−52.5	−48	−27	+20.5	−48
Resurrection	−36	−62	−52	−18.5	−42
St Paul's	N/A	+7	−49	+64	−42
St Matthias	−45	−57	−42	−6.8	−56

Sources: Synod reports; vestry books; census 1961, 1981.

Table 19
Percentage Changes in Membership, Attendance, and Offerings in Four
Parishes, 1971–88

	Membership 1971–88	Attendance 1971–86	Offerings 1971–88	From Peak of Total Offerings (in Constant Dollars) to 1988
Grace	−72	−41	−15	−45
Resurrection	−32	+9	−2	−12
St Paul's	−16	no change	+28	−33
St Matthias	−64	−25	−14	−41

Sources: Synod reports; vestry books.

Table 20
Ratios of Membership to Easter Communicants: Canada and the Dioceses of
Montreal and Toronto, 1961–86

Year	Canada	Montreal	Toronto
1961	2.85	2.51	2.98
1962	2.80	2.51	2.85
1963	2.25	2.71	2.85
1964	2.80	2.77	2.80
1965	2.90	3.02	2.76
1966	2.91	3.04	2.72
1967	2.85	2.97	2.74
1968	2.85	3.10	2.67
1969	2.96	3.06	2.67
1970	2.93	2.86	2.83
1971	2.78	2.55	2.61
1972	2.91	2.93	2.58
1973	2.92	2.87	2.58
1974	2.77	2.74	2.41
1975	2.79	2.80	2.35
1976	2.72	2.61	2.32
1977	2.58	2.61	2.14
1978	2.60	2.77	2.29
1979	2.48	2.54	2.01
1980	2.34	2.50	1.85
1981	2.27	2.40	1.83
1982	2.19	2.39	1.81
1983	2.26	2.47	1.91
1984	2.16	2.36	1.79
1985	2.01	2.33	1.65

Source: Annual Synod reports.

Table 21
Membership in Four Parishes, 1961–88

Year	Grace	Resurrection	St Paul's	St Matthias
1961	1,060	1,506	525	2,700
1966	1,100	1,250	590	3,050
1971	1,000	1,090	645	2,200
1976	600	816	580	1,850
1981	550	584	560	1,160
1986	330	750	700	800
1988	285	750	750	800

Source: Synod reports.

Table 22
Average Weekly Attendance at All Services at Four Parishes, 1961–86

Year	Grace	Resurrection	St Paul's	St Matthias (est.)
1961	171 ('65)	305	172	400
1966	154	199	148	370
1971	120	148	141	210
1976	129	161	103	120
1981	124	108	87	223
1986	71	162	141	263 ('85)

Source: Vestry books.

Table 23
Open, Regular, and Special Offerings at Four Parishes, 1966–88
(in constant 1981 dollars, in 000's)

Year	Grace	Resurrection	St Paul's	St Matthias
1961	35	**90**	31	220
1962	30	81	22	230
1963	35	79	38	**231**
1964	28	81	42	230
1965	30	75	33	209
1966	24	66	32	211
1967	23	64	40	214
1968	32	63	35	202
1969	20	66	39	191
1970	23	59	45	194
1971	27	52	43	182
1972	23	59	45	164
1973	25	55	46	149
1974	26	52	40	166
1975	23	50	45	161
1976	21	**56**	48	**263**
1977	24	49	39	**240**
1978	**30**	55	76	**216**
1979	**33**	48	82	**234**
1980	32	46	53	194
1981	**42**	40	51	205
1982	24	37	51	177
1983	33	49	58	210
1984	31	58	60	211
1985	24	56	61	203
1986	**38**	55	55	175
1987	23	53	55	172
1988	23	51	55	156

Source: Synod reports.
Note: Peak values in bold print.

Table 24
Offerings per Member at Four Parishes, 1961–88 (in constant 1981 dollars)

Year	Grace	Resurrection	St Paul's	St Matthias
1961	32.88	32.66	59.40	80.53
1971	26.81	47.94	65.93	82.69
1976	35.37	68.28	81.28	139.76
1981	76.71	68.62	119.09	176.34
1986	115.28	73.98	73.86	218.42
1988	82.59	86.40	72.79	195.20

Sources: Synod reports; vestry books.

Table 25
Average Weekly Offerings per Person Attending Services at Four Parishes,
1961–86 (in constant 1981 dollars)

Year	Grace	Resurrection	St Paul's	St Matthias
1961	3.33 ('65)	5.69	3.51	10.60 est.
1971	4.28	6.80	5.80	16.70 est.
1976	3.18	6.64	8.88	23.05 est.
1981	6.53	7.12	11.32	17.63
1986	10.32	6.59	7.56	14.80

Sources: Synod reports; vestry books.

Table 26
Average Attendance as a Percentage of Membership* in Four Parishes, 1961–86

Year	Grace	Resurrection	St Paul's	St Matthias
1961	16	20	33	15
1966	14	16	25	12
1971	12	14	22	10
1976	22	20	18	14
1981	23	19	16	19
1986	22	22	20	23

Sources: Synod reports; vestry books.
* Attendance calculated as total of all services, divided by 52 for a "weekly" average.

Table 27
The Ratios of Easter Communicants to Average Attendance in Four Parishes,
1961–89

Year	Grace	Resurrection	St Paul's	St Matthias
Averages				
1961–66	3.24 ('65)	2.98	2.89	2.76
1966–71	2.79	2.87	2.97	3.64
1971–76	2.06	2.21	2.98	2.78
1976–81	2.09	2.09	2.86	2.50
1981–86	2.32	1.71	2.10	2.21
1983–89	2.19	1.61	1.60	–

Sources: Vestry books

Table 28
Distribution of Church Members: Percentage Living at Variable Distances from
the Church

Distance	La Nativité	Resurrection	St Paul's	Grace	St Matthias
2 km	8	75	61	46	77
5 km	39	92	79	65	88
10 km	82	100	91	84	95
Total No. of Addresses on Parish Rolls	160	209	159	158	391

Source: Parish rolls.

APPENDIX B: FIGURES

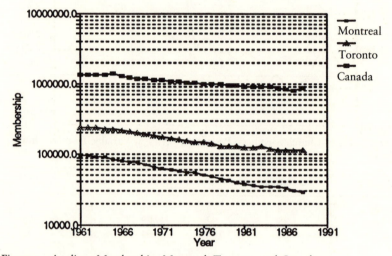

Figure 1   Anglican Membership, Montreal, Toronto, and Canada
Source: National Synod reports.

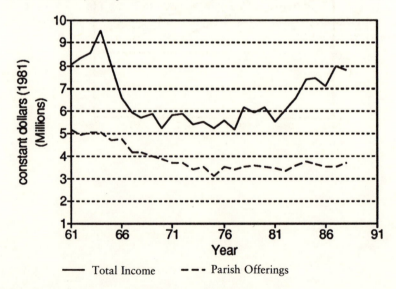

Figure 2   Total Parish Income and Offerings, Montreal
Source: Synod reports.

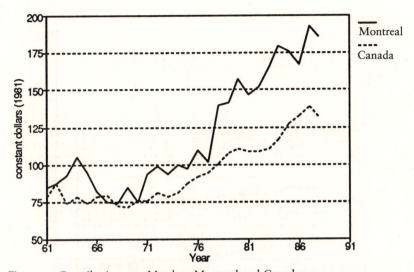

Figure 3   Contributions per Member, Montreal and Canada
Source: National and Montreal Synod reports.

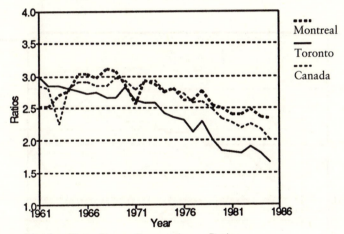

Figure 4   Membership to Easter Communicants Ratios
Source: National Synod reports.

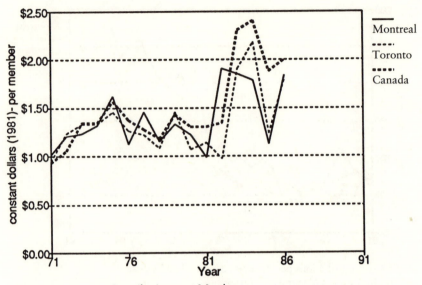

Figure 5   PWRDF, Contributions per Member
Source: National Synod.

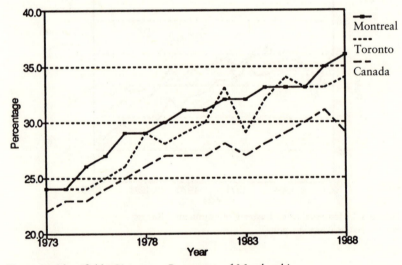

Figure 6   Identifiable Givers as a Percentage of Membership
Source: National Synod reports.

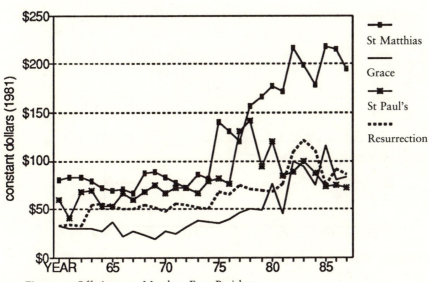

Figure 7   Offerings per Member, Four Parishes
Source: Parish records.

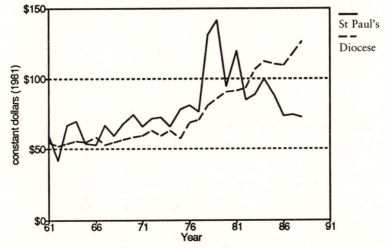

Figure 8   Offerings per Member, St Paul's and Diocese
Source: Parish records.

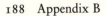

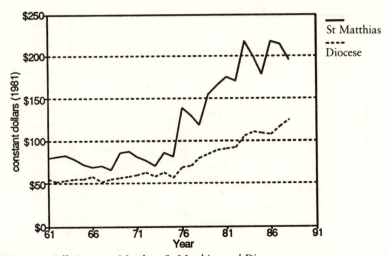

Figure 9   Offerings per Member, St Matthias and Diocese
Source: Parish records.

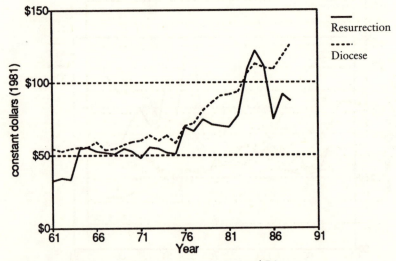

Figure 10   Offerings per Member, Resurrection and Diocese
Source: Parish records.

189   Figures

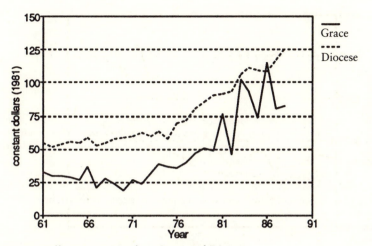

Figure 11   Offerings per Member, Grace and Diocese
Source: Parish records.

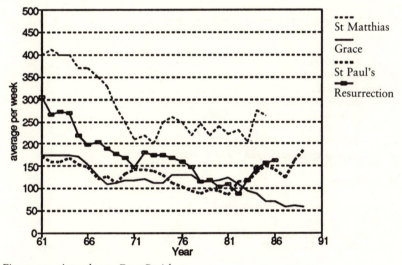

Figure 12   Attendance, Four Parishes
Source: Parish records.
Notes: Attendance averages were calculated by the summation of attendance figures for all
Sunday services recorded in vestry books, divided by 52 weeks.
Easter and Christmas services were excluded.

APPENDIX C: THE SURVEYS

The national *Parish Questionnaire on the Use of the Book of Alternative Services* was an eleven-page questionnaire sent out in 1987 to all parishes in the country. Of these, 1,282 were returned, representing 40.5 per cent of the total. From Montreal Diocese there were 36.5 per cent returned.

The *Questionnaire for Montreal Diocese*, which I conducted in March 1988, received a 77 per cent return and was one page in length, as shown here.

Parish –
Church –
Rector –
Assistant –
Questionnaire: New Initiatives in the Anglican Church

For each congregation in your parish, please record the situation as it presently exists:

A) *Book of Alternative Services*

Do you own enough copies for your congregation?	yes	no
Do you use the B.A.S.?	yes	no
a. only for Holy Communion?	yes	no
If yes, number of times per month		
b. all regular services?	yes	no
c. other occasions? Mention:		
d. Do most members attend BAS service(s)?	yes	no

B) *Lectionary*

Do you use the ecumenical lectionary?	yes	no
If yes, exclusively?	yes	no
If no, is it being considered?	yes	no

C) *Children Admitted to Communion*

Do you admit pre-confirmation children to communion as an operating principle?	yes	no
If no, are you considering doing so?	yes	no
Do you expect to do so in 1988?	yes	no

APPENDIX D: SOME MEASURES OF ANGLICAN COMMITMENT

TOTAL MEMBERSHIP – This figure reflects the parish roll, and its reliability varies according to the efficiency/administrative interests of the rector and/or parish secretary. It includes all individuals and families who are regular attenders; identifiable and regular financial contributers; and, possibly, people who have been married or baptized in the church.

PARISH INCOME – All parishes have audited statements recording the sources of annual income, which are sent to the diocese, compiled, and sent on to the national office. Approximately half of the total income is from "envelopes"; another portion is from "identifiable givers"; and the balance is from the women's association, hall rentals, and interest from endowment funds. As discussed in my study, the women's accounts frequently are not included in the financial statement and may not be part of the audited records.

ENVELOPE CONTRIBUTIONS – Each year parishioners are given a box of envelopes if they request them, one for each week of the year, plus ones for Easter and Christmas. In some churches there are also "pledge cards" that indicate to the corporation and the treasurer what the financial commitment is for the coming year. In other churches the "pledge" is taken to be the amount in the first envelope each year. These are important indicators for budget planning.

IDENTIFIABLE GIVERS – These include everyone who has received a receipt for contributions to the church. While they may include one-time contributers, most often they are people who habitually donate money once a year. Often these people do not attend regularly, and have long family connections with the church.

AIM – As noted in the definitions, this initiative of the national church sought to ensure the long-term financial support of mission. It was a professionally run campaign reaching into the individual parishes, extending over a three-to-five year period.

EASTER COMMUNICANTS – This figure, collected at the parish level and recorded in the vestry books, is regarded as important by Anglicans because attendance at Easter is the most important expression of commitment for the church. For this reason I have used it rather than the Christmas figure. Another consideration was that attendance at Christmas is affected by weather and by the day of the week on which Christmas happens to fall.

AVERAGE SUNDAY ATTENDANCE – Available for most of Canada, this figure is not collected for Montreal Diocese after 1977, and therefore my data have been derived directly from vestry books. While it is generally reliable, there were some adjustments that I made in order to ensure comparability. In the case of St Matthias, the rector recorded only the numbers attending Eucharist services, excluding morning prayer and evensong. In this case I "estimated" attendance by multiplying actual figures by 190 per cent, assuming fewer people at the non-communion services. At Grace Church for several years the rector, who was active in the Masonic Order, had well-attended services that did not involve his own congregation. Therefore I excluded these figures from the data. Other minor adjustments had to be made to ensure that weddings were not included; baptisms were included, however, since they are often part of the regular service.

APPENDIX E: DEFINITIONS OF SOME ANGLICAN TERMS

ADMINISTRATION STRUCTURE – Canada is divided into four ecclesiastical "provinces" (Canada, Ontario, Rupert's Land, British Columbia), each of which has an archbishop. The provinces in turn are subdivided into dioceses, of which there are thirty in the country, led by a bishop. Montreal Diocese was led by Bishop Reginald Hollis from 1975 until November 1990, when Bishop Andrew Hutchison was elected by the joint "houses" of clergy and lay representatives. Montreal Diocese is one of six in the Province of Canada. The Anglican Church of Canada is headed by a primate, Archbishop Michael Peers. There is no formal connection to either the Church of England or the American Episcopal Church.

ADVISORY BOARD/SELECT VESTRY/PARISH COUNCIL – All these terms refer to a board of the parish that meets from four to twelve times a year and usually includes representatives of each of the organizations in the church such as the ACW (Association of Women), Sunday school chairperson, etc.

AIM – Anglicans in Mission: an initiative of the national church taken in 1983, through which it was hoped enough money could be raised to ensure a long-term fund for the support of "assisted" parishes and remote "missions" in the Canadian Arctic. It was originally intended to be a three-year campaign in which parishes were asked to commit (pledge) an additional amount of money for use beyond parish and diocesan borders. The suggested target was one-third of present parish income. If parishes had not met their commitment in the three-year period, they were encouraged to continue until it had been realized.

BAS – Book of Alternative Services: the new and "provisional" prayer book, introduced by the National Synod of the Anglican Church of Canada in 1983 and published for distribution in 1985. It was introduced as a "trial" for ten years, after which time a decision would be made as to the precise form a new prayer book should take.

BCP – Book of Common Prayer: the 'traditional' prayer book used in the Canadian Anglican, American Episcopal, and the Church of England until the introduction of the new "alternative" prayer book.

CELL GROUPS/HOME CHURCH – Introduced in recent years in a few Anglican churches in the diocese, they have been part of the Catholic practice for much longer. People meet in small gorups of ten to twelve once a week for spiritual, personal, and social sharing of their faith. They have been successfully integrated into one of my study parishes, St Paul's in Knowlton.

CHARISMATIC RENEWAL – A movement more prominent in the Catholic church, it has also touched the Anglican church. It is viewed with suspicion and even hostility by many Anglicans because it incorporates 'speaking in tongues' as one of the 'gifts of the spirit'; healing; and lively services with non-traditional music.

CORPORATION – This is the group of three people, clergy and two wardens, who have the legal responsibility for the parish. Their decisions are legally binding, and they are answerable to the congregation and to the bishop. The people's warden is elected at the annual vestry meeting by a quorum of all "active" members of the congregation. The rector's warden, usually considered to be the senior position, is appointed by the rector. There are no fixed terms of office.

CURSILLO – This is a lay movement, not restricted to the Anglican Church. It derives from the Spanish word meaning "short course" and is a two-or three-day live-in course about christianity. About eight hundred Montreal Anglicans have attended. It has been a source of division in some churches because of its evangelistic tendencies.

ENVELOPE SECRETARY – This person is responsible for recording financial commitments and weekly envelope contributions and for issuing all receipts.

THE PEACE – Following reconciliation in the service, this is a greeting exchanged by all members of the congregation. It has been introduced into the Anglican Church only with the new prayer book, and it has been the source of a great deal of tension in some congregations. David Martin's *Breaking of the Image* discusses the implictions of these new elements in the church in both cultural and theological terms.

SYNOD – This is a meeting of bishops, priests, and laity that takes place annually at the diocesan level; every three years at the province and national levels. The purpose of these meetings is to discuss and make policies to guide the church in Canada. Some of the controversial issues in recent years have been the ordination of women; admittance of young children to communion before confirmation; the new prayer book; acceptance of an ecumenical lectionary (the calendar of biblical readings); and involvement in social issues such as the refugee question.

TREASURER – This person is appointed by the corporation at the annual vestry meeting, held in January each year.

Notes

CHAPTER I

1 Guindon, *Quebec Society*, 138.
2 Marc V. Levine, *The Reconquest of Montreal*, 216.
3 Mann, *The Sources of Social Power*, 27.
4 Baum, *Religion and Alienation*, 104.
5 Durkheim, *Sociology and Philosophy*, trans. Pocock, 80–97.
6 Wilson, Bryan R., *Religion in Sociological Perspective*, 2.
7 Berger, *The Sacred Canopy*, 106.
8 David Martin, *A General Theory of Secularization*, 3.
9 Bryan R. Wilson, *Religion*, 148.
10 Ibid., 151.
11 Eliade, *The Sacred and the Profane*, 17.
12 Ibid., 20.
13 Kern, *The Culture of Time and Space*, 17.
14 Ibid., 24.
15 Luckmann, *The Invisible Religion*, 81.
16 Berger and Luckmann, *The Social Construction of Reality*, 40.
17 Berger, *The Sacred Canopy*, 155.
18 Ibid., 153.
19 Ibid., 107.
20 Geertz, *The Interpretation of Cultures*, 20.
21 Scherer, *Contemporary Community*, 1.
22 Greeley, *Unsecular Man*, 148.
23 Sopher, *Geography of Religions*, 138.

24 Wilson, *Religion in Sociological Perspective*.
25 Baum, *Religion and Alienation*, 252–3.
26 Lane, *Landscapes of the Sacred*, 188.
27 David Martin, *The Breaking of the Image*, 85.
28 Clift, *The Secret Kingdom*, 116.
29 Charles Taylor, *Sources of the Self*, 113.
30 Lowenthal, *The Past Is a Foreign Country*, 197.
31 Taylor, *Sources of the Self*, 203.
32 MacIntyre, *After Virtue*, 221.
33 Hall, *Thinking the Faith*, 123.

CHAPTER 2

1 Levine, *The Reconquest of Montreal*, 45.
2 Ibid., 10.
3 McRoberts, *Quebec*, 3.
4 Guindon, "The Social Evolution of Quebec Reconsidered," 546.
5 Marc V. Levine, *Reconquest*, 33.
6 Ibid., 39.
7 Arnopoulos and Clift, *The English Fact in Quebec*, 61.
8 McRoberts, *Quebec*, 95.
9 Renaud, "Quebec's New Middle Class," 61.
10 Ibid, 97.
11 Waddell, quoted in Handler, *Nationalism and the Politics of Culture*, 188.
12 Arnopoulos and Clift, *The English Fact*, 120.
13 Guindon, *Quebec Society*, 63.
14 Arnopoulos and Clift, *The English Fact*, 49.
15 Dufour, *Le Défi Québécois*, 120.
16 Guindon, *Quebec Society*, 90; originally published in D. Glenday, H. Guindon, and A. Turowitz, eds., *Modernization and the Canadian State* (Toronto, 1978).
17 Alliance Quebec, *Brief on Immigration*.
18 Baillargeon, *Evolution et caractéristiques*.
19 Maheu, "L'émigration des anglophones."
20 Alliance Quebec, *Brief on Immigration*.
21 Statistics Canada study, quoted in ibid.
22 Henripin, *La Population Québécoise*, 53.
23 Alliance Quebec, *Brief on Demographic Tendencies*, 58.
24 Grant, *The Church in the Canadian Era*, 232.
25 Ibid., 230.
26 Bibby, *Fragmented Gods*.
27 Ibid., 83.

28 Grant, *The Church*, 242.
29 Bibby, *Fragmented Gods*, 87.
30 Ibid. 12.
31 Ibid., 87–9.
32 Ibid., 99.
33 Anglican Church of Canada, "National Long Range Planning Report."
34 Mol, *Faith and Fragility*, 212.
35 Clifford, "His Dominion."
36 Mol, *Faith and Fragility*, 217.
37 Porter, *The Vertical Mosaic*, 515.
38 Anglican Church of Canada, *"National Long Range Planning Report."*
39 Percentage over 50 and 65 years: Montreal Diocese, 36 and 16 per cent; Quebec Diocese, 35 and 13 per cent; Toronto Diocese, 30 and 18 per cent; Canada, 29 and 10 per cent. Percentage of non-movers 1976–81: Montreal, 55 per cent; Quebec, 68 per cent; Toronto, 52 per cent; Canada, 53 per cent. (Anglican Church of Canada, *"National Long Range Planning Report."*)
40 Wm. Wolf, ed. *Anglican Spirituality* (Conn.: Morehouse-Barlow Co., 1982), 105, quoted in Marshall, *The Anglican Church*, 112.
41 Garvey, 31.
42 Ibid.

CHAPTER 3

1 Ross, "French and English Canadian Contacts and Institutional Change."
2 Clifford, "His Dominion," 28.
3 The *Montreal Churchman* was the monthly newspaper for Montreal Diocese for eighty years. Its name was changed in December 1992 to the *Montreal Anglican.*
4 Synod, *Proceedings*, 1963.
5 *Montreal Churchman*, December 1963.
6 *Montreal Churchman*, October 1963.
7 *Montreal Churchman*, September 1967.
8 Lee, *October Crisis to Referendum*, 62.
9 Quoted in ibid., 62.
10 Synod, *Proceedings*, 1970.
11 Synod, *Proceedings*, 1971.
12 *Montreal Churchman*, October 1975.
13 *Montreal Churchman*, December 1976.
14 Williams, *Canadian Churches and Social Justice*, 195.
15 *Montreal Churchman*, February 1977.
16 *Montreal Churchman*, May 1977.

17 Synod, *Proceedings,* 1977.
18 Ibid.
19 *Montreal Churchman,* June 1977.
20 Ibid.
21 *Montreal Churchman,* December 1977.
22 Ibid.
23 Ibid.
24 *Montreal Churchman,* February 1978.
25 *Montreal Churchman,* April 1978.
26 *Montreal Churchman,* February 1978.
27 *Montreal Churchman,* May 1978.
28 *Montreal Churchman,* September 1978.
29 Many of the clergy were retiring, but there were also some who sought parishes in other parts of the country.
30 *Montreal Churchman,* January 1979.
31 *Montreal Churchman,* June 1980.
32 Synod, *Proceedings,* 1980.
33 *Montreal Churchman,* December 1981.
34 *Montreal Churchman,* March 1982.
35 Ibid.
36 *Montreal Churchman,* May 1990.
37 Kern, *The Culture of Time and Space,* 3.
38 "Gleanings" (unpublished), Parish of Vaudreuil, 1987.
39 *Montreal Churchman,* March 1988.
40 Parish of Vaudreuil, January 1988.
41 Personal interview, 21 February 1988.
42 Personal interview, 20 March 1988.
43 *Daily Telegraph,* January 1987, quoted at the meeting of the Prayer Book Society, October 1988.
44 Personal notes, 18 October 1988.
45 Bibby, *Fragmented Gods*; Ley, "Pluralism and the Canadian State."
46 Ley, "Pluralism and the Canadian State."
47 *Montreal Churchman,* May 1982.
48 Westfall, *Two Worlds,* 174.

CHAPTER 4

1 Samuel Martin, *An Essential Grace,* 97.
2 *Montreal Churchman,* October 1979.
3 *Montreal Churchman,* October 1979.
4 Samuel Martin, *An Essential Grace,* 120.
5 Ibid, 185.

6 Deeg, "How and What Canadians Contribute to Charity."
7 Kitchen, "Some New Evidence on the Distribution of Charitable Donations by Families in Canada."
8 Samuel Martin, *An Essential Grace*, 215.

CHAPTER 5

1 Gretta Chambers, in *Montreal Gazette*, 12 December 1991.
2 Bellah, *Habits of the Heart*, 227.
3 Mead, *Mind, Self and Society*
4 Tuan, *Space and Place*, 281.
5 Buttimer and Seamon, *The Human Experience of Space and Place*, 167.
6 Ibid., 86.

CHAPTER 6

1 Meeting on stewardship, September 27, 1988.
2 Meeting on stewardship, October 11, 1988.
3 Advisory board meeting, October 24, 1988.
4 Meeting on stewardship, November 28, 1988.
5 Ibid.
6 Special choir meeting, February 14, 1989.
7 Ibid.
8 Personal interview, February 1988.

CHAPTER 7

1 "Down through the Years" (unpublished history of Grace Church, 1982).
2 Statistics Canada, 1989.
3 March 1988.
4 "Down through the Years."
5 Notre-Dame-de-Grace (N.D.G.) is a community to the northwest of Pointe St Charles, to which many parishioners moved as their financial means improved. St Matthews was the Anglican church built to serve the newly emerging community.

CHAPTER 8

1 *Montreal Gazette*, letter to the editor, 1988.
2 *Globe and Mail*, 15 August 1990.
3 January 1989.

CHAPTER 9

1 April 1989.

CHAPTER 10

1 He "didn't receive a very warm welcome right from the beginning."
2 "It is important to mention that active women constitute about 90 to 95 per cent of the regular participants. They are the backbone of the parish. Their age varies from 25 to 50 years. While some of them are unwell and others are office secretaries, the vast majority work in factories. Men are between 25 and 60 years of age, and are all married. They work in factories. The young are imprinted with Quebecois culture. Children are those between a few months and 14 years. They have been born in Canada. They speak French but understand Creole."
3 "This is a community that wants to continue the rituals of faith begun in Haiti. The beginning of this parish was marked by a need to come together to share new experiences, to identify together the challenges and to surmount them, to meet obstacles in solidarity together in a new country."
4 "I would like to see the actors becoming real 'actors' and not merely spectators."
5 "One finds a totally anglo-saxon culture there and a British ecclesiastical vision."
6 "The paternalistic socio-political system of Haiti has influenced the mentality and the attitude that one meets in the ecclesiastical milieu."
7 "They must espouse new values."
8 "They think they can continue the work of their fathers and especially to be the link with the deceased Anglican parents and grandparents."
9 "Within the diocese, the practising faithful of La Nativité have more a sense of foreigners than they do within their parish. They are very reticent when they have to participate in diocesan activities because of the cultural and linguistic barriers mentioned above. They feel like strangers ... therefore, there is no communication between them and the rest of the diocese. Everything is done according to English Canadian and British ways."

CHAPTER 12

1 Charles Taylor, *Sources of the Self*, 36.
2 Ibid., 204.
3 Ley, "Pluralism and the Canadian State."
4 Kern, *The Cultre of Space and Time*, 45.
5 Mannheim, *Ideology and Utopia*.
6 David Martin, *The Breaking of the Image*, 85.
7 Giddens, *The Constitution of Society*, 367.

Bibliography

Adams, James Luther. *Paul Tillich's Philosophy of Culture, Science and Religion.* New York: Harper & Row, 1965.

Acquaviva, S.S. *The Decline of the Sacred in Industrial Society.* Trans. Patricia Lipscomb. New York: Harper & Row, 1979.

Alliance Quebec. *Brief on Demographic Tendencies.* Presented to the Standing Committee on Culture of the National Assembly. Quebec, 1984.

– . *Brief on Immigration.* Presented to the Commission Permanente sur la Culture de l'assemblée nationale. Quebec, 1987.

Anglican Church of Canada. *Mutual Responsibility and Interdependence in the Body of Christ.* Toronto, 1963.

– . "National Long Range Planning Report." Toronto, 1986. Unpublished report prepared for the 1986 General Synod, based on specially compiled data from the 1981 census.

Arnopoulos, Sheila McLeod, and Dominique Clift. *The English Fact in Quebec.* Montreal and Kingston: McGill-Queen's University Press, 1980.

Baillargeon, Mireille. "Évolution et caractéristiques linguistiques des échanges migratoires interprovinciaux et internationaux du Québec depuis 1971." 1983. Unpublished report (édition provisoire), Conseil de la Langue Française.

Barnes, Trevor, and Michael Curry. "Towards a Contextual Approach to Geographical Knowledge." *Transactions, Institute of British Geographers,* N.S. 8 (1983): 467–82.

Baum, Gregory. "Catholicism and Secularization in Quebec." *Cross-currents,* Winter 1986–87, 436–58.

– . *Communication in the Church.* New York: Seabury Press, 1978.

– . *Religion and Alienation*. New York: Paulist Press, 1975.

– . "Sociology and Theology." In *The Church as Institution*, 22–31. ed. Baum and Greeley.

– . "The Survival of the Sacred." In *The Persistence of Religion*, ed. A. Greeley and G. Baum, 11–22. New York: Harper & Row, 1973.

– . *Theology and Society*. New York: Paulist Press, 1987.

Baum, Gregory, and & A. Greeley, eds. *The Church as Institution*. New York: Herder & Herder, 1974.

Behiels, Michael, ed. *Quebec Since 1945: Selected Readings*. Toronto: Copp Clark Pitman, 1987.

Bellah, Robert. "Christianity and Symbolic Realism." In *The Social Meaning of Religion*, ed. Newman, 111–22.

Bellah, Robert, et al. *Habits of the Heart*. New York: Harper & Row, 1985. Originally published by University of California Press.

Berger, Peter. *The Sacred Canopy*. New York: Doubleday, 1967.

– . "Sociology of Religion and Sociology of Knowledge." In *The Social Meaning of Religion*. ed. Newman, 99–110.

Berger, Peter, and Thomas Luckmann. *The Social Construction of Reality*. New York: Doubleday, 1966.

Bernstein, Richard J. *The Restructuring of Social and Political Theory*. Philadelphia, Pa: University of Pennsylvannia Press, 1978.

– , ed. *Habermas and Modernity*. Cambridge, Mass.: MIT Press, 1985.

Bibby, Reginald W. *Fragmented Gods: The Poverty and Potential of Religion in Canada*. Toronto: Irwin Publishing, 1987.

Bienvenue, Rita M., and Jay E. Goldstein, eds. *Ethnicity and Ethnic Relations in Canada*. Toronto: Butterworths, 1985.

Blumer, Herbert. *Symbolic Interactionism*. Englewood Cliffs, N.J.: Prentice-Hall, 1969.

Breton, Raymond. "The Production and Allocation of Symbolic Resources: An Analysis of the Linguistic and Ethnocultural Fields in Canada." *Canadian Review of Sociology and Anthropology* 21 (1984): 123–44.

– . "Reflections on the French Presence in Canada. "In *Ethnicity*, ed. Greeley and Baum, 42–7.

– . "Stratification and Conflict between Ethnolinguistic Communities with Different Social Structures." In *Ethnicity and Ethnic Relations in Canada*, ed. Bienvenue and Golstein, 45–59.

Breton, Raymond, et al. *Ethnic Identity and Equality*. Toronto: University of Toronto Press, 1990.

Brown, David, and Raymond Boyce. "Study of Downtown Churches: Montreal." Unpublished study, Urban Planning Program, McGill University, 1975.

Buttimer, Anne. "Grasping the Dynamism of the Lifeworld." *Annals, Association of American Geographers* 66, no. 2 (1976): 277–92.

– "Social Space in Interdisciplinary Perspective." *Geographical Review* 59 (1969): 417–26.

– . "Home, Reach and Sense of Place." In *The Human Experience of Space and Place*, ed. Buttimer and Seamon.

– . "Social Space in Interdisciplinary Perspective." *Geographical Review* 59 (1969): 417–26.

Buttimer, Anne, and David Seamon, eds. *The Human Experience of Space and Place*. New York: St Martin's Press, 1980.

Caldwell, Gary. *A Demographic Profile of the English-Speaking Population of Quebec, 1921–1971*. Quebec: International Centre for Research on Bilingualism, 1974.

– . *Outmigration of 1971 English Mother Tongue High School Leavers*. Quebec: Institut Québécois de recherche sur la culture.

– , and Eric Waddell, eds. *The English of Quebec: From Majority to Minority Status*. Quebec: Institut Québécois de recherche sur la culture, 1982. Also in French as: *Les anglophones du Québec*.

Canadian Centre for Philanthropy. *Canada Gives: Trends and Attitudes towards Charitable Giving and Voluntarism*. Ed. Allan Arlett et al. Toronto, 1988.

Clarke, Colin; David Ley; and Ceri Peach, eds. *Geography and Ethnic Pluralism*. London: Geo. Allen & Unwin, 1984.

Clifford, Keith, N. "His Dominion: A Vision in Crisis." In *Religion and Culture in Canada*, ed. Slater, 23–42.

Clift, Dominique. *The Secret Kingdom: Interpretations of Canadian Character*. Toronto: McClelland & Stewart, 1989.

Coleman, James S. "Social Theory, Social Research, and Theory of Action." *American Journal of Sociology* 91, no. 6 (1986): 1309 – 35.

Cybriwsky, Roman A. "Social Aspects of Neighbourhood Change." *Annals, Association of American Geographers* 68, no. 1 (1978).

Decima. "Nation-wide Survey of Attitudes towards Philanthropy." Unpublished study sponsored by the Canadian Centre for Philanthropy, October 1987.

Deeg, J.F. "How and What Canadians Contribute to Charity." *Philanthropist* 4, no. 1 (1984): 3–31.

Deffontaines, Pierre. *Géographie et Réligions*, Paris: Gallimard, 1948.

– . "The Religious Factor in Human Geography." *Diogenes* 2 (1953): 24–37.

Demerath, N.J. *Social Class in American Protestantism*. Chicago: Rand McNally, 1965.

de Villiers-Westfall, Wm. E. "The Sacred and the Secular: Studies in the Cultural History of Protestant Ontario in the Victorian Period." Unpublished PhD thesis, University of Toronto, 1976.

Dufour, Christian. *Le Défi Québécois: A Canadian Challenge*. Lantzville,

B.C.: Oolichan Books and Institute for Research on Public Policy, 1990.

Duncan, James S. "The Superorganic in American Cultural Geography." *Annals, Association of American Geographers* 70, no. 2 (1980): 181–98.

Durkheim, Émile. "On the Process of Change in Social Values." In *Theories of Society* vol. 2, ed. Parsons, 1305–11.

– . *Sociology and Philosophy*. Trans. Pocock. London: Cohen and West. 1953.

Eisenstadt, S.N., ed. *Max Weber: On Charisma and Institution Building.* Chicago and London: University of Chicago Press, 1968.

Eldridge, J.E.T. *Max Weber: The Interpretation of Social Reality.* London: Michael Joseph, 1971.

Eliade, Mercea. *The Sacred and the Profane.* New York: Praeger Palo, 1957.

Emmet, Dorothy, and A. MacIntyre, eds. *Sociological Theory and Philosophical Analysis.* London: Macmillan, 1970.

Eyles, John. *Senses of Place.* Warrington, England: Silverbrook Press, 1985.

– , ed. *Research in Human Geography*, London: Basil Blackwell, 1988.

Falardeau, Jean-Charles. "Évolution des structures sociales et des élites au Canada français." In *Structures sociales du Canada français*, ed. G. Sylvestre, 3–13. 1966. Toronto: Les Presses de l'université Laval et University of Toronto Press.

Faris, R.E.L. *Chicago Sociology, 1920–32.* Chicago: University of Chicago Press, 1967; reprint, San Francisco: Chandler, 1970.

Fickeler, P. "Fundamental Questions in the Geography of Religions." In *Readings in Cultural Geography*, ed. P.L. Wagner and M.W. Mikesell, 94–117. Chicago: University of Chicago Press, 1962.

Firey, W. "Sentiment and Symbolism as Ecological Variables." *American Sociological Review* 10 (1945): 140–8.

Frye, Northrop. *Creation and Recreation.* Toronto: University of Toronto Press, 1980.

Gale, Nathan, and R.G. Golledge. "On the Subjective Partitioning of Space." *Annals, Association of American Geographers* 72, no. 1, (1982): 60–7.

Gauvreau, Michael. "History and Faith: A Study of the Evangelical Temper in Canada, 1820–1940." Unpublished PHD thesis, University of Toronto, 1985.

Gay, J.D. *The Geography of Religion in England.* London: G. Duckworth, 1971.

Geertz, Clifford. *The Interpretation of Cultures.* New York: Basic Books, 1973.

Gibson, Edward. "Understanding the Subjective Meaning of Places." In *Humanistic Geography*, ed. Ley and Samuels, 138–53.

Giddens, Anthony. *Central Problems in Social Theory*. Berkeley: University of California Press, 1979.

– . *The Constitution of Society*. Berkeley and Los Angeles: University of California Press, 1984.

Glasner, P. *The Sociology of Secularisation*. London: Routledge & Kegan Paul, 1977.

Goode, Erich. "Class Styles of Religious Sociation." *British Journal of Sociology* 19, no. l (1968): 1–15.

– . "Social Class and Church Participation." *American Journal of Sociology* 72 (1966): 102–11.

Gowdy, Kenneth. "Communities and Urbanization." In *Christian Perspectives on Sociology*, ed. Grulan and Reimer, 362–84.

Grand'Maison, Jacques. *Nationalisme et Religion*, vol. 2. Montreal: Librairie Beauchemin, 1970.

Grace Church. "Down Through the Years." Unpublished history of Grace Church, 1990.

Grant, John W. *The Church in the Canadian Era*, vol. 3 of *A History of the Christian Church in Canada*, ed. J.W. Grant. Toronto: McGraw-Hill Ryerson, 1972; rev. ed. Burlington, Ont.: Welch Publishing Co, 1988.

– . "A Decade of Ferment: Canadian Churches in the 1960's." In *Religion in Canadian Society*, ed. S. Crysdale and L. Wheatcroft, 207–18. Toronto: Macmillan of Canada, 1976.

– . "Religion and the Quest for a National Identity: The Background in Canadian History." In *Religion and Culture in Canada*, ed. Slater, 7–21.

Greeley, Andrew. *The Denominational Society*. Glenview, Ill.: Scott, Foresman. 1972.

– . "The Persistence of Community." In *The Persistence of Religion*, ed. A. Greeley and G. Baum, 23–35. New York: Herder & Herder, 1973.

– . *Unsecular Man*. New York: Schocken Books, 1972.

Greeley, Andrew, and G. Baum, eds. *Ethnicity*. New York: Seabury Press. 1977.

Gregory, Derek. "Human Agency and Human Geography." *Transactions, Institute of British Geographers*, N.S. 6 (1981): 1–18.

Gregory, Derek, and J. Urry. *Social Relations and Spatial Structures*. London: Macmillan Education, 1985.

Grulan, Stephen A., and Milton Reimer, eds. *Christian Perspectives on Sociology*. Grand Rapids, Mich.: Zondervan, 1982.

Guindon, Hubert. *Quebec Society: Tradition, Modernity, and Nationhood*. Toronto: University of Toronto Press, 1988.

– . "The Social Evolution of Quebec Reconsidered." *Canadian Journal of Economics and Political Science* 26 (1960): 533–51.

Hall, Douglas. *The Canada Crisis: A Christian Perspective.* Toronto: Anglican Book Centre, 1980.

– . *Thinking the Faith: Christian Theology in a North American Context.* Minneapolis: Augsburg, 1989.

Hammersley, M., and P. Atkinson. *Ethnography: Principles in Practice.* New York: Tavistock, 1983.

Hammond, Phillip E., ed. *The Sacred in a Secular Age.* Berkeley: University of California Press, 1985.

Handler, Richard. *Nationalism and the Politics of Culture in Quebec.* Madison: University of Wisconsin Press, 1988.

Heatwole, Charles A. "Exploring the Geography of America's Religious Denominations: A Presbyterian Example." *Journal of Geography* 76 (1977): 99–104.

Henripin, Jacques. "La population québécoise de la langue anglaise: une projection démolinguistique, 1971–2001." Unpublished study prepared for Alliance Quebec, 1984.

Herberg, Edward N. *Ethnic Groups in Canada: Adaptations and Transitions.* Scarborough, Ont.: Nelson, 1989.

Hillery, G.A. "Definitions of Community." *Rural Sociology* 20 (1955): 111–23.

Houston, James M. "The Concepts of 'Place' and 'Land' in the Judaeo-Christian Tradition." In *Humanistic Geography*, ed. Ley and Samuels, 224–37.

Isaac, E. "Religious Geography and the Geography of Religion." *University of Colorado Studies, Series in Earth Sciences*, 1–14. 1965.

Jackson, Peter. "Principles and Problems of Participant Observation." *Geografiska Annaler B* 65 (1983): 39–46.

– . "Social Geography: politics and place." *Progress in Human Geography* 11, no. 2 (1987): 286–92.

– . "Social Geography: The rediscovery of place." *Progress in Human Geography* 10, no. 1 (1986): 118–24.

Jackson, Peter, and Susan Smith. *Exploring Social Geography*, London: Geo. Allen & Unwin, 1984.

– . *Social Interaction and Ethnic Segregation.* Don Mills, Ont.: Academic Press, 1985.

Johnston, R.J. "On the Nature of Explanation in Human Geography." *Transactions, Institute of British Geographers* 5, (1980): 402–12.

– . "The State and the Study of Social Geography." In *Social Interaction and Ethnic Segregation*, ed. Jackson and Smith, 205–22.

Jones, Emrys. "Cause and Effect in Human Geography." *Annals, Association of American Geographers* 46, no. 4 (1956): 369–77.

– , ed. *Readings in Social Geography.* London: Oxford University Press, 1975.

Jones, Emrys, and J. Eyles. *An Introduction to Social Geography*. London: Oxford University Press, 1977.

Kennedy, Eugene. "Religious Faith and Psychological Maturity." In *The Persistence of Religion*, ed. A. Greeley and G. Baum, 119–27. New York: Herder & Herder, 1973.

Kern, Stephen. *The Culture of Time and Space, 1880–1918*. Cambridge, Mass.: Harvard University Press, 1983.

Kitagawa, Joseph M., and Charles H. Long. *Myths and Symbols: Studies in Honor of Mircea Eliade*. Chicago: University of Chicago Press, 1969.

Kitchen, Harry. "Some Evidence on the Distribution of Charitable Donations by Families in Canada." *Philanthropist* 6, no. 1 (1986).

– . "Some New Evidence on the Distribution of Religious Charitable Donations by Families in Canada." *Philanthropist* 6, no. 3 (1986): 40–55.

Kobayashi, Audrey, and S. MacKenzie. *Remaking Human Geography*. Winchester, Mass.: Unwin Hyman, 1989.

Kuriyan, G. "Geography and Religion." *Indian Geographical Journal* 36, no. 1 (1961): 46–51.

Lachapelle, Réjean. "Démographie et langues officielles au Canada." Unpublished report for a colloquium "Vers la coexistence équitable et la réconciliation: droits et politiques linguistiques," Queen's University, Kingston, Ontario, December 1989.

Lachapelle, Réjean, and J. Henripin. *The Demolinguistic Situation in Canada*. Report prepared for Alliance Quebec, Montreal, 1982.

Lane, Belden. *Landscapes of the Sacred: Geography and Narrative in American Spirituality*. New York: Paulist Press, 1988.

Lee, John. "October Crisis to Referendum: Ideological elements in the discourse of English Protestant churches concerning the socio-political evolution of Quebec, 1970–1980." Unpublished M.A. thesis, Faculty of Religious Studies, McGill University, Montreal, 1984.

Lenski, Gerhard E. *The Religious Factor*, Garden City: Doubleday, 1963.

Levine, Gregory James. "In God's Service: The role of the Anglican, Methodist, and Presbyterian and Roman Catholic Churches in the Cultural Geography of Late Nineteenth Century Kingston." Unpublished PhD thesis, Queen's University, Kingston, Ont., 1981.

– . "On the Geography of Religion." *Transactions, Institute of British Geographers*, N.S. 11, no. 4 (1986): 428–40.

Levine, Marc V. *The Reconquest of Montreal*. Philadelphia: Temple University Press, 1990.

Levi-Strauss, C. *The View from Afar*. New York: Basic Books, 1985.

Ley, David. "Behavioural Geography and the Philosophies of Meaning." In *Behavioural Problems in Geography Revisited*, ed. Kevin Cox and R.G. Golledge. New York: Methuen 1981.

– . "Cultural/Humanistic Geography." *Progress in Human Geography* 7, no. 2 (1983): 267–73.

– . *Geography Without Man: A Humanistic Critique.* Research paper no. 24, University of Oxford, 1980.

– . "Pluralism and the Canadian State." In *Geography and Ethnic Pluralism*, ed. Colin Clarke, David Ley, and Ceri Peach. London: Geo. Allen & Unwin, 1984.

– . "Social Geography and Social Action." In *Humanistic Geography*, ed. Ley and Samuels, 41–57.

– . "Social Geography and the Taken-for-Granted World." *Transactions, Institute of British Geographers* N.S. 2 (1977): 498–519.

Ley, David, and M. Samuels, eds. *Humanistic Geography: Prospects and Problems.* Chicago: Maaroufa, 1978.

Licate, J. "The Geographic Study of Religion – A Review of the Literature." Unpublished MA thesis, University of Chicago, 1967.

Lovell, George. "The Mission of the Church and Community Development." In *The Social Sciences and the Churches*, ed. Mitton. 208–220.

Lowenthal, David. "Geography, Experience and Imagination: Towards a Geographical Epistemology." *Annals, Association of American Geographers* 51, no. 3 (1961): 241–60.

– . *The Past Is a Foreign Country.* Cambridge, Mass.: Cambridge University Press, 1985.

– . "Past Time, Present Place: Landscape and Memory." *Geographical Review* 65, no. 1 (1975): 1–36.

Lowenthal, David, and Martyn J. Bowden, eds. *Geographies of the Mind.* New York: Oxford University Press, 1976.

Luckmann,Thomas. *The Invisible Religion: The Transformation of Symbols in Industrial Society.* New York: Macmillan, 1967.

MacIntyre, Alasdair. *After Virtue.* Notre Dame, Ind.: University of Notre Dame Press, 1981.

McIntosh, Wm. Alex, and Jon P. Alston. "Lenski Revisited: The Linkage Role of Religion in Primary and Secondary Groups." *American Journal of Sociology* 87, no. 4 (1982): 852–67.

McRoberts, Kenneth. *Quebec: Social Change and Political Crisis.* 3d ed. Toronto: McClelland & Stewart, 1988.

Maheu, Robert. "L'émigration des anglophones québécois." *Cahiers québécois de démographie* 12, no. 2 (1983).

Mair, N.H. "Les églises protestantes." In *Les anglophones du Québec*, ed. Caldwell and Waddell, 219–32.

Mannheim, Karl. *Ideology and Utopia.* New York: Harcourt, Brace and World, 1936.

Mann, Michael. *The Sources of Social Power*, vol. 1. Cambridge: Cambridge University Press, 1986.

Marshall, Michael. *The Anglican Church: Today and Tomorrow.* Wilton, Conn.: Morehouse-Barlow, 1984.

Martin, David. *The Breaking of the Image.* Oxford: Basil Blackwell, 1980.

– . *The Dilemmas of Contemporary Religion.* Oxford: Basil Blackwell, 1978.

– . *A General Theory of Secularization.* Oxford: Basil Blackwell, 1978.

Martin, Samuel. *An Essential Grace.* Toronto: McClelland & Stewart, 1985.

– . *Financing Humanistic Service.* Toronto: McClelland & Stewart, 1975.

Mead, George H. *Mind, Self and Society.* Chicago: University of Chicago Press, 1934.

Meinig, Donald W. "The Mormon Culture Region: Strategies and Patterns in the Geography of the American West, 1847–1964." *Annals, Association of American Geographers* 55 (1965): 191–220.

– , ed. *Interpretation of Ordinary Landscapes.* Oxford: Oxford University Press, 1979.

Meyer, Judith W. "Ethnicity, Theology, and Immigrant Church Expansion." *Geographical Review* 65 (1975): 180–97.

Meyers, G.C. "Patterns of Church Distribution and Movement." *Social Forces* 40 (1962): 354–63.

Mikesell, Marvin W. "Tradition and Innovation in Cultural Geography." *Annals, Association of American Geographers* 68, no. 1 (1978): 1–16.

Mitton, C.L., ed. *The Social Sciences and the Churches.* Edinburgh: T.T. Clark. 1972.

Mol, Hans. *Faith and Fragility.* Oxford: Basil Blackwell, 1985.

– . *Identity and the Sacred.* Oxford: Basil Blackwell, 1976.

Nelson, H.M., and R.A. Clews. "Geographic Mobility and Religious Behaviour." *Sociological Review,* n.s. 21, no. 1 (1973): 127–35.

Nelson, H.M., and H.P. Whitt. "Religion and the Migrant in the City: A Test of Holt's Cultural Shock Thesis." *Social Forces* 50 (1971): 379–84.

Newman, Wm. M., ed. *The Social Meaning of Religion.* Chicago: Rand McNally, 1974.

Nock, David A. "Patriotism and Patriarchs: Anglican Archbishops and Canadianization." *Canadian Ethnic Studies* 14, no. 3 (1982): 79–93.

Norton, Wm. "Humans, Land and Landscape: A Proposal for Cultural Geography." *Canadian Geographer* 31, no. 1 (1987): 21–30.

O'Dea, Thomas. "Five Dilemmas in Institutionalization of Religion." In *The Social Meaning of Religion,* ed. Newman, 271–86.

– . "Pathology and Renewal of Religious Institutions." In *The Church as Institution,* ed. Baum and Greeley, 119–27.

Park, R.E. "The Concept of Social Distance." *Journal of Applied Sociology* 8 (1924): 339–44.

– . "Human Nature and Collective Behaviour." *American Journal of Sociology* 32 (1926): 733–41.

Parsons, Talcott. *Structure and Process in Modern Societies.* Glencoe, Ill.: Free Press, 1960.

Parsons, Talcott, et al., eds. *Theories of Society,* 2 vols. New York: Free Press of Glencoe, 1961.

Pickering, W.S.F. "The Persistence of the Rites of Passage." *British Journal of Sociology* 25 (1974): 63–78.

Piggott, Charles. "A Geography of Religion in Scotland." Unpublished PHD thesis, Department of Geography, University of Edinburgh, 1977.

Pillsbury, Richard. "The Religious Geography of Pennsylvannia: A Factor Analytic Approach." *Proceedings, Association of American Geographers* 3 (1971): 130–4.

Porter, John. *The Vertical Mosaic.* Toronto: University of Toronto Press, 1965.

Powles, Cyril. "The Anglican Church and Canadian Culture." In *Church and Canadian Culture,* ed. VanderVennen.

Pred, Allan. "Place as Historically Contingent Process: Structuration and Time-Geography of Becoming Places." *Annals, Association of American Geographers* 74, no. 2 (1984): 279–97.

Raffestin, Claude. "Religions, relations de pouvoir et géographie politique." *Cahiers de Géographie du Québec* 29, no. 76 (1985): 101–7.

Rawlyk, George A., ed. *The Canadian Protestant Experience, 1760–1990.* Burlington, Ont.: Welch Publishing Company, 1990.

Reed, Bruce D. "The Local Church as Institution." In *The Social Sciences and the Churches,* ed. Mitton. (51–61).

Reitz, Jeffrey G. "Language and Ethnic Community Survival." In *Ethnicity and Ethnic Relations in Canada,* ed. Bienvenue and Goldstein, 105–23.

Relph, E. *Place and Placelessness.* London: Pion, 1976.

– . *Rational Landscapes and Humanistic Geography.* London: Croom Helm, 1981.

– . "Seeing, Thinking and Describing Landscapes." In *Environmental Perception and Behaviour,* ed. T.F. Saarinen, D. Seamon, J.L. Sell, research paper no. 209, 209–23. Chicago: University of Chicago Press, 1984.

Renaud, Marc. "Quebec's New Middle Class in Search of Social Hegemony." In *Quebec Since 1945,* ed. Behiels, 48–79.

Resnick, Philip. *Letters to a Quebecois Friend.* Montreal and Kingston: McGill-Queen's University Press, 1990.

Robertson, Roland. *The Sociological Interpretation of Religion.* New York: Schoken Books, 1970.

Roof, Wade Clark. *Community and Commitment: Religious Plausibility in a Liberal Protestant Church.* New York: Elsevier, 1978.

Ross, Aileen. "French and English Canadian Contacts and Institutional Change." *Canadian Journal of Economics and Political Science* 20, no. 3 (1954): 231–95.

Rowntree, Lester B., and Margaret W. Conkey. "Symbolism and the Cultural Landscape." *Annals, Association of American Geographers* 70, no. 4 (1980): 459–74.

Rudin, Ronald. *The Forgotten Quebecers: A History of English-speaking Quebec, 1759–1980.* Quebec: Institut québécois de recherche sur la culture, 1985.

Scherer, Jacqueline. *Contemporary Community: Sociological Illusion and Reality.* London: Tavistock Publications, 1972.

Schmalenbach, Herman. "The Sociological Category of Communion." In *Theories of Society*, vol. 1, ed. Parsons et al., 331–47.

Schutz, Alfred. "Concept and Theory Formation in the Social Sciences." In *Sociological Theory and Philosophical Analysis*, ed. Emmet and MacIntyre, 1–19.

Schutz, Alfred, and T. Luckmann. *The Structures of the Lifeworld.* Evanston: Northwestern University Press, 1973.

Seamon, David. "Philosophical Directions in Behavioural Geography with an Emphasis on the Phenomenological Contribution." In *Environmental Perception and Behaviour*, ed. T.F. Saarinen, D. Seamon, and J.L. Sell eds., research paper no. 209, 167–78. Chicago: University of Chicago Press, 1984.

Shibutani, Tomatsu. "Reference Groups as Perspectives." *American Journal of Sociology* 6 (1955): 562–9.

Shils, Edward. *Tradition.* Chicago: University of Chicago Press, 1981.

Shippey, F.A. "The Variety of City Churches." *Review of Religious Research* 2 (1960): 8–19.

Shortridge, James R. "Patterns of Religion in the United States." *Geographical Review* 66 (1976): 420–34.

Siefor, Gregor. "Ecclesiological Implications of Weber's Definition of Community." In *The Church as Institution*, ed. Baum and Greeley, 148–60.

Simmel, Georg. "A Contribution to the Sociology of Religion." *American Journal of Sociology* 60 (1955): 1–18.

Simpson, John. "Ethnic Groups and Church Attendance in the United States and Canada." In *Ethnicity*, ed. Greeley and Baum, 16–22.

Slater, P., ed. *Religion and Culture in Canada.* Waterloo, Ont.: Wilfrid Laurier University Press, 1977.

Smith, Rebecca L. "Activism and Social Status as Determinants of Neighborhood Identity." *Professional Geographer* 37, no. 4 (1985): 421–32.

Smith, Susan J. "Practicing Humanistic Geography." *Annals Association of American Geographers* 74, no. 3 (1984): 353–74.

Soja, Edward W. "The Socio-Spatial Dialectic." *Annals Association of American Geographers* 70, no. 2 (1980): 207–25.

Sopher, David E. "Geography and Religions." *Progress in Human Geography* 5, no. 4 (1981): 510–24.

– . *Geography of Religions*. Englewood Cliffs, N.J.: Prentice-Hall, 1967.

– . "The Landscape of Home." In *The Interpretation of Ordinary Landscapes*, ed. Meinig, 129–49.

Spradley, James P. *Participant Observation*. New York: Holt, Rinehart & Winston, 1980.

Stackhouse, John G. Jr. "The Protestant Experience in Canada Since 1945." In *The Canadian Protestant Experience, 1760–1990*, ed. Rawlyk, 198–252.

Stark, W. *The Sociology of Religion*, 5 vols. London: Routledge, 1966–72. (Especially vol. 5, *Types of Religious Culture*.)

Stein, Michael. "Changing Anglo-Quebecer Self Consciousness." In *The Anglophones of Quebec*, ed. Caldwell and Waddell, 109–25.

Suttles, Gerald D. *The Social Construction of Communities*. Chicago: University of Chicago Press, 1972.

Taylor, Charles. *The Malaise of Modernity*. Concord, Ont: Anansi Press, 1991.

– . *Philosophy and the Human Sciences*. Cambridge: Cambridge University Press, 1985.

– . *Sources of the Self*. Cambridge, Mass.: Harvard University Press, 1989.

Taylor, Donald, M., and Ronald J. Sigal. "Defining 'Quebecois': The Role of Ethnic Heritage, Language, and Political Orientation." In *Ethnicity and Ethnic Relations in Canada*, ed. Bienvenue and Goldstein. 125–137.

Thielbar, Gerald. "Localism – Cosmopolitanism: Social Differentiation in Mass Society. Unpublished PhD dissertation, University of Minnesota, 1966.

de Tocqueville, Alexis. *Democracy in America*, vol. 2. 1840; reprint, New York: Vintage Books, 1990.

Toennies, Ferdinand. "Gemeinschaft and Gesellschaft." In *Theories of Society*, vol. I, ed. Parsons et al., 191–201.

Towler, R. *Homo Religiosus*. London: Constable, 1974.

Troeltsch, Ernst. *Protestantism and Progress*. New York: G.P. Putnam & Sons, 1912.

Tuan, Yi-Fu. "Geopiety: A Theme in Man's Attachment to Nature and to Place." In *Geographies of the Mind*, ed. Lowenthal and Bowden, 11–39.

– . "Sign and Metaphor." *Annals, Association of American Geographers* 68, no. 3 (1978): 363–72.

– . *Space and Place: The Perspective of Experience*. Minneapolis: University of Minnesota Press, 1977.

– . "Thought and Landscape." In *The Interpretation of Ordinary Landscapes*, ed. Meinig, 89–102.

Turpin, Reginald. "The Church in Quebec." Unpublished report to General Synod on French-English relations, the Anglican Church in Canada, August 1977.

Upton, Graham J.G. "Factors Affecting Religious Participation." *Sociological Methods and Research* 10, no. 3 (1982): 327–35.

Vachon, R., and J. Langlais. *Who Is Québécois?* Ottawa: Tecumseh Press, 1983.

van der Laan, Lambert, and Andries Piersma. "The Image of Man: Paradigmatic Cornerstone in Human Geography." *Annals, Association of American Geographers* 72, no. 3 (1982): 411–26.

vanderVennen, Robert E., ed. *Church and Canadian Culture.* New York: University Press of America, 1991.

van Wright, Georg Henrik. *Explanation and Understanding.* Ithaca, N.Y.: Cornell University Press, 1971.

Warren, Roland L. *The Community in America.* 2d ed. Chicago: Rand McNally College Publishing Company, 1972.

Watson, L.C., and M.B. Watson-Franke. *Interpreting Life Histories.* New Brunswick, N.J.: Rutgers University Press, 1985.

Watson, W. "The Soul of Geography." *Transactions, Institute of British Geographers,* N.S. 8 (1982): 385–99.

Weber, Max. *The Methodology of the Social Sciences.* Trans. Edward Shils and Henry Finch. 1904; New York: Free Press, 1949.

– . *The Protestant Ethic and the Spirit of Capitalism.* Trans. Talcott Parsons. 1920; New York: Charles Scribner's Sons, 1958.

– . "Religion and Social Status." in *Theories of Society,* vol. 2, ed. Parsons, 1138–61.

– . *The Sociology of Religion.* Trans. E. Fischoff. 1922; Boston: Beacon Press, 1963.

– . "Types of Social Organization." In *Theories of Society,* vol. 1, ed. Parsons et al., 218–29.

Werblowsky, R.J. Zwi. *Beyond Tradition and Modernity.* London: Athlone Press, 1976.

Westfall, Wm. *Two Worlds: The Protestant Culture of Nineteenth Century Ontario.* Montreal and Kingston: McGill-Queen's University Press, 1989.

Westley, Margaret W. *Remembrance of Grandeur, The Anglo-Protestant Elite of Montreal.* Montreal: Éditions Libre Expression, 1990.

Williams, John R., ed. *Canadian Churches and Social Justice.* Toronto: Anglican Book Centre, 1984.

Wilson, Bobby. "The Influence of Church Participation on the Behaviour in Space of Black Rural Migrants within Bedford-Stuyvesant." Unpublished PhD dissertation, Clark University, Worcester, Mass., 1974.

Wilson, Bobby. "Social Space and Symbolic Interaction." In *The Human Experience of Space and Place,* ed. Buttimer and Seamon, 135–47.

Wilson, Bryan R. "The Anglican Church and Its Decline." *New Society*, 5 December 1974.

– . *Religion in Sociological Perspective.* Oxford: Oxford University Press, 1982.

Winch, Peter. *The Idea of a Social Science and Its Relation to Philosophy.* London: Routledge & Kegan Paul, 1958.

Wirth, Louis. "Localism, Regionalism and Centralization." *American Journal of Sociology* 42 (1936): 493–509.

Wuthnow, Robert. "Recent Patterns of Secularization: A Problem of Generations?" *American Sociological Review* 41 (1976): 850–67.

– , ed. *The Religious Dimension: New Directions in Quantitative Research.* New York: Academic Press, 1979.

Wuthnow, Robert, et al. *Cultural Analysis: The Work of Peter Berger, Mary Douglas, Michel Foucault, and Jurgen Habermas.* London: Routledge & Kegan Paul, 1984.

Yinger, J.M. *Religion, Society and the Individual.* New York: Macmillan, 1957.

– . *The Scientific Study of Religion.* New York: Macmillan, 1970.

Zelinsky, Wilbur. "An Approach to the Religious Geography of the U.S.: Patterns of Church Membership in 1952." *Annals, Association of American Geographers* 51 (1961): 139–93.

– . "The Demigod's Dilemma." *Annals, Association of American Geographers* 65, no. 2 (1975): 123–43.

Zimmer, B.G., and A.H. Hawley. "Suburbanization and Church Participation." *Social Forces* 37, no. 4 (1959): 348–54.

Documents and Data Sources

Annual Synod *Proceedings*, Montreal Diocese, 1961–90.

National Synod reports, 1961–92.

Vestry Books: records in individual parishes.

Surveys:

1. Unpublished national survey on the use of the Book of Alternative Services, conducted in 1988.

2. Author's survey of parishes in Montreal Diocese, letter and questionnaire sent to regional deans in March 1989.

Montreal Churchman, monthly Anglican newspaper. Renamed in December 1992, *Montreal Anglican*.

Special accounts compiled by the national treasurer on request of the author, relating to mission and outreach.

Parish bulletins, newsletters, and minutes of meetings.

Index

DATE DUE